C000136202

2 -99

8

NEW DIRECTIO...

Editors

Françoise Audouze
Centre de Recherches Archéologiques, Meudon, France
Richard Bradley
Department of Archaeology, University of Reading
Joan Gero
Department of Anthropology, University of South Carolina
Tim Murray
Department of Archaeology, La Trobe University, Victoria, Australia
Colin Renfrew
Department of Archaeology, University of Cambridge
Andrew Sherratt
Department of Antiquities, Ashmolean Museum, Oxford
Timothy Taylor
Department of Archaeology, University of Bradford
Norman Yoffee
Department of Anthropology, University of Arizona

THE USES OF STYLE IN ARCHAEOLOGY

THE USES OF STYLE
IN ARCHAEOLOGY

EDITED BY

MARGARET W. CONKEY
University of California, Berkeley

and

CHRISTINE A. HASTORF
University of Minnesota

CAMBRIDGE
UNIVERSITY PRESS

For Elden Johnson

Published by the Press Syndicate of the University of Cambridge
The Pitt Building, Trumpington Street, Cambridge CB2 1RP
40 West 20th Street, New York, NY 10011-4211, USA
10 Stamford Road, Oakleigh, Melbourne 3166, Australia

© Cambridge University Press 1990

First published 1990
Reprinted 1992
First paperback edition 1993

Printed in Great Britain at the Athenaeum Press Ltd,
Newcastle upon Tyne

British Library cataloguing in publication data

The uses of style in archaeology. – (New
directions in archaeology)
1. Cultural processes. Sources of evidence.
Artefacts. Style
I. Conkey, Margaret W.
II. Hastorf, Christine A.
III. Series
306

Library of Congress cataloguing in publication data

The uses of style in archaeology / edited by
Margaret W. Conkey and Christine A. Hastorf
    p.   cm. – (New directions in archaeology)
Bibliography.
Includes index.
ISBN 0-521-35061-1
1. Indians – Pottery – Congresses.
2. Mogollan culture – Pottery – Congresses.
3. Pottery – Themes, motives – Congresses.
I. Conkey, Margaret Wright, 1944–
II. Hastorf, Christine Ann, 1950–
III. Series.
E59.P8U84   1989
970.01-dc20   89-35782   CIP

ISBN 0 521 35061 1 hardback
ISBN 0 521 44576 0 paperback

CE

CONTENTS

CONTRIBUTORS

Margaret W. Conkey, University of California, Berkeley
Whitney Davis, Northwestern University, Illinois
Warre, R. DeBoer, Queens College, City University of New York
Timothy Earle, University of California, Los Angeles
Christine A. Hastorf, University of Minnesota
Ian Hodder, University of Cambridge
William K. Macdonald, New Jersey, USA
Stephen Plog, University of Virginia
James R. Sackett, University of California, Los Angeles
Polly Wiessner, Max Planck Institut für Humanethologie

PREFACE

This volume on the uses of style in archaeology grew out of a conference of the same title sponsored by the Department of Anthropology and the University of Minnesota, Minneapolis the weekend of January 25–26, 1985. There six archaeologists, who have long been concerned with this issue, along with two commentators and a guest speaker, discussed the problem of style. As this volume will demonstrate, the subject is rich and multidimensional, with many varying points of view, from the functional use of style by archaeologists, to the interpretation by art historians, to the use of style by those in past cultures themselves.

The inception of the conference was a bit like the subject, diverse and eclectic. One year before the visit of a traveling exhibit of ceramic pieces from the prehistoric Mimbres culture of the southwestern United States to the University Art Museum, I was approached by the chairman of the Anthropology Department, Elden Johnson, to consult on several archaeological exhibits that would accompany the pottery, which were being organized by Lyndel King and Susan Brown of the museum, and to coordinate an associated conference with Dr. Christy Caine. The Anthropology Department had periodically held a small conference in honor of the late archaeologist Dennis Puleston, and Johnson suggested we think about organizing a departmental conference linked to the Mimbres pottery, because the department houses the largest collection of this ceramic tradition in the world.

Upon thinking about the pottery and its complex style, I had to move beyond seriations, art history, and the southwestern U.S. space-time traditions: the designs on the pottery were expressing relationships and communicating social messages that archaeology should be pursuing, I felt.

I realized that in order to talk about the Mimbres designs and styles with a cultural connection to the humans who conceived of them, produced them, and perceived them, we would have to begin with a wider debate on style in general. And so we abandoned the idea of a conference on Mimbres culture and ceramics, and turned to the underlying issue of style itself, though it is a very broad intellectual vista.

The number of scholars interested in the subject was increasing each year, yet there were only a few archaeologists who had expressed the major views on this subject in the archaeological literature. We invited seven archaeologists to come to Minnesota, present a paper, and join a round-table discussion on the uses of style in archaeology. Six agreed to attend, despite the fact that the proposed date was in the heart of winter in Minnesota! The six speakers were Margaret Conkey, Timothy Earle, Ian Hodder, Stephen Plog, James Sackett, and Martin Wobst. In addition, University of Minnesota colleagues Sheila McNally, an art historian, and Guy Gibbon, an archaeologist, each commented on three of the papers. To tie the conference on style to the exhibit we invited a keynote speaker on the pottery itself. James Brody of the

Maxwell Museum at the University of New Mexico came to speak on the pottery. The auxiliary exhibits were completed by Barbara Lass Withrow, and were on display in conjunction with the nationally traveling Mimbres pottery exhibit.

The conference was funded by the University of Minnesota including monies from the Vice-President for Academic Affairs, the College of Liberal Arts Committee for Conferences, the Center for Ancient Studies, and the University Arts Museum in addition to special departmental funds in honor of Dennis Puleston. In addition to thanking them for their support, I would also like to thank all who helped, especially Elden Johnson, Joan Carothers, Christy Caine, Lyndel King, Susan Brown, and Barb Withrow.

As the conference commenced, the enthusiasm of the participants, the amount of heated debate and critical issues raised, as well as the opportunity to have so many interested parties together in one place convinced me to take the time to bring these papers together in a volume on the uses of style in archaeology. Having moved quite far afield from my own current research, I asked Margaret Conkey to join me in editing the volume to help gain a more complete and sophisticated range of contemporary viewpoints on style. All but one of the invited speakers have contributed revised papers to this volume. We solicited several other chapters, from Whitney Davis, Warren R. DeBoer, and William K. Macdonald, that fill out the volume by providing additional views and approaches to the uses of style in archaeology. In addition, we have written an introduction to the volume that is a brief overview on the subject of style in archaeology. The final chapter in the volume is a commentary by Polly Wiessner, who discusses her own views on the uses of style based on her work and in light of the volume's contributions.

This volume is not a compendium of all perspectives, approaches, or debates on the uses of style in archaeology; it is merely a first attempt to face directly such an amorphous but fundamental aspect of archaeology: style is in all things, yet it is almost undefinable. The fact that the discipline is willing to address this very complex and multifaceted thorn in interpretation makes the subject and these papers timely and important. As we become more conscious of the issues debated in this volume, and can incorporate, criticize, and build on them, we should be moving closer to more full cultural interpretations of all cultural artifacts, including Mimbres pottery.

Christine A. Hastorf
1989

ACKNOWLEDGMENTS

The editors would like to thank the authors for their patience, the Cambridge University Press for its encouragement, and the many individuals who made the volume possible. In particular, our acknowledgments go to the Center for Advanced Study in the Behavioral Sciences for its support (BNS 84–11738) of Christine Hastorf during 1986–87 and to the following staff and students at the University of California, Berkeley for their extensive editorial and clerical work on the manuscript and for compiling the composite 'References cited' section: Marcia-Anne Dobres, Eric Kettner, and Avis Worthington. Finally, thanks go to Ian Bapty for compiling the index.

Chapter 1

Introduction

Margaret W. Conkey and
Christine A. Hastorf

Why a volume on style in archaeology?

This volume addresses the use of style in archaeological inquiry. What we think of as style is pervasive in human society, no matter how we may define it. And style is involved in all archaeological analysis, whether it is covertly or overtly discussed. It is style that creates and defines artifact types, culture types and even types of evolutionary trajectories. Style is at work and can be studied at the level of the individual, a group, or a society. Style is rooted in both time and space. Style is opinionated: an object or event can have good style, bad style, old style, new style, or can even be a combination of styles. Style is not separate from the social contexts that give the cultural materials in question their social values. It is no wonder that style has been referred to as elusive, controversial, and the proverbial "black box." It is no wonder that many debates in the archaeological literature are over the use of style in analysis, in interpretation, and in legitimation of specific archaeological viewpoints. For all of these reasons, the study of style and its place in research and interpretation in archaeology is central and determining.

As recently as twenty years ago, Hans Georg Gadamer, "one of the founding fathers of modern hermeneutics, could still write without hesitation: ' the notion of style is one of the undiscussed self-evident concepts upon which our historical consciousness is based'" (Gadamer 1965: 466, as cited by Sauerländer 1983: 253). Given the scholarly "earthquakes"

that have affected archaeology since then, this statement of Gadamer's is now open to question. But to dismantle the concept of style itself is a major historical and epistemological endeavor. Although there are several explicitly historical essays in this volume (e.g., chapter 2, by Conkey and chapter 4, by Sackett), and although all of the essays have epistemological implications, the in-depth and comprehensive historical and epistemological essays on the uses of style in archaeology remain to be written. To write such essays, we must at least return to our roots in the culture-history "paradigm," where style was so inherent in archaeological interpretation; in some ways, we are still there, in this volume.

What we have tried to do here is to present chapters with differing perspectives on style in archaeology, particularly in the context of how a concept of style may be *used* in archaeological analysis and interpretation. This volume presents views of the mid-1980s; style here is not reducible to an "undiscussed, self-evident concept" or to a set of agreed-upon attributes or topics. Rather, style is now taken as "a highly conditioned and ambivalent hermeneutical 'construct' worked out at a distinct moment in social and intellectual history" (Sauerländer 1983: 254).

Our closest intellectual neighbor in the use of style for the analysis of cultural materials has been art history (Schapiro 1953). As in art history (Sauerländer 1983), archaeology has used style as a mirror, if not also as a key, in order to make all the cultural materials of the past accessible to us. Stylistic types (as defined by Krieger 1944) created the time–space divisions of the past and the archaeological "cultures." By our style types and definitions, we create the past. Some of the effects of this have been the detachment of the types from their past; and, in addition, the past has become our own creation. As in art history, archaeologists have used style in a way that detaches from these cultural materials "what may have been their original message and function . . . reducing them to patterns, samples . . ."(Sauerländer 1983: 254). Yet our style types and definitions have provided us with a link to the past, and have yielded new insights into it.

What this volume shows is that these uses of style in archaeology (as in art history) have neither gone away *nor* gone unquestioned. Rather, these approaches as well as the outcomes are being contested and provide the basis for substantive debate about the concepts and uses of style in archaeology.

Despite the necessity of style in archaeological research, archaeologists remain frustrated in their pursuit of the role and use of style. Style, like ideology, remains elusive, implicit, and ambiguous. Stylistic inferences in archaeology are, to many, unsettlingly underdetermined. Without a unified theory of style and its methodological program, and without any real possibility of one in the future, why do we have a volume on the uses of style in archaeology?

Style is *unavoidable* in all archaeological interpretation, from the style of the analyst or from the style in which artifacts were made, to the style of the prehistoric cultural materials, even to the style of our narrative accounts about the past. Style is pervasive and unavoidable because there is nothing to discuss or be interpreted without assigning or inferring style. Without style we have little or nothing to say. In some ways, it is this diverse and thorny issue of style as both subject and object that has generated this volume, as it generates archaeology.

Can there be a unified concept of style?
In an early and classic article on style for anthropologists, Schapiro (1953: 288) suggested three dimensions of style:
  (1) form elements, motifs;
  (2) form relationships;
  (3) qualities.

Of these three dimensions, only the first relates directly to the physical, material world. The other two dimensions derive from and produce context and cultural meaning through use. It is through action and reaction that these cultural qualities, the elements, forms, and form relationships, are culturally mediated; without these cultural qualities, the elements or forms do not exist.

The very processes of cultural transmission are through "the style of things," through social actions (e.g., a way of farming), through the recognition and use of materials (e.g., a stone hoe). As that hoe may be found in different archaeological contexts (in a burial, or in fields), the hoe provides the archaeologist with different cultural meanings.

Style is always grounded in some cultural context or frame of reference. From this, it should not be surprising that style is diverse, multivalent and elusive, especially when in another context.

The diverse uses of style in archaeology remain unsatisfying and only partial because, in part, archaeologists have preferred a materialist approach. Objects and materials from past activities are the focus of our interpretation; the elements, shapes, and distributions have been taken as style, as culture. But this approach alone is not sufficient to understand style and one cannot use the same approach for all questions. Style is also ideas, intentions, and perceptions. Because these are highly variable, polysemic, and ambivalent, there are many possible styles for objects and actions.

Any specific stylistic analysis must therefore outline the styles involved and must provide support for the choices. This area has become the locus of much debate in interpretation. These are the "qualities" of Schapiro's definition. Involving all three of Schapiro's dimensions in an analysis forces the archaeologist beyond material analysis. This is one tension that makes a style hard to define and hard to use.

Most would agree that, at its most delimited and fundamental level, style is some sort of a "formal statement of the particular ways in which different artifacts are similar to each other" (Davis 1986c: 124). This would be a stylistic description which – as Davis goes on to point out – in and of itself says nothing about sources of variation, rates or kinds of change, nor about history, society, meaning, use, or culture. In order to make any further statements about variation, causality, rate, or direction of change, or about any correlations so that style may be used as an archaeological descriptive or as an historical "tool," archaeologists must draw upon a wide range of further assumptions. Any general or inclusive theory of style must include these assumptions and any archaeological *use* of style necessarily goes beyond the formal statement and invokes various further assumptions that may or may not be made explicit by the analyst. If only because the range of these assumptions can be so great, and if only because the use of stylistic descriptions in the service of these assumptions can be so ampliative, it is hard to imagine how there could be any single, general, comprehensive theory of style.

In his critique of the emergence of a "symbolic anthropology," Spiro (1969) made a point that may be applicable to any attempts to formulate an inclusive theory of style for archaeologists. As he saw how widely and, to him, how loosely the term "symbolic" was being used, and how so many events, behaviors, or objects were being considered "symbolic," Spiro suggested that this "new" symbolic anthropology was little more than a revitalization movement for cultural anthropology, and that symbolism was being used so inclusively that it was not much different from "culture." Any general theory of style that is so inclusive as to cover the range of assumptions noted above (and perhaps more) may also be not much different from a general notion of culture.

We have come to think that if only a single, unified

theory of style could be agreed upon, with a specific set of stages and procedures for analysis and interpretation, then we could answer most archaeological questions more easily and with much agreement. But there is not nor will there be *a* theory or method to "capture" style. We should not concern ourselves with trying to define *a* concept of style or with specifying *one* way to do stylistic analysis.

The use of style must remain flexible *and* problematical. It will also remain ambiguous and underdetermined. Archaeologists will have to accept both ambiguity and the relatively underdetermined nature of our archaeological inferences.

To abandon the hope for a unified theory of style does not necessarily deny that there can be a conceptual and analytical unity to the *use* of style in archaeology. In the concluding chapter of this volume, Wiessner suggests that many of the ways in which she and others have been "defining" and using style are not disparate but complementary. She suggests that there are some fundamental features of style that *we can agree on* and that could structure our use of style in analysis and interpretation.

However, these features may only be applicable in certain contexts and with certain kinds of archaeological materials, and Wiessner herself gives these features much more universality than we would. She does not, however, propose her views as a unified general theory of style that can transcend context and analyst; rather she proposes a consensual base of understanding that, we would argue, must be situational or contextual to be efficacious.

On the uses of style in archaeology

Perhaps most of the tension in the archaeological uses of style derives from the very nature of what archaeological research is all about. By definition, we are analysts, and we are trying to "make sense" out of cultural materials and cultural representations that are no longer enmeshed in their former context. As analysts, we use style as a "tool" to help us make sense out of the materials and out of the past. Often, style can be used in a passive way to serve as a mirror that reflects to us certain ideas or characteristics about the past.

But while there is this analytical, "outsider's" view, where style in material objects is used *by us* to write prehistory, there is also the perspective that there were active human beings who thought up, made, used, re-used and often discarded that which we have as archaeological materials. For these past human actors, there were styles of making, of using, of knowing, and ever-changing contexts that these styles derived from and defined. As archaeologists, we often claim that we want to "get at" these active uses of style by prehistoric peoples, yet in the process of trying to access these, we all too easily slide into the "outsider's" role, where style becomes *our* analytical tool. Some archaeologists have taken an explicit stand on this, preferring, for example, to use style in archaeological research only as an analytical tool that tells us

about such things as society or ethnicity in the past (see Sackett, chapter 4, this volume).

The most problematic way in which this tension is manifest is when archaeologists unwittingly slip back and forth between these two postures: from seeking clues as to the meanings of and contexts in which the styles of cultural materials were "at work" in that culture, to the manipulation of attributes or patterns in these materials as measures of certain cultural phenomena that we want the styles to "reveal" to us. There is no way to eliminate the analytical, "outsider's" posture, but the tension between what the materials were about in the past and what we have made them out to be in the present can be mediated somewhat by a more self-aware perspective on our archaeological practice (e.g., Shanks and Tilley 1987).

This slippage between the two "faces" of style as it is used in archaeology is certainly a source of tension but it is also a source of dynamism. There is no doubt that the two perspectives on what style is (a tool to us; a potential source of meaning to prehistoric peoples) are part of, are embedded in, and define wider debates and tensions in archaeological theory and method. The cultural materials are simultaneously artifacts/tools and texts (Derrida 1974).

Some historical observations

There has been a sequence of alternative perspectives on what style is about and what, therefore, it can tell us about the past. Although many of these perspectives are reviewed in more detail in chapter 2, by Conkey (as well as in less detail in other chapters), a brief review here will serve as a reminder that there has been a diversity in the uses of style, even when archaeologists have agreed, for example, that style is formal variation, or that style is communication. There are many ways we could categorize the predominant views on style of the last two decades; this diversity is striking in contrast to the agreed-upon use of style by the culture historians prior to the 1960s.

To culture historians (e.g., Krieger 1944) style was in the service of chronology and the typologies that were developed were explicitly time-sensitive. Here, as Sauerländer describes it for art history, "stilus" (style) and "chronos" (time) intersect. Certainly Gadamer's observation – on style as a self-evident concept upon which historical consciousness is based – applies to the archaeological practice of the culture-historical "school." And yet we are still working with the results created by this approach, despite all the impact of successive waves of theoretical "earthquakes" since the 1960s.

We still depend upon the products of the culture-history approach and its concept and use of style. Foremost among these products are the divisions of the past into named spatial and temporal units, the definitions of archaeological "cultures," and above all, what follows from these, namely, the very unquestioned periodizations (e.g., the Neolithic) that are based on and thus privilege certain tools, technologies, "styles" of ceramics or of other materials.

Any overview of alternative uses of style since the mid-1960s, with the advent of the New Archaeology, would certainly include the following: there were those uses that saw style as a "measure" in the service of defining bounded spatial and temporal distributions; style was an analytical tool of the archaeologist (e.g., Whallon 1968). At first, it was an analytical tool that could be used explicitly to locate social units and to chart changes in those units (e.g., Deetz 1965). Then came a concern for style as a measure of more specific social processes, especially social interaction and social exchange (see Plog 1978 for a review).

Style has always been seen as formal variation but there is debate as to what that formal variation refers to or derives from. In the mid-1970s, style was both formal variation and communication; it was about information exchange and about the establishment and maintenance of social boundaries (Wobst 1977). There was debate over the relation between style and function, and style came to take on communication as one of its functions. There was also the idea that style was no longer the residual that "we" could find once we had identified the function of an object (Wobst 1977; Sackett 1982). This had been the view promoted by the partitive approach of the New Archaeology, especially as charted out by Binford (1965) and as guided by the hope that we could "isolate" relevant variables.

With the 1970s development of the notion that style had a function, and that style could be thought of as formal variation that referred to processes of information exchange, there was more possibility for understanding the active aspect of style. Although early attempts at using style in this way produced quite functionalist interpretations, where style was assumed to be "adaptive" (e.g., Conkey 1978a), further analyses have suggested how, in some cases, a materialist view on the uses of style *in* past societies – as a means for political manipulation, for example – can be put to work (see Earle, chapter 8, this volume).

And, despite the strong proclamations against a normativist conception of archaeological materials that were launched in the 1960s (e.g., Binford 1965), it is perhaps not surprising that "style as a way of doing" has recently re-surfaced (see Wiessner, chapter 10, this volume). But this view on style is more complex than a passive normativism; a close reading of Hodder (chapter 5, this volume) and Wiessner (chapter 10, this volume) illustrates how two analyses, starting from some similar fundamental assumptions – style as a way of doing – reach very different, if not incompatible, concepts of style. Wiessner's view retains some functionalism – style as social communication. Hodder's view retains some passive aspects – style involves the relational referral of an individual event to a general way of doing. Style as more than a way of doing is a view that holds style and material culture to be part of the means by which humans make sense of their world and with which cultural meanings are always in production.

On the chapters in this volume

There are nine chapters here that cover a range of theoretical positions and methodological approaches to the uses of style in archaeology. Although there are two possible sections to the volume, we have chosen not to make an organizational division. The first chapters are obviously more theoretical and historical in scope and intent; the later chapters are obviously more about specific attempts to use style with specific archaeological or ethnoarchaeological materials. The final chapter by Polly Wiessner was designed as an overview paper, and she does draw upon most of the chapters in the volume, especially the latter group, but in doing so, she uses them to present her own views and to make a case for a consensual and unified approach to style.

This volume on style does not take a particular stand or present a set of papers that will reinforce any particular programmatic for the uses of style in archaeology. It is not intended as a manifesto. The conference that provided the basis for the volume (see the Preface) was intended to survey the field, and to take in a fuller spectrum. Because there is no one way to view an artifact, a site, or a human culture, issues of style will remain fundamental in all archaeological research. As in all of archaeology, with more styles of archaeological research, there will be more uses of style in archaeology.

Chapter 2

Experimenting with style in archaeology: some historical and theoretical issues

Margaret W. Conkey

In the introduction to this chapter, the author points out that, after many years of critical thinking, archaeologists still continue to debate what style is and what its use may be in cultural interpretation. Towards this end, the chapter outlines the last century of American archaeology. In the historical outline, the author highlights the major issues that have prompted so much debate. She then turns to some analytical implications of these theoretical orientations. Through her analysis of the use of style in archaeology and in related disciplines, Conkey provides the reader with a presentation of how philosophers, art historians, critical theorists, ethnographers, and archaeologists have grappled with the study of material culture. Ultimately, the issue revolves around the concept of culture and the place of materials and material culture in the anthropological study of human culture.

Introduction

More than ever, archaeologists are grappling with the concept, the theory, and the uses of style in archaeological analysis and interpretation. This is not only healthy but provocative. This chapter is an attempt to probe the underside of the archaeological study of style by assessing our intellectual history of the past two decades, and by exploring some emergent theoretical issues relevant to the use of style in archaeology. Thus, in favor of intellectual history and theoretical issues, this chapter will *not* address measures of style, nor provide an analysis of style or predictive models of style, which can be found elsewhere in this volume.

Archaeologists have always been concerned with

identifying and interpreting similarities, differences, homogeneity, and heterogeneity among the artifacts and cultural products of the human past. According to Dunnell's account of the past fifty years of American archaeology (1986; see also 1982), it was during the culture-history phase – which has predominated throughout the twentieth century, up until the late 1960s – that the archaeological record itself came to be described primarily in terms of styles. The kind of style that was being employed was one that aimed to find homologous similarities. These similarities, and the resultant definition of "types," were in the service of chronologies, which were the agreed-upon goal of culture-historical archaeology. "No effort was made to explain why stylistic types displayed the distributions in time and space that proved so useful. That they did was enough" (Dunnell 1986: 32).

The use of style became a more explicit and discussed method of archaeological inquiry with the methodological program of the New Archaeology in the 1960s.[1] The definition of styles was no longer confined to the identification of "types," and new kinds of stylistic analysis have become prominent and privileged endeavors in the archaeological research of the past two decades. There are at least two general reasons for the elevation of certain kinds of stylistic studies.

First, if one accepts Dunnell's characterization (1986) of the New Archaeology as having shifted the search from homologous similarities to analogous similarities, then one could make the case that new conceptions and uses of style were not only necessary but perhaps central to the new task of making analogical inferences. These inferences, it was hoped, would (to paraphrase Flannery 1967) reveal the adaptive cultural system – rather than the Indian or the cultural norms – behind the artifact. Secondly, the early and very compelling first case studies in New Archaeology (e.g., Deetz 1965; Hill 1966, 1970; Longacre 1963) all employed a concept of style and an explicitly stylistic analysis as the central method to render analogous inferences about prehistoric social life.

Since then, a variety of explicit conceptual frameworks for the study of style have been proposed and tried out. In retrospect, these varying approaches since the 1960s (e.g., Conkey 1978a; Sackett 1982; Wiessner 1983, 1984; Wobst 1977) seem to have been presented to us as contrastive or as replacements for previous approaches. We seem to have tried one, then another alternative approach, suggesting each time how the current view supersedes the earlier approach and corrects for what appear to have been its weaknesses. To a great extent, this has promoted an either/or perspective on stylistic analysis: one should adopt either one approach or another, often regardless of context or data.

Thus, it is not surprising that there appears to be a typology for the study of style. Each new perspective is identified with its own tenets and advantages, and is presented after a review of preceding approaches. For example, the debut of the "isochrestic" approach (Sackett 1982) is accomplished following an intellectual history that charts each of its conceptual ancestors. As with many typologies, we have named the differing approaches with labels that are not immediately understood, such as "iconological" or "isochrestic."

There may be another reason why the recent history of the study of style appears to be typological. There is little doubt that archaeologists have always thought style to be a grand concept, one that has explanatory value in and of itself; and yet it is also "elusive" (DeBoer and Moore 1982: 147). As archaeologists we have tried to grasp the concept of style in a way that we know best from all of our archaeological work – by typing it and by classifying it. Although we often refer to the various conceptual frameworks as different dimensions or different approaches, we have tended to treat them as mutually exclusive. There are at least two immediate problems that result from this.

First, the studies and assumptions that one of us might consider under a given approach – e.g., the iconological – are not necessarily the same as those that someone else might include. As a result, we may not be working with a common vocabulary nor with a set of shared understandings, which makes communication and, above all, evaluation difficult. Second, because the literature has presented various approaches as named "types" of stylistic analysis (e.g., in S. Plog 1980), students all too often take these types as givens and as starting points for sorting out how to do stylistic analysis, rather than going back to original papers and studies, looking

for continuities, and deciding for themselves what is involved in various approaches and perspectives. Often these approaches are individualized and associated with specific researchers or proponents, which has led in some instances to critiques that are more *ad hominem* than substantive (e.g., Binford 1986; Sackett 1986a).

These aspects of the study of style have structured our perception of its recent history, which appears to be one of contrastive types of stylistic analysis, each one expanding upon, if not replacing, what had been widely held. Although this view of our history – as a linear sequence of approaches to style – may have insulated us, until recently, from serious confrontation with why and how we study style, I would argue that two fundamental and related theoretical challenges are the more important factors in accounting for our current encounters and engagement with style.

The first challenge is that posed by developments in critical and social theory (e.g., Leone, Potter and Shackel 1987; Wylie 1985a), which demand that archaeologists confront not only history and context but also our predominantly naive and simplistic notions about human social formations and groups. This challenge is particularly relevant in the archaeological study of style because if there is any one thing we have had in the back of our minds for the use of stylistic analyses, it has been to find or to reveal social units or specific historical entities.

The second challenge is to become more intensely concerned and knowledgeable about design theory and artifact production systems: that is, what processes bring forms and all material culture – from endscrapers to landscapes – into existence in the first place. Although there are many other reasons (some of which will be argued in the concluding sections of this chapter), minimally we need to study design and production processes because at the base of any stylistic analysis lie assumptions about how to provide stylistic descriptions for the materials we study. For example, we may employ formal analysis (e.g., Washburn 1977) or iconographic analysis (e.g., Donnan 1978). An anthropological and archaeological knowledge of production may be one of the few ways in which we can confirm, on independent grounds, the very "measures" we have assumed to be relevant and valid for providing stylistic descriptions (see Davis, chapter 3, this volume).

These introductory observations are only some outlines of the current state of the study of style. Given these, the discussion to follow has two goals: (1) to provide an historical account of the study of style over the past two decades, which will try to avoid the typological and linear characterization in favor of one that can elucidate continuities and probe the agendas of stylistic analysis; and (2) to outline some conceptual expansions of the past few years that signal that there could be an emergent reconsideration of why and how we use style in archaeological inquiry.

The intent here is not to propose yet another concept of style; rather, it is to rethink how we have used style and what we think we are doing in our interpretations of the past. The very word "style" has perhaps been more of a barrier than a facilitator to our understanding of humans and material culture. With the many definitions that we have paraded before ourselves, it is no wonder that style has been considered "elusive," "intractable", "multifaceted," and a veritable "black box." What we have lumped together and labelled as "style" may have these characteristics, but they are not inherent in the label "style," just as style itself is not inherent in artifacts or behavior. The word "style," like the rest of language, works by difference, and we certainly have used the study of style as our *access to difference*. Style, as a term (which itself is derived from a descriptor of writing, "stilus" [see Sauerländer 1983]) – like the rest of language – is not just a medium for description but a medium of social practice (see Hodder, chapter 5, this volume). But the emphasis on the definitions of "style" has led to more concern with what style is or is not at the expense of inquiry into "why style?" and "how style?"

Some cultural factors

Most of the following sections are devoted to tracing the study of style within the context of American anthropological archaeology. But first I would like to inject a few notions drawn from analyses of wider social and intellectual contexts within which anthropology has been situated. These notions *may* have something to do with how the archaeological study of style has emerged as a prominent concern. Historians of western culture have charted the emergence and elaboration of – and now decline, or least reaction to – "modernism," which came in with the social, political, and technological revolutions of the twentieth century (Burgin 1986; Jameson 1984). The rise of Americanist archaeology (Sabloff and Willey 1980) certainly coincides with modernism, and two aspects attributed to modernism seem intriguing and relevant to an inquiry into the history of the use of style in archaeology.

First, it seems that the very idea of style as an entity, and of style as a unique and personal phenomenon that can be linked to a centered subject has been a central feature of modernist thought,[2] and one that has influenced all sorts of cultural practices of the twentieth century: music, architecture, painting, sculpture, literature, etc. This is not the place to elaborate on how this emphasis on "unique style" has been manifest in cultural production (see, e.g., Jameson 1984; Burgin 1986; Williams 1961), but an emphasis on style analysis in all these domains (sculpture, literature, even in archaeology) can be seen as part of the predominant *visualist* ideology of modernism (Ong 1967, 1977). This ideology has emphasized not only that knowledge can be described, compared, classified, and generalized, but also that ways of knowing are visually rooted. For example, when one comes to understand an idea, the usual response is "I *see* what you mean."

Second, the archaeological emphasis on style can also be seen as an example of what Derrida (e.g., 1974) has referred to as "logocentrism," another characteristic feature of modernist

thought. He coined this word, claims Burgin, to refer to "our tendency to refer all questions of meaning of 'representations'" – e.g., novels, films, paintings, even artifacts or archaeological features – "to a singular founding presence which is imagined to be 'behind' them, whether it be 'author', 'reality', 'history', 'zeitgeist', 'structure', or whatever" (Burgin 1986: 32).[3] In stylistic studies, logocentrism is at work when the meaning of an artifact is referred to its "style," when the style of an artifact is referred to its (social) "group."

These ways of thinking (visualist, logocentric) should be investigated not merely out of historical interest, but because they still affect the way we talk and think; they are endemic throughout western history (Burgin 1986; Gombrich 1972). Since this kind of thinking underlies the archaeological study of artifacts and other cultural productions, it is no wonder that archaeological practitioners have themselves often mused about the reification of style, how it may be an instance of Whitehead's "fallacy of misplaced concreteness" (Sackett: personal communication) or, more strongly, as Davis notes (chapter 3, this volume: 23): "without style we have nothing to talk about, no problem to solve."[4]

One historical path

The history of inquiry into style is historical.[5] What the earlier studies did should be viewed in their own context, only some of which I can account for here. When we find the approaches pursued one or more decades ago to be inadequate or underdetermined, this is because we are now neither asking the same questions nor conceiving of the archaeological record in the same way. The alternatives drawn upon by previous workers to account for their materials and styles, those that they ruled out, and those that they felt they could support are different from the alternatives we now work with (David P. Braun: personal communication). Thus, this account is not intended to dismiss past uses of style because we have developed "better" ones; we are developing different ones, drawing upon different conceptions of the record, considering different alternatives, and for different intellectual and sociopolitical purposes.

One intellectual thread running through this historical account of the uses of style in archaeology involves the idea that the analysis of pattern(s) came to be a central concern of archaeology. One simplistic view of the post-evolutionary twentieth-century anthropology – in which the archaeological study of style has been situated – suggests that archaeological research and social anthropology diverged from each other in several ways. An early divergence is placed with the well-known reaction against early evolutionism and the peripheralization of objects and material culture within ethnography and social anthropology. A second divergence comes in the 1960s when the "New Archaeology" leans towards Leslie White's evolutionary and systematic view (White 1959) on culture and artifacts in human life (see Keesing 1974 for a general review of this and other views on culture). Although I will take quite a few paragraphs to develop the historical implications, one result has been the primacy of pattern-recognition and the reverence of the (archaeological) object in archaeological research.

Earlier approaches

As Miller (1983) has insightfully suggested (and develops further than I will here), the relationship of twentieth-century anthropology to the culture being studied was to be a direct relationship that was mediated through language – ethnographic fieldwork, informant interviews, etc. – and not through objects. Miller suggests that cultural objects – masks, spears, bows-and-arrows – *had* been a central vehicle through which the nineteenth-century evolutionists (e.g., Tylor 1865) encountered and classified the non-western world. These objects could "stand for" certain groups, certain cultural roles, and certain stages of cultural development. Even though the objects in anthropology began by "standing for" or being symbolic of the peoples we wanted to study, objects – and the study of material culture – were, as Miller (1983) suggests, peripheralized in the twentieth-century ethnographic endeavor.

In archaeology, the peoples we wanted to study – such as the Hohokam, the Maya, the Aurignacians – became *labels* for artifacts that, in turn, have monopolized our attention. The objects-as-artifacts, and the patterns among and between them, became the immediate subjects of our inquiry. The artifacts became the objects of our scientific inquiry *and* the objects of our knowledge (which are not always isomorphic [Tagg 1985]).

This conflation of the objects of inquiry with objects of knowledge is particularly apparent when, on the one hand, the artifact styles or assemblages were equated with social/historical entities (e.g., the "red-on-buff culture" [Gladwin and Gladwin 1935]), or, on the other hand, the artifact takes on an autonomous role to the point that the spread or change in artifacts alone appears to cause cultural changes. Such is the case in the anthropomorphizing of artifacts, which have been portrayed as capable of breeding and diffusing on their own (see Gruber 1986; Sackett 1983).

Burgin (1986), among others, suggests deep roots for the writing of art history as a history of objects, which can be extended to archaeology: ever since the commodity connoisseurship of the Renaissance the idea of art as object has been a core concept. We have internalized this idea such that, even in prehistoric/archaeological contexts, when we talk about cultural production it is the production of objects, of materials.[6] The practice of culture in the past is both limited to and equated with the production of cultural materials – ceramics, stone tools, and all the things we investigate for style. This practice-as-production was thus defined as an artisanal activity: "a process of crafting [fine] objects in a given medium" (Burgin 1986: 39). Thus what we, in turn, produce in our archaeological narratives is a history of objects and a decontextualized notion of artisanal activities: stone tool-making, basketmakers. There are, however, other histories to be written and other views on these cultural practices.

During most of the twentieth century (up until the late 1960s), culture-history has been the dominant sense-making model for archaeology (Dunnell 1982). The archaeological record came to be described primarily in terms of styles, and the definition of artifact types was based on styles (e.g., Krieger 1944). Furthermore, as Dunnell suggests, given the archaeological record described in this way, and given that the kind of style being used was one designed to record homologous similarities, the only process that could explain the record as it had been conceptualized and described are "processes that explained homologous similarities: diffusion, trade, persistence, migration" (Dunnell 1986: 31).

To the culture-historian, style was to be used in the service of chronology. The significance of variation was that it would be a record of change: "it allowed the culture-historians to tell time" (Dunnell 1986: 31). Because artifact style was conceptualized as expressive – expressive of a maker's mind, of a world view, of a historical entity – the use of style by culture-historians was a straightforward attempt to read history from style, to read history from stylistic description, and – as Sauerländer (1983) has suggested – "stilus" and "chronos" intersected. We have come to appreciate, however, that "expression is not the (only) cause of style," even if expression could be easily identified with any well-defined historical entities (Davis, chapter 3, this volume: 24). Style, we have learned, is more than expression (more than time, more than history); but as conceived by most culture-historians, style-as-expressive was seen as the explanation for similarities among artifacts. In this view, style matters simply because it has explanatory value (see Davis, chapter 3, this volume: 23).[7]

From the rootedness of style inquiry in culture-history, and thus in the history of our archaeological practice, it is not surprising to see – despite subsequent reconceptualizations of the archaeological record and of the uses of style in archaeology – the persistence of attempts by archaeologists to try to account for "similarity-relations" that appear to obtain among artifacts and cultural products. As Davis (chapter 3, this volume) points out, we have remained "forever hopeful" that such similarity-relations may be taken as evidence for historical and cultural relatedness of artifacts – and, by extension, of their makers – so that we might read history, if not culture, from style.

Style and the New Archaeology

With the challenges of the "New Archaeology" to culture-history, the archaeological record came to be conceived in new ways; the kinds of style that archaeologists described were more oriented towards the recording of analogous, rather than homologous, similarities (see Dunnell 1982), and thus the *alternatives* being considered that might account for variation in the archaeological record are different from those considered by culture-historians. But as this New Archaeology emerged with a concept of culture-as-adaptive-system as its core guiding concept, a particular view of material culture and artifacts was to accompany the culture concept – a view that would strongly influence the concept and especially the use of style in archaeological inquiry. This view would continue to emphasize the primacy of artifacts and of pattern-recognition as central to the new objective: the explanation of cultural processes (that was to replace the chronicling of culture-history).

There is no doubt that the cultural evolutionary views of Leslie White had a deep influence on the New Archaeology's concept of culture-as-adaptive-system (Binford 1965; Leone 1972). In these systemic views (of White and New Archaeologists), the artifacts made and used by humans were cultural products in the sense of being outputs of cultural and behavioral systems. Although material culture was certainly considered to have been used somehow in the now-extinct cultural systems, the participation or active role of artifacts was not the emphasis of inquiry; rather, material culture was more often thought about as adaptive components of a functioning cultural system.

Archaeological correlates for various cultural subsystems (e.g., technoenvironmental) or processes (e.g., population growth, urbanization) were expected to be identified. From the patterning of archaeological data, the "artisanal activities" – such as stone tool-making or basket-making – could not only be identified, but could be used to make analogical inferences about the functioning of these activities within the wider cultural system. In the vocabulary of the adaptive-systems approach, patterns in archaeological data could be treated as coded information about variability in and the functioning of past cultural systems.

Thus, stylistic – or any other – patternings in artifacts and archaeological materials were conceived of as cultural products that comprise codes for *us* to read. From this, it followed that there was a methodological emphasis on strategies for pattern-*recognition*, because the patterns are said to inform us about style, its spatiotemporal contexts, and its role in the cultural system. By implication, style is taken to be an inherent property of (certain) archaeological materials to be "discovered" by us. Sackett, for example, has been quite explicit about this: style is a passive aspect of material culture that *speaks to us* about such things as social groupings or ethnic geography. He has advocated viewing style from the "outside," as an analyst; he once stressed that his goal was to identify style rather than to explain it (Sackett 1977: 372; see also chapter 4, this volume).

The logic that has allowed us to accept the idea that artifact patterns are readable and can speak to us about the past in ways that culture-historians never thought possible involves at least three implicit assumptions. First, it has been assumed that variation in artifacts, including stylistic variation, can be considered *as if* it were a language; recall Miller's suggestion (1983) that language had become the acceptable anthropological medium for elucidating the "other." That is, patterning as language is a patterning that can be read, as if it were a language to be decoded or a text to be translated. Second, material culture traits are treated as products of extinct cultural systems more than as active participants produced and used by different human actors. As products of specific,

potentially identifiable cultural subsystems, artifacts are thus material correlates; as such, they *reflect* various sociocultural phenomena. If, as was postulated, artifact style is referable to the "social context of manufacture and use" of an item (Binford 1965: 208), once artifacts are characterized in terms of their stylistic patterns these patterns can be said to reflect certain sociocultural phenomena (such as ethnic groups or post-marital residence patterns) or certain stages in the evolution of cultural systems (such as craft-specialization or tribalization). Although, as will be discussed below, we have moved into new conceptual terrain from that of the New Archaeology, it is relevant here to discuss in more detail the analytical and interpretive implications of the approaches developed during the productive years of the New Archaeology.

Some analytical implications

One of the primary proposals of the New Archaeology to counter the skepticism and antiquarianism they perceived traditional archaeology to be (Wylie 1981) was the theoretical proposal that cultural phenomena must be understood in materialist (not mentalist) terms. And one of the unifying aspects of the New Archaeology was its insistence upon a testing program (a hypothetico-deductive strategy) that invited methodological elaborations in order to make compelling linking arguments between hypothetical statements about the past and the data that could inform on the past.

As is well known, what accompanied this methodological emphasis was a shift in the concept of culture to the adaptive-systems approach. The *analytical consequence* of this view was the notion that there were behavioral and thus material (i.e. archaeological) correlates to the different subsystems. As early as 1965, archaeologists were advised to "partition our observational fields" (Binford 1965: 207) in order to gain access to the different axes of variation in the archaeological record and, by extension, of the past cultural systems.

The Binfordian programmatics of the early 1960s (e.g. Binford 1962, 1965) set a certain polemic tone and an advocacy style (Salmon 1982) for archaeological research. The directives called for eradicating one approach (normativist), and replacing it with another specific approach (the systemic). At the operational level – i.e., how to analyze the archaeological record – the directives were that we search for what Binford called "formal variability" (more properly, formal variation).[8] Despite the attempt to eradicate normativism in archaeological analysis – e.g., the assumption that people held certain shared ideas about how to make and use artifacts – the call for the study of formal variation paradoxically advocated and stimulated the archaeological study of style – which had been a centerpiece of traditional archaeology – in the New Archaeology.

However, as Wobst (1977) points out, it was only *residual* formal variation that was stylistic: "formal variability that relates to the social contexts of manufacture and use *other than* that related to function" (Binford 1965: 208, emphasis added). Despite Wobst's pertinent critique (1977) of this residual concept of style, he (and others, including myself [Conkey 1978a]) retained the phrase and the object of study – "formal variation." Thus Wobst's 1977 concept of style was stated to be "that formal variability that is related to the participation of artifacts in the processes of information exchange" (Wobst 1977: 321).

These concepts of style are characterized by considering formal variation *as if* it were equivalent to style.[9] This was an appealing methodological way to deal with the complexity, "elusiveness" and mentalist (normative) aspects of style. With the benefit of hindsight, it is easy to see what we missed by conceptualizing and using style and formal variation as equivalents, *as if* formal variation were style. For example, this tends to bypass the inquiry into the production processes that brought the formal variation into existence in the first place. Pattern-recognition studies were favored over those of pattern-generation. And, concomitant with this emphasis on patterns in the archaeological record as the immediate subjects of analysis, we too easily overlooked the contexts within which the variation arose, how the artifacts in question were used, and that they were part of the production of meaning to prehistoric peoples just as much as being a part of the way *we* produce meanings about the past. Although analogous similarities were sought through the study of style, the study of formal variation provided primarily *de*contextualized analogues for particular – especially social – aspects of human behavior.

Analytical priority, then, was given to the search for formal variation, and certain attributes of formal variation (e.g., non-functional ones such as painted designs on ceramics) became archaeological correlates of past behavior (e.g., stylistic behaviors operant in the social subsystems of artifact manufacture and use). What promoted this analytical priority of "formal variability"? Certainly the archaeological uses of style were embedded in the systematic concept of culture which, analytically, was subject to a methodological dissection into subsystems, each with its own archaeological correlates. Style was separated from function; the technological domain was separated from the social, and from the ideological (see note 8, below).

But above all, formal variation had analytical priority because it was perceived as a way to access social groupings or social units (such as post-marital residence units) that were thought to be reflected by patternings in the archaeological data. Thus we could "know" prehistoric social life, and the limits on interpretation imposed by traditional archaeology could be transcended. Social groups, social boundaries and social interactions were considered knowable and given considerable research priority; stylistic analysis and the use of style was in the service, not of chronologies, as with traditional archaeology, but of this version of social anthropology.

To view style as formal variation reinforced that long-standing belief (see above, page 8) in the production of cultural materials as artisanal activity, and the belief that style

is inherent in materials: if we just "partition our observational fields," that which is stylistic and which will inform on social contexts can be "discovered." We could do more than read a history of objects from style; we could read "group" from style. Style was necessarily the index or symptom of a social entity. These notions were part of an extremely optimistic and productive period of archaeological research.

Style, function, and communication
One of Binford's concerns (e.g., 1965) about normativism as an account for human behavior was its very logocentricity (although he did not use this term; see above, page 7). To normativists (as described by Binford 1965), the source of cultural behavior, including stylistic expression, was to be found in a single, undifferentiated source, which was ideas or norms about how to do things (for an original critique of normativism, see Aberle 1960). Although, as will be indicated below, normativism did not "go away," the sources for style in archaeological materials became increasingly more specific and processual aspects of human behavior: social interaction, social communication, social "marking," social comparison.

But certain aspects of normativism are retained, which is not, I would argue, a bad or naughty thing. To the extent that we recognize that style *is* a way of doing things and that there are parameters or limits on the design process, there is a normative component to anyone's concept of style. Certainly normativism took on a more active aspect in the 1970s. It was defined specifically as cultural processes, such as enculturation and acculturation. It also became more complex and less monolithic. For example, we recognized that there could be different *levels* of patternings because the contexts for learning or being exposed to "ways of doing things" could be varied – from the individual or household level to the regional (e.g., S. Plog 1980, 1983; in Flannery 1976; Lechtman 1977; Whallon 1968).

And, more than being enculturation or acculturation, style came to be defined as having a function, and one that was in the domain of cultural information and communication systems. There is an expanded approach to style here, which conceives of style as *more than* formal variation and *more than* a code to be deciphered by archaeologists about social contexts: style, decoration, and stylistic forms are viewed *as* communication, as social marking, as cultural signals at work in certain social contexts.

Style and communication
Yet when these concepts are used in archaeological analysis, it is usually from the perspective of style *as if* it were communication, *as if* it were social marking. This is only a subtle difference – between style *as* communication and style *as if* it were communication – but the latter usage has several important implications. First, the "as if" approach generates a certain kind of analysis in which a questionable literary metaphor is perpetuated. This metaphor promotes a methodological dependence upon "reading" the data and its

patterns and on viewing the materials to be analyzed as "text," as if they were a form of discourse in another language to be decoded. Again the patterns become the object of our inquiry, and the stylistic patterns or "texts" tend to be taken as givens, and with this view comes some sense of absoluteness of (archaeological) interpretation. But texts – and stylistic patterns – are not given, but made:

> The "authors" of the texts we wish to "read" were enabled or constrained through specific social and cultural structures and we – as "readers" – are similarly embedded in our contexts, both enabled and restrained by social structures that include conceptual notions, vocabulary, and language.
>
> (Rowntree 1987: 5; see also La Capra 1983: 19–26)

The stylistic texts we think we are reading are not merely a medium for us to access stylistic and thus social descriptions; they were in the past – as in our present archaeological use of them – a medium of social practice (Giddens 1979: 245). That style could be amenable to a reading – as if communication, as if a text – and that style was also amenable as a measure, an aspect or artifact or tool, embodies the wider intellectual tension in archaeological inquiry between the historical mode (reading/interpreting the past) and the scientific mode (measuring/explaining the data).

This literary metaphor – style *as if* communication – thus encourages and perpetuates both analysis and interpretation that emphasizes style as speaking to us, rather than also encouraging our inquiry into the particular historical contexts of how and why style may have been not just a means whereby social marking may have taken place (as is assumed in the first place), but how and why style *was* social marking in those contexts, and in the particular media, forms, or attributes so observed.

Now there was some leaning in this direction towards context but it was not directed very much towards particular historical contexts except in the most general and evolutionary terms. This "leaning" came in the form of such works as Wobst's (1977) predictions about the kinds of artifacts that would have borne stylistic messaging (e.g., highly visible artifacts that were regularly entered into social contexts), and about the kinds of contexts that any good adaptationist approach would consider: when would it have been adaptive to send stylistic messages about groups, and what form would such messages take? There was a powerful analytical appeal to the use of style as information/communication, particularly with the specified predictors (Wobst 1977).

Despite this replacement of the Binfordian, non-functional, residual concept of style, the conceptual roots in adaptive systems persisted. My own article is a classic example of this approach (Conkey 1978a) and illustrates one of the major concerns with this kind of adaptationist thinking, which is its *post hoc* accommodative nature. We think we ought to see style or marking via material culture and we then look at what possibilities there are in the particular archaeological record at hand. We only have to be moderately clever to find a good, especially evolutionary, "reason" for such marking via style.

The 1970s work on style led to increasingly specified conceptual frameworks and a concomitant set of more specified and interesting alternatives to explore in our attempts to account for patterning in archaeological materials. There were increasingly more explicit statements that we were trying to use style to access social proximity and/or social distance. Above all, the use of style in archaeology has come to center more explicitly on what stylistic studies have always been about: the interest in style *as if* it "reveals" group or entity – ethnic identity, social identity, social units, historical entities.

By trying to break down the social phenomena "behind" style into a range of more specified social processes (e.g., interaction [S. Plog 1978, 1980]; social comparison [Wiessner 1984]; power negotiations [Hodder 1982b]), and spurred on by details available from ethnoarchaeological studies (e.g., DeBoer and Lathrap 1979; Wiessner 1983), recent archaeological work has to confront the problematic notion that we have tried to use the concept and analysis of style as a way to reveal "group" as if it (the social unit) were a continuous, integrated entity, and an entity that changes transformationally and gradually (such as in the process of "tribalization").

On the one hand, this has led to some important critiques as to what inferences are not warranted by the establishment of similarity relations (or lack thereof) among artifacts (e.g., Davis 1986c, and chapter 3, this volume). This concern for why and when style and group do not necessarily intersect (Franklin 1986) has also led to some ethnoarchaeological "tests" of the predictors (after Wobst 1977) for style-bearing artifacts that call such predictors into question (e.g., DeBoer and Moore 1982). With an increasing concern for style as meaning*ful* or meaning-bearing to those who made and used the materials in question, the complexities of the relationships between stylistic messaging and varying social contexts are apparent (see DeBoer, chapter 9, this volume; Macdonald, chapter 6, this volume). To find style as meaning-bearing does not mean that is is necessarily messag*ing*, but, more challengingly, that style in materials – because it is meaningful – has only the *potential* to be received (as messages), as in the case of the projectile points discussed by Wiessner (1983).

On the other hand, the problematics raised by style-as-if-it-revealed-group demand some increased methodological work and, above all, redefinitions of some deep conceptual formations. For example, once it is fully accepted[10] that correlations between stylistic descriptions and any kind of entities (historical, cultural, chronological, or social) cannot in and of themselves reveal the *cause* of the relation nor be taken as evidence for relatedness, the methodological requirement is that such correlations and such social processes assumed to lie behind them (e.g., interaction) must be supported by an *independent* archaeological argument (see Davis, chapter 3, this volume: 20). But even more serious a challenge is the revision of theoretical presuppositions about social theory and archaeological practice.

Emergent conceptual shifts

A critical and self-reflective posture is increasingly manifest in the archaeology of the 1980s (e.g., Hodder 1985; Leone, Potter and Shackel 1987; Wylie 1985a, 1985b; P.J. Watson 1986). Certainly this has roots from well over a decade ago,[11] when Clarke (1973) – in suggesting archaeology's "loss of innocence" – argued that an on-going, self-directed critical consciousness had to happen if we were to really admit theory – cultural theory – into our archaeology. But as Wylie (1985b) has argued, this 1970s loss of innocence was radically incomplete and it is not surprising to find not just the eclecticism and less unified practice of 1980s archaeology, but also what Wylie has identified as a "second crisis" (see also Kohl 1985).

The emphasis on the testing program of the New Archaeology contributed to an overemphasis on epistemological (and methodological) concerns about how we can verify the claims we make about the past, *at the expense of* getting more involved in considering substantive issues about the nature of our archaeological models of the human past (Bray 1985). What is now happening, with this 1980s critical posture, is that "for the first time, questions about the nature and limits of archaeological knowledge are beginning to be raised as truly open and problematic and not as ground-clearing preliminaries to the assertion of authoritative solutions" (Wylie 1985b: 3). This same general idea is put more metaphorically by Kohl: the critical process of self-examination by contemporary Anglo-American archaeology involves the casting-off of "the heavy positivist armor which protected the soft theoretical underside of the New Archaeology" (1985: 105).

Here is where I think the contemporary concerns with style fit in, with this direction in which we are more critically self-conscious about what we are doing, are more aware of the unexamined presuppositions that we bring to our research and theorizing, and are less concerned with either formulation of or following assertive, programmatic statements. Rather, to paraphrase Wylie as cited above, we are beginning to raise questions about the nature and limits of archaeological knowledge about style and social group, which is seen as problematic, ambiguous, and underdetermined.

Of direct relevance to concepts and uses of style in archaeology would be a serious examination of our assumptions not just about social groups but about human culture. What if we question the assumption that groups are continuous integrated bounded entities that can be stopped in their time-space tracks as traditional ethnography has led us to believe? (For a critique, see, e.g., Fabian 1983.) What if we question the assumption that social groups in the past changed transformationally and gradually, as the pervasive kind of evolutionary theory has led us to believe: that there was tribalization or complexification of a "progressive" sort? (See, e.g., Dunnell 1980 for a critique.)

At a minimum, we should recognize the weight of our own particular historically contingent world view that has emphasized social and cultural boundaries. Even those stylistic studies that work with inferences about social interaction, as a process, are dependent upon the demonstration (or hypothesized existence) of social boundaries:

> . . . if we interpret stylistic similarity as indicating social interaction among the producers of artifacts, then we must simultaneously interpret it as *also* indicating a "social boundary" – for where similarity decreases, by hypothesis we are seeing less social interaction, and at the extreme, a social boundary between producers.
>
> (Davis 1986c: 124)

At a very fundamental level, questioning these taken-for-granted notions about the inherent boundedness of groups or the inevitable transformations of social units through time should lead to a radical change not just in the way we conceptualize culture but in how we practice cultural description or representation. The recursive implications of such conceptual reorientations would alter two fundamental components of archaeological practice: (1) what material culture and artifacts were all about; and (2) how we use stylistic studies of them.

A reconceptualization of culture would challenge the notion of culture as an adaptive system with material culture as its output, as its products to be decoded. One quite radical view (see, e.g., Clifford 1986) proposes that "culture" must first be deleted from the list of entities, of "things," of "its"; it (*sic*) is not an object to be described or an entity to be revealed by our analyses. In this critique, there is no fundamental difference between the cultural descriptions of the normativists/ traditionalists and those cultural systems of the new archaeologists. Instead of being conceived of as object or entity, culture, if there is such a thing at all, can be conceived of as a constitutive process, "a series of productive and individual acts aimed at the construction of meaning" (Dougherty and Fernandez 1981: 415). Culture, Drummond has suggested, is always "in production"; "stated radically, cultures do not exist, but are always in the process of formation" (Drummond 1981: 638). Taking this further, Clifford (1986: 19) argues that culture is not even a unified corpus of symbols that can be definitively interpreted. Culture, he proposes, is "contested," "temporal," and "emergent."

The implications of such views are at least twofold. On the one hand, given these notions, culture and our view of "it" are produced historically,[12] and are actively contested. Thus there is a strong role for critical and self-reflexive questioning in archaeological inquiry; this should not be a critical thinking that is merely ground-clearing for "getting on" with normal archaeological inquiry, but an integral and continuous part of inquiry itself. On the other hand, as extensions or consequences of such reconceptualizations of "culture" are reconceptualizations of the social "groups" that we think comprise cultures: they too, are in production, produced historically, are contested and emergent. What does this mean for the archaeological study of style and material culture?

Most simplistically, this challenges the notion of material culture as a product, as an output that reflects social entities at any or all levels. Material culture is itself an active constitutive element of social practice (see, e.g., Csikszentmihalyi and Rochberg-Halton 1981; Hebdige 1979; Wolff 1981) and style is more about context than about group (as DeBoer, in chapter 10 in this volume, illustrates so well). What we can learn about from the study of style is the contexts in which groups, or other sociocultural phenomena, are brought into existence. What style can "reveal" (if this is admissible any more) is the mobilization of group as process (James Moore: personal communication), but it also means that we are not limited to "group" in the study of style.

One well-known study of style (Wiessner 1983) may be helpful here in grasping how style may be more about context than group and how, in its representation (i.e., a re-presentation, which implies a present*er*), style is also contested, temporal, and emergent. In the ethnoarchaeological study of stylistic variation of the projectile points made by Kalahari San, Wiessner shows how it is difficult to identify stylistic variation that reveals "group" at any level but the most inclusive – that of language groups. One aim of the study was to try an ethnoarchaeological "test" of the common archaeological goal, to identify style (especially in a form of material culture – projectile points – that often occurs in archaeological contexts) that actively communicates ethnic or group identity. In his response to Wiessner's study, Sackett (1985a) suggests that, for the most part, the kind of style she has identified is not really "iconological" in the sense of actively communicating identity. Rather, he suggests that the stylistic variation that she describes is more the passive style that he calls "isochrestic," which results from just doing things/making objects in a certain way. One implication of his discussion is that there is still an either/or approach to understanding style: is it iconological or isochrestic?

What is, however, really interesting about the Wiessner study and the resultant debate is that there *does* appear to be a recognition among the San of stylistic differences at the level of the language groups, and at this level it *is* an us/them kind of recognition. Here it seems to be that what is passive style in certain and most contexts can become active or identity-recognition style in other contexts. This is what is interesting if we are to understand the processes underlying or generating style: how and when it comes into existence, and how it is used. It seems as if the variation in San projectile points has the "unintended consequences" of becoming iconic – or identifying – style in certain contexts of social comparison. And furthermore, in this particular case, these contexts of social comparison may actually have been generated (or at least set off) by Wiessner, the ethnographer, by eliciting the responses of the San to the showing of other projectile points!

Although I can agree with the view that much of what we call style exists as a result of traditional ways of doing things – that there is a normative component to style – this alone, as a definer of style, does not lead us to very interesting or anthropological understandings. Rather, the questions should be along the lines of: why that style? how did it come into

existence? what is "done" with it? by whom and how? Wiessner has shown how the San projectile points vary and how they do not. Sackett has drawn our attention to the source of this variation – traditional ways of doing things. But this does not account for how or why the traditional way came into existence or to what extent it may also be part of the means by which individuals and groups identify or compare themselves.

Questions such as these require not only more explicit (if not more developed) cultural and social theory, but an understanding of design, in its broadest sense. Design is much more than that which is applied to a pot; it is the most essential set of processes that bring form into existence. All artifacts and all cultural production are the result of a series of – or a "pathway" through – mental and manual processes set in and defined by a historical and social framework. In any given prehistoric situation there *are* ways of doing things, but these don't just happen; they are taught, reinforced, modified, if only through the trial and error that is inherent in the design process. That is, even isochrestism is active.

Certain choices are made in the making and using of material culture. One way to characterize painting pots, engraving bones, or making bronze earspools would be as sets of probabilities that certain raw materials, elements, techniques and so forth would be selected and would occur in certain contexts. There are, as Lechtman (1977) has so succinctly argued, "technological styles." And, as Hosler (1986) has demonstrated with her study of the technology and social construction of metallurgy in West Mexico, material culture is a symbolic system whose meaning is communicated through culturally specific aspects, such as shapes, colors, textures, or sounds, which are, in turn, achieved through processing regimes that select and enhance such properties. The probability that certain attributes will be selected and used is not universal but relative to the specific contexts and to past histories of use and manufacture.

As an extension, then, of reconceptualizations of culture-as-production, our notions about cultural representations, objects, and artifacts will shift also. We need to grasp the objects as praxis (after Bourdieu 1977), as productions, as symbolic acts in their own right – not as reflections of such nor as only texts about such praxis or about productions to be "read" by us depending upon how clever we are at pattern-recognition (Faris 1983). Production itself – or, in archaeologically compatible terms, pattern-generation – is a constitutive endeavor:

> One way of reconstructing the initial situation to which the work is somehow a response is by stressing the raw materials, the initial content, which it confronts and which it reworks, transforms, and appropriates.
>
> (Jameson 1984:6)

Artifact production systems have long been an implicit factor behind the identification of style: "style . . . is the result of the common descent of a group of artifacts from an artifact-production system" we can identify in the historical record of the past (Davis, chapter 3, this volume: 26). But, as Davis goes on to note, there has been little work on understanding what an "artifact production system" is and how artifacts "descend" from it. Because style is embedded in and produced by human cultural practice, these artifact production systems or design systems warrant further theoretical, methodological, and analytical attention.

Although recent archaeological inquiry has begun to push at the interpretation of objects that involves symbolic, structural, and institutional components (e.g., Hodder 1982a; Kohl 1985; Leone 1982), another interpretive perspective would include certain historical aspects, such as authorship or detailed knowledge of production systems (e.g., Hosler 1986; Lechtman 1984). These perspectives may be two sides of the same interpretive coin – as in Lechtman's (1984) detailed elucidation of the Andean metal-working processes *as* symbolic economy, *as* ideology – and both are just as central to a full stylistic description and understanding as is formal variation. Knowledge of production systems alone might lead us to see how objects could belong to different styles, despite apparent similarities in formal attributes, or vice versa. As Davis argues (chapter 3, this volume: 21) *independent* archaeological and anthropological knowledge of production may be one of the few ways in which we can access not only a more robust stylistic description but also the "relevant original cultural categories" for the making and using of artifacts (for a discussion of how this approach is being applied in Paleolithic "art," see Conkey 1987).

Needless to say, we are just beginning to explore and develop satisfactory accounts for the making of objects, especially not as objects *per se* but as cultural representations. As Davis shows (chapter 3, this volume: 26 and also 29), there are several different kinds of accounts for artifact production systems, each with its own metaphors and assumptions, such as production-as-language or production-as[-artisanal]-activity. Each of these can be closely aligned with and are implicit in differing concepts of style (e.g., the former with style-as-information; the latter with style-as-isochrestic), but few approaches to style have made explicit their assumptions about artifact production systems or integrated these into a more inclusive concept of style (but see Lechtman 1977; Smith 1978 for some important early developments), as well as drawing from theories of cultural production (but see Leone 1973, 1977).

As discussed above, the archaeological concepts and uses of style have been greatly influenced by the long-standing cultural premises of modernism, including the privileging of commodity- connoisseurship since the Renaissance. Our work has been dominated by the study of cultural products, by the reification of the object and its patterns, by a definition of the production of cultural materials as artisanal activity. And we have produced a history of objects in which technologies (in their widest sense) and production systems have come to be viewed as only a way of mediating between humans and their environments in the evolution of adaptive cultural systems.

But, following Burgin (1986, and all the literature that he draws upon) there is both another history and another view on those practices. Rather than just a history of objects, there is the history of representations. Rather than artisanal activity, there is the view that the production of cultural materials and representations can be seen as "a set of operations performed in a *field of signifying practices*, perhaps centered on a medium but not bounded by it" (Burgin 1986: 39, emphasis added).

It is this "field of signifying practices" that brings us back to the current state of the archaeological study of style, for such a view implies two things. First, this view asks us to consider not merely new conceptualizations about "culture," about "group" and about sociohistorical entities, especially as they relate to stylistic descriptions, but also the productive contexts within which the artifacts we study were, and are today, embedded (see, e.g., Handsman 1987; Leone 1977). By productive contexts we mean not just the production of form, of object, but the ongoing production and negotiation of meaning.

Second, if style is, at least in part, about the production of cultural representations seen as a set of operations performed in a field of signifying practices (see Hodder, chapter 5, this volume) then it should not be surprising to see the (intellectual) diversification of approaches to and uses of style in archaeology. This both entails and is manifested by – to recall Wylie's (1985b) observations – serious inquiry into the nature and limits of archaeological knowledge and the raising of substantive issues about the nature of our archaeological models of the human past.

Some conclusions

This chapter has tried to present some views on the history of the use of style in archaeological inquiry, of style as a concept and method for making inferences not just about artifacts but also about the human past. I have tried to consider what style has been "about" and how it has been used – from the very general twentieth-century premises of modernism, with its concerns for logocentrism, visualist thinking, and style as a unique and founding presence, to the consensus paradigm of culture-history and to the unfolding of New Archaeology and the current eclectic state of 1980s archaeology.

One theme that appears throughout and that is very much integral to the concept and use of style in archaeology has been the primacy and priority of the analysis of patterns of material culture and the almost autonomous nature of the artifact/object. That this theme took form while material culture studies were peripheralized in sociocultural anthropology has reinforced a divergence between archaeology and sociocultural anthropology.

One could perhaps make the case that with a reification of object and the deep roots of an intellectual tradition for the writing of culture (or art) history as a history of objects, the practice of culture (in the past) came to be conceived of as both limited to and equated with the production of materials, of objects.[13] Despite the shift within archaeology away from culture-history to a New Archaeology, this perspective on cultural practice did not go away but was elaborated to a view on cultural practice as the adaptive production of materials for use in functioning cultural systems.

With the culture-history paradigm, style was central but as a basis for artifact types and as a way to tell time. Style was in the service of chronology and it was both the basis for and a means of identifying homologous similarities. With the New Archaeology there was a new conception of the archaeological record, which was to be conceived of in materialist, not mentalist terms. There was the new concept of culture as an adaptive system with material outputs and specific archaeological correlates. There was an entirely new concept of what the archaeologist's enterprise was to be about and the research has been productive and stimulating. The analysis of style was undertaken in the service of identifying – or more properly, making – analogous similarities, drawing upon more rigorous models for reasoning and analysis.

The material record was conceived of as a code to be read by archaeologists, as coded information about variability in and the functioning of past cultural systems. Thus, pattern-recognition as an emphasis was given priority. Formal variation became the definer of style, although style was at first a residual kind of formal variation that later was argued to be a functional component of the cultural systems under scrutiny. This view of style, as if it were communication, led to a view on stylistic patternings as if they were a text to be read. The literary metaphors that have been invoked have led to a view on style that emphasized how it "spoke" to us about the past,[14] at the expense of inquiry into how style itself was emergent, temporal, contested, and manipulated by prehistoric peoples.

Out of the thoughtful critiques of the concepts and uses of style has come a more specified conceptual framework with more specified and interesting alternatives to explore in our attempts to account for patterning in archaeological materials – social interaction, social comparison, social negotiation. Despite (or because of?) these more specified processes, it has been concomitantly more explicit that we have been using style to access social phenomena, if not aspects of social "group" or social entity. And, as I tried to argue, it is the problematics raised by style-as-if-it-revealed-group, in the context of a 1980s critical and more self-reflexive archaeology, that has contributed to an important eclecticism and open questioning in style studies.

I have here discussed only two emergent conceptual shifts as relevant to the current situation in style research. First, I discussed the serious examination of assumptions about culture and, by extension, about "group," drawing on some reformulations about culture as an object of inquiry which challenges the view of culture as an adaptive system that has material culture as its outputs, as products to be decoded. Instead, the view of material culture as an active, constitutive element of social practice is supported here, a view that implies, by extension, that what style can "tell" us about is *not* culture or groups *per se*, but the contexts in which group or other social/cultural phenomena are mobilized as process.

Second, I have suggested that with the notions on objects as praxis, and as production, there is an emergent concern for design and production processes as integral to any study of style and as something that is just as important as the study of formal variation (as traditionally defined) – if not more so – to the endeavor to identify similarity-relations among objects or whatever. With a concern for the production of cultural representations (rather than an emphasis on material culture as outputs) as a constitutive practice, the archaeological study of pattern-*generation* and of the productive contexts within which materials and technologies (*sensu lato*) are embedded become more crucial to the archaeological engagement with style.

Our history of the use of style has indeed been one of experimentation, although there have been certain unifying and consistent concerns. There is little doubt that we will remain "forever hopeful" that we might read history or culture from style; we have always read a history of objects from style. As Davis reminds us (chapter 3, this volume: 19), style is not *in* the material: it must be "discovered" and written up by someone. But since there are no inherent measures or definitions, our history can *only* be one of experimentation, and one of trial and error. On the surface, it appears as if we have been seeking *a* way to study style, *a* programmatic. But from the experimentation of past decades – only some of which has been presented here – it has become clear that such a programmatic is not forthcoming, nor should it be.

Our insights have perhaps come just as much from trying, refining, or abandoning one "measure" or one use after another. This is all the more reason why it is the theoretical framework that must be a focus for our intellectual energies, and, above all, why the current probing into the nature and limits of archaeological knowledge must be sustained.

Acknowledgments

As with many other papers in this volume, the original impetus for this chapter was the conference on the uses of style in archaeology organized by Christine Hastorf and her associates at the University of Minnesota in January 1985. I am grateful to them for the conference and to the University of Minnesota for its support, which brought many of us together for the first and only time explicitly to discuss our ideas about style.

The metamorphoses of that 1985 paper into the one that is presented here cannot entirely be accounted for. I am surely indebted to a variety of people for their comments and criticisms, including David Braun, Christopher Carr, Whitney Davis, and James Moore, and especially to Christine Hastorf for her sharp editorial mind and pen.

Notes

1. Although practicing culture-historians employed style as a fundamental concept, it took the form of a concern with artifact "types," which were dominantly stylistic (Krieger 1944). Thus it is not surprising that although much ink was spent on the explicit discussion of types and typology during the 1940s and 1950s, when it came to an explicit discussion of style in anthropology, it was often an art historian who was called upon. This can be seen most clearly, for example, in the 1953 compendium *Anthropology Today*, edited by Alfred L. Kroeber, in which the chapter on "Style" was authored by the art historian – albeit an anthropologically sympathetic one – Meyer Schapiro (Schapiro

1953). Among Schapiro's primary characteristics of what style refers to is an idea that is most compatible with the culture historical *use* of style: styles exhibit a constancy of form and expression over measurable and often considerable periods of time or geographic distance.

2. Davis (in a personal communication to me) has suggested that this central tenet of modernism – the centered subject (cf. Stadler 1982) – "may not be all that closely associated with the emphasis on the individual and on the intentionality of producers as revealed by their habitual idiosyncrasies in production, that is, with stylistic criticism or connoisseurship" (although, I would argue, this is only one part of the archaeological agenda in stylistic studies). Davis suggests that a deeper intellectual history would link the connoisseurship concept to Giovanni Morelli, who was working out his ideas *before* modernism (cf. Wollheim 1974), but it should come as no surprise to us that modernism (or any other "ism") derives from certain historically prior interests (in the case of modernism, from the interests of early-nineteenth-century Romantics). One point of invoking the influence of modernism here is not only to remind ourselves as relatively narrowly concerned archaeologists that our practice is rooted in much wider cultural concepts than we usually think about, but also to suggest that perhaps the *decentering* of the modernist subject (which is being undertaken in current criticism) will (or should) lead to a decentering in style studies.

3. Some original texts that develop the concept of "founding authority" would include Derrida (1970), Foucault (1979), and Bloom (1973).

4. In this same essay (Davis, chapter 3, this volume: 30) suggests that everything that we do is "stylistic description"; even "history" is a stylistic description specially privileged in a given archaeological analysis. This view reminds me of the story that the anthropologist Clifford Geertz is reported to tell (Sass 1986):

> An Indian tells an Englishman that the world sits on the back of an elephant which, in turn, sits on the back of a turtle. Hoping to get to the bottom of things, to discover the foundation of the world, the Englishman asks, "And what does that rest on?"
> "Another turtle," is the Indian's answer.
> "And *that* turtle?"
> "Ah, Sahib," is the final answer; "after that it's turtles all the way down."

The analogy here is that our stylistic descriptions are like the turtles: it's stylistic description all the way down . . .

5. Although much of the following section was originally presented at the Minnesota conference that this volume is based upon, many of these historical thoughts were included in a subsequent paper on the use of diversity measures in stylistic analysis, which has been recently published (Conkey 1989); thus there is some overlap between this paper and that one.

6. In a recent paper presented at a conference on Symbolic and Structural Archaeology, Sperber (1987) reminds us how our root classifications are based on material-ness; that material is the baseline. We talk about things as being material or immaterial.

7. Taken to its logical extreme, this concept of style allowed the *use* of style to write culture-history: the stylistic description could be taken to reveal the history (e.g., diffusion, migration, etc.) which explains the style! Despite the obvious tautology of such a proposition this kind of reasoning from style-to-history allowed the culture-historians a long enough interpretive leash to flesh out their chronicles of the past, which were otherwise quite restrained by empirical preferences and a general fear of speculation (Wylie 1981). Recognizing the limits of all three practices – reading history from stylistic description, dependence upon empiricism, and avoidance of theory and speculation – Kluckhohn (e.g. 1939) was one of the most astute and articulate critics, anticipating, as Wylie (1981) demonstrates, much of what the New Archaeology came to promote three decades later.

8. Certainly these programmatics of the 1960s did try to generate a new, unassailable foundation for how we think about culture, and thus about culture in the past. It is deeply embedded in our western intellectual history for us to generate such systems of thought, which are based upon a first principle and upon which a whole hierarchy of meaning may be constructed. First principles of this kind (e.g., culture as an adaptive system) can be deconstructed and shown to be *products* of a particular system of meaning rather than to be what props it up from the outside. These first principles are, moreover, commonly defined by what they exclude (e.g., normativism).

It is almost ironic that, in advocating a holistic systems approach, the method was explicitly partitive: "we must *partition* our observational fields . . . isolate relevant variables" (Binford 1965: 207, emphasis added). The parative vocabulary permeates such programmatic statements as Binford's (1965).

9. Although more structurally minded archaeologists (e.g., Conkey 1978b; Friedrich 1970) replaced "formal variation" with "design structure" as the equivalent of style – *as if* design structure were style – the kinds of reasoning and linking arguments between artifacts and behaviors were essentially the same. Similar to the way in which formal variation as style was considered an index or symptom of social entities, patternings and variablity in design structure became an index, a symptom, or a reflection of socially interacting units (see also Washburn 1977, 1983).

10. The concern over whether and how style may be equated with social entities is long-standing despite our being "forever hopeful" that something so simple and straightforward might obtain. Particularly noteworthy among the theoretical considerations is David Clarke's treament in his *Analytical Archaeology* (1968: especially 365–78). A recent ethnoarchaeological analysis that tries to show how complex any correlations might be is Hodder's (1978) study of Baringo District artifact style and social units. Most recently, this issue has been taken up again by Franklin (1986) in her attempt to show that there is *not* necessarily a correlation between distinctive styles and specified social entities; this time the data are Australian rock art styles. Franklin proposes to deal with this by differentiating between what she calls "stochastic" and "emblemic" style. Unfortunately, she sets up these two genres in contradistinction to each other despite arguing that one cannot distinguish, at least archaeologically, between the two types of style, at least not without extensive further contextual analysis and more elaborated archaeological models.

11. It is important to note again that an articulate concern for theory and the implications of putting theory to work in archaeology goes back at least as early as Kluckhohn (1939), whose writing embodies much of the critique and programmatics to be put forth by the New Archaeologists (see also Steward and Setzler 1938; see Wylie 1981 for a full exposition on this early and articulate call for a "loss of innocence"): "Unless archaeologists treat their work quite firmly as part of a general attempt to understand human behavior, they will, before many generations, find themselves classed with A. Huxley's figure who devoted his life to writing a history of the 3-pronged fork" (Kluckhohn 1940: 43).

12. One might even argue that these kinds of views on culture – open-ended, emergent, contested – are particularly well suited to the particular historical contingencies of the 1980s and beyond, in which the presumed bounded cultural entities that have so long been the object of anthropological inquiry are being (have been) rapidly transformed by globalization. However, this shift

in thinking – which itself is, of course, contested – is of considerable relevance to archaeology and it is a way of thinking that has come not only into anthropology but into most domains in which cultural representation and cultural production are of concern (e.g., art history, literary theory). These intellectual movements have contributed to what Clifford (1986: 22) has aptly described as a dislodging of the ground from which groups and persons (such as you and I) securely represent others: "there is no longer a mountaintop from which to map human ways of life." This kind of conceptual shift is said to be *tectonic* in its implications: "we ground things now on a moving earth" (Clifford 1986:22). And this is why it is only now that the kind of "loss of innocence" proclaimed by Clarke for archaeology in 1973 is emergent, although in a radically different form, as Kohl (1985) describes.

13. In referring to the different approaches to the study of early civilizations, Flannery said something very much related to this view, in a much more entertaining and yet accurate way: "To read what the 'ecologists' write, one would often think that civilized peoples only ate, excreted and reproduced, to read what the humanists write, one would think that civilizations were above all three and devoted their energy to the 'arts'" (1972: 399).

14. One might argue that our "reading" of style tells *us* something: we consume the meaning that we produce. Following some ideas advanced by Burgin with regard to what a critic does with a work of art or any other cultural product, we could think that to have archaeologists explain and evaluate the archaeological record (as a critic might do with a film) takes the audience – the student, the public – out of the uncomfortable position of themselves being *producers* of meaning and allows them the "easier position of *consumer*" (Burgin 1986: 33). The literary metaphors of archaeological interpretation contribute directly to this role for the archaeologist.

Chapter 3

Style and history in art history

Whitney Davis

The author of this chapter is an art historian who has worked with archaeological materials including Paleolithic art, rock art of Africa, and Egyptian artifacts. Here he presents the art historian's perspective on style and provides extensive references to literature that grapples with style but which is not well known among most archaeologists.

Davis begins with a tripartite concept of style that he dissects and evaluates. Central to his chapter is an important discussion of the possibilities of and differences between reading history from style and reading style from history. Throughout the chapter, Davis argues for the necessity of independent confirmation and of context. Lastly, Davis discusses the centrality of the study of artifact production systems. In our theory of style, he argues, it is an archaeology of production – of language, of making – that will be the context for control upon and explanation of style.

Introduction

Most working art historians probably still believe that "style is an indispensable historical tool; it is more essential to the history of art than to any other historical discipline" (Ackerman 1963: 164). Many are also more and more intrigued by the possibility that "style descriptions can be written and rewritten unconstrained by anything except prevailing art historical interests" (Wollheim 1979: 140). There would be no need to worry about this possibility if we had a clear idea of our "interests," historical and theoretical – but we do not. As we will see, the concept of style itself does not and should not commit us to any particular way of writing history. Today

consensus about the proper concerns and central concepts of art history seems difficult to achieve and perhaps even undesirable.

I cannot pretend to offer a complete statement of the concept of style in art history, or even of an art historical concept of style. Today it hardly seems possible to imitate the treatments of Meyer Schapiro (1953), James Ackerman (1963), or Ernst Gombrich (1968). Furthermore, I cannot say what tools other disciplines should or should not take from art history. Instead, I pursue an argument which I take to be intrinsically important; it leads to some descriptive and some prescriptive claims about art history and related disciplines, but also, I think, to necessary skepticism about any such claims.[1]

Style in history

The definition of style offered here captures some aspects of the practice of working art historians. More important, it suggests how the concept of style ideally or logically should function. That in practice it sometimes cannot function this way is not a problem for the theory of style itself; it is a problem of evidence or interpretation. The definition is built to take account of some matters of special interest to art historians, but it must also be able to comprehend many phenomena, some of them hardly ever studied by art historians; we may want to be able to talk about the style of chimpanzee scribbles, the monolith in *2001: A Space Odyssey*, driftwood, Polykleitos' *Doryphoros*, forged Vermeers, Duchamp's bottle-racks, ordinary bottle-racks, rocks in a Japanese garden, Mousterian scratchings.

For the art historian's purposes, (a) "style" is a description of a polythetic set of similar but varying attributes in a group of artifacts, (b) the presence of which can only be explained by the history of the artifacts, (c) namely, common descent from an archaeologically identifiable artifact-production system in a particular state or states. In the discussion which follows I shall refer to these elements of a definition of style in the shorthand form (a), (b), (c).

This definition requires a good deal of explanation and clarification of its several ambiguities. The key elements – e.g., polythetic classification, similarity-relations, phylogenetic explanation, and production systems – are in themselves independent of one another but are brought together here in a single statement. Although the definition seems general, flexible, and circumspect, the concept of style is significantly restricted. In particular, it makes no statements or predictions one way or another about many aspects of works of art – like sequence, distribution, rates of change, or causes of variability – of great interest to art historians and to archaeologists.

The art historian

The art historical concept of style (clauses (a)–(c)) is derived from a more inclusive concept – that of (a) alone, or the concept of "format," maintained by critics of the arts, teachers, artists, and others, enshrined in most dictionary definitions of style.

Under the more inclusive definition (a), historical statements are not the only substantive or permissible statements about style. Thus, a critic points to the striking similarity between an ancient Egyptian drawing of a house and a modern architectural blueprint, and remarks – contrasting them with Vermeer's *View of Delft* – that they are "in the same style." Inclusive statements like this often serve as a prolegomenon or provocation for art-historical or archaeological research, for similarities are not always due to chance factors but may result from relations of influence, shared methods, and so forth.

Strictly speaking, statements of the inclusive form (a) are inadmissible in art historical discourse unless and until they can be shown to satisfy the further clauses (b) and (c). However, in much writing about artifacts this specification is never actually carried out. The visible validity of (a) – the recognition of similarities in "format" – is often used as a *proof* of (b) and (c).

"Style"

Although style is a primary classificatory concept in art history, it is not the only one. Stylistic descriptions are often coupled with non-stylistic classifications of artifacts, for example, by the date, technique, function, or "meaning" of a work (see further Ackerman 1963: 182). In particular, as we will see in more detail, the "fateful interconnection of *Stilus* and *Chronos*" (Sauerländer 1983: 266) – the real underpinning of art history – does not derive wholly from the theory of style but also from theories of change, evolution, or progress.

Logically, the taxonomies founded on non-stylistic statements about artifacts may vary independently of stylistic description. For example, the term "Greek sculpture" may be taken as a monothetic statement about date and medium rather than as a stylistic description. However, in practice, attributions of date or function are sometimes *derived from* stylistic descriptions. Conversely, stylistic descriptions are often *produced for* "a group of artifacts" pre-classified by chronological, technical, or other criteria. Although the informativeness of a stylistic description will be strongly affected by any coupled and sometimes cross-cutting classifications, the theory of style is not committed one way or another to any coupling.

Statements about style are very different from other kinds of descriptive or historical statements art historians make. To ask whether a painting is by Velazquez is very different from asking whether it is in Velazquez' style. The one question can be answered directly and empirically while the other requires a complex polythetic description. Stylistic statements are related to these non-stylistic statements in many ways. Statements about morphology, similarity, and synonymy are preliminary to stylistic analysis. Statements about representation, "meaning," or value may be but are not *necessarily* involved in stylistic descriptions. Statements about tradition and fashion follow upon stylistic analysis.

A description

Style is not "in" the material, the matter of artifacts or works of art. Style must be discovered and written up by someone. No rigid protocols seem to be available for writing stylistic descriptions. Art historians prefer densely descriptive expository prose, perhaps impressionistic or subjective but often more subtle, flexible, and informative than simple checklists of attributes (see Schapiro 1953: 289; Kroeber 1956: 330–31; Sibley 1959; Baxandall 1979, 1985). Metaphorical description ("warm," "fluid") may suit continuously varying attributes not easily broken into units or quantified. Non-initiates may be puzzled by the logical structure, weight, or value of the complex art-historical descriptions coupling stylistic and non-stylistic classifications.

A polythetic set

In a fully polythetic group of artifacts, (1) each artifact possesses a (large) number of the attributes of the group; (2) each attribute may be found in a (large) number of the artifacts in the group; and (3) no single attribute is found in every artifact in the group. (For the general definition of polytypic aggregation or a polythetic set, see Beckner 1959: 22, Simpson 1961: 94–96; Sneath and Sokal 1973: 21–22; Needham 1983.) It follows that no single attribute is both necessary and sufficient for membership in the group (Clarke 1983: 36). The polythetic character of stylistic description is one of its most important features. Therefore it is worth making three supplementary points.

First, the numerical quantities in (1) and (2) above are

unspecified, but by definition are greater than one and less than the total. Art historians often tend to prefer high average quantities, that is, groups in which *many artifacts share many attributes*. This preference can be justified by a secondary assumption, namely, that many of the artifacts assigned to the same category in monothetic classifications (by date, author, etc.) will tend to share many attributes. However, this assumption sometimes breaks down: being-by-Picasso does not automatically give us being-in-Picasso's-style, and, conversely, being-in-Vermeer's-style does not automatically give us being-by-Vermeer. As we will see in more detail, this possibility strikes a fatal blow at correlations between stylistic descriptions and historical, cultural, or chronological entities and phases unsupported by an independent archaeological argument.

Second, in practice many stylistic descriptions can only be pseudo-polythetic. They must describe some attributes as being possessed by all artifacts in the group as it has been constituted for analysis. Some of these "universal" properties – e.g., objecthood, materiality – are not usually meaningful and need not be treated as taxonomic characters (Hennig 1979: 7). However, some may be treated operationally as diagnostic when they are discovered (or believed) not to be "universal" beyond the group. Insofar as diagnostic attributes are used to define and discriminate styles, the power and flexibility of polythetic classification has been forfeited. Moreover, an artifact might always be discovered that does not possess the diagnostic attribute but which clearly belongs to the polythetic group by virtue of its other attributes.

Third, by our definition it is not possible to write a *stylistic* description of *one* unique attribute of an artifact. In theory, style is a description of a set of attributes distributed in a certain way in a set of artifacts. However, in practice art historians may not explicitly cite the whole distribution or group, although stylistic analysis of single artifacts is implicitly informed by it.

The polythetic nature of stylistic description implies that ultimately it is fruitless to look for neat or absolute boundaries for and between styles. "Almost any style can be convincingly described as transitional" (Gombrich 1968: 357).

Furthermore, it is fruitless to hope for stylistic descriptions of uniform scale, complexity, and resolving power. Focusing on individual clusters of attributes, we can always extract sub-sets from any polythetic set, and a polythetic set can always be nested within larger sets, and conversely, any well-defined polythetic set can be derived from sub- or mega-sets. The principles and procedures of stylistic description do not in themselves tie us to any particular level of historical or other particularity. To reveal historical particulars – e.g., artists' identities, workshops, traditions – the resolving-power of stylistic description must be carefully regulated. The criteria used have to be defended on independent grounds. Unfortunately they are not often stated in the text of a stylistic description itself. In art history, "explanation" is often the expansion, contraction, nesting, and mutual self-reinforcing

derivation of stylistic descriptions of varying scales: as we will see in more detail, style has been regarded as its own cause, history, and context.

Similar but varying

The attributes of different artifacts in the group cannot be identical. In a material sense, no action can be repeated in exactly the same way every time. There will always be minor and sometimes major variations in the morphology of a type of artifact as it is repeatedly made. In a logical sense, even two identical or "indiscernible" (Danto 1981) morphologies may have different stylistic values. Therefore, the attributes studied in a stylistic description are not identical but similar.

The definition and measurement of similarity poses as many problems in the study of style as it does in the study of perception, biological species, and elsewhere (see Goodman 1972b). Art historians have evolved a complex vocabulary for this element of their work. Here only a few comments are possible.

First, as a statement about the distance of the relation between two attributes, similarity has many degrees. Mass-produced artifacts, duplicates, replicas, copies, quotations, and forgeries are very close to each other or to the template, original, master, or prototype (discussion in Hermerén 1975: 50–89). Parallels and allusions are more distant, as are many productions separated by literal distance, that is, by a chronological hiatus or spatial barrier. However, it is important to note that similarity is not necessarily a good measure of the *distance* of the relation between two attributes, as cases of "negative influence" or "antithetical similarities" suggest (Hermerén 1975: 45).

Second, although many of our similarity-terms ("copy," "quotation") prejudge the case, a similarity-relation of whatever degree does not in and of itself necessarily reveal the *cause* of the relation between two attributes – e.g., parallelism, convergence, analogy, mimicry, etc. (Simpson 1961: 78–79). From a similarity-relation alone it is not possible to determine which of two artifacts is an original and which a copy, or whether an artifact distantly alludes to or quotes from another or merely resembles it fortuitously. These judgements must be rendered on independent grounds.

Third, we have already seen that, in the inclusive definition of style (a) (see p. 19), similarity-relations can be used to propose non-historical statements about the relatedness of artifacts. Moreover, although the presence of a similarity-relation may be evidence of the historical relatedness of artifacts (a matter proved independently), the *absence* of a similarity-relation is *not* evidence of their historical *un*relatedness. For this reason, stylistic description alone can always miss historical relations between artifacts.

Fourth, because of the polythetic character of stylistic description, analysis of similarity-relations between *whole* artifacts, each with many attributes, becomes a matter of weighting (1) measures of shared to unique attributes, and (2) degrees or strengths of similarity between shared attributes. An overall measure of the intensity of similarity between artifacts with some identical, indiscernible, or very similar attributes and some very different or unique attributes has proved quite elusive. Art historians often employ intuitive judgements, although some formalizations have become available (such as Tversky and Gati's [1978] "weighted difference of the measure of the common and distinctive features").

Fifth, like style itself, similarity is not "in" the material. All artifacts are similar to all other artifacts in some respects, and a well-defined statement about similarity must be a statement about the nearness of the positions of attributes *in a particular order* set up by the observer. Art historians sometimes do not make explicit statements of quality-orders and their measurement in digital or analogical units. Descriptions produced by different writers therefore become very difficult to compare, and new observations are not easily integrated into the existing body of descriptions.

Furthermore, art historians often favor the study of certain particular quality-orders using certain particular measures – namely, visible surface qualities using the unaided eyes, hand, and body as measuring devices and anthropocentric and highly social or cultural categories as units. These preferences have led variously to the drift of stylistic analysis toward what might be called visual or optical formalism, connoisseurship, and metric historicism. Justification for these preferences has not been highly articulate. These visible qualities, simple unscientific devices, and special metrics are often assumed to have been those self-consciously manipulated by artisans in the past. However, in and of itself stylistic description cannot be a proof of such assumptions; they must be confirmed by independent archaeological and anthropological knowledge of production. Although anthropologists suggest we should use the relevant original cultural categories in our analysis, it is often stylistic analysis that enables us to see what these categories might have been, and not the other way around.

Strictly speaking, *no* particular quality-orders or metrics of and for similarity are uniquely inherent in the definition of style (see also Hermerén 1975: 49). Advances have been achieved precisely by abandoning one quality-order or metric for another.

Attributes

In keeping with the polythetic character of stylistic description, "no fixed catalogue of the elementary properties of style can be compiled" (Goodman 1978: 32). *All* attributes of an artifact are potentially stylistic; however, in any single artifact in a polythetic classification, not all attributes *are* stylistic in practice. The several implications and difficulties of this statement should be outlined.

Which attributes of an artifact are picked out for inclusion in a stylistic description? Art historians tend to use visible, material, "formal" attributes, like line, color, or surface texture, which are supposed to be "intrinsically expressive" and

form a coherent whole, "apart from denoted meanings" (Schapiro 1953: 291, but cf. 304, 309).

Nevertheless, despite occasional assertions that it is "something essentially concerned with form" (Kroeber 1957: 26), style should not be reserved just for optically visible morphology or just for those perceptible or palpable attributes we believe to be "non-functional," "aesthetic," and so forth. Not only visible formal but also "unexhibited" (Dickie 1974) functional, symbolic (e.g., denotational, expressional, exemplificational) (Goodman 1972a), and institutional properties of the artifact are *potentially* stylistic. To represent the Virgin Mary in-the-style-of-Raphael in 1500 would be to use an already somewhat conservative, deeply spiritual, idealizing or classicizing style; to represent the Virgin in-the-style-of-Raphael – that is, with the visible morphology of a Raphael – in 1989 would be to use some kind of radical, perhaps even ironic or satirical style (see further Gombrich 1960: 313). A description encompassing only formal attributes would group the visually indiscernible Virgins of 1500 and 1989 together. A description encompassing the contemporary connotations of subject-matter, the institutional functions of the artifacts, and so forth, might group them in different categories – although, of course, it might not.

Although material morphologies can be stable, social functions, attributed meanings and other unexhibited properties of the artifacts might be volatile. Conversely, artifacts might possess closely similar functions or meanings and yet appear to be formally remote – for example, because of decay, because we do not possess a chain of variants connecting them, or because they were once used together in a single context now lost to us. (Who would know from visual inspection alone that caterpillar and butterfly belong to the same species?) Evidently different classes of formal and unexhibited attributes may vary independently of each other. We know very little about the full range of these relations.

Just as with material formal attributes, the functions and meanings of different artifacts – the unexhibited attributes – are not identical but only similar in varying degrees. Although all formal and unexhibited attributes are potentially stylistic, we want to know how to *recognize* the stylistic attributes of any single artifact or within any single group of artifacts. As Goodman (1978: 23) says, "not all differences [between artifacts] . . . are differences in style."

Briefly, a stylistic attribute is one for which a match or similar can be found elsewhere in the group. By the terms of our definition, style is always a relational, comparative, or statistical description (clause (a)); moreover, this match or association must be explained by the history of the artifacts (clauses (b), (c)). Although any attribute may enter into the "functioning of the work as a symbol or as such" (Goodman 1978: 35), if it cannot be matched or associated with attributes of other artifacts, a description of it remains a purely morphological rather than a stylistic characterization. Therefore all formal and unexhibited attributes of an artifact are also potentially *non*-stylistic (morphological) insofar as they may not be entered into a polythetic classification.

By this definition, an attribute may be without style or style-less, but no artifact can be without style or style-less, for an artifact for which *no* matches or associations can be found anywhere for any attributes is unthinkable. Although some attributes remain unmatched or unassociated, all artifacts can be brought under a stylistic description of some kind. As we have seen, strictly speaking there is no need to prefer a high number of matches or associations for the attributes of our artifacts: "many objects we deal with are not as uniform, not as patterned, briefly not as stylized, as our notions of style would like to have them" (Sauerländer 1983: 167).

All stylistic description requires morphological characterization but is certainly not identical with it. The residuum of "unique" morphology that cannot be taken up in a stylistic description may be the result of decay, or "random" (if nonetheless informative or even diagnostic) variation in motor or manufacturing habits (Hill 1977). Insofar as it is unique, it may serve as a defining description of the artifact or a defining trace of its particular history. Inter-artifactual style may be successfully anchored to history through infra-artifactual morphology, some proportion of which is always non-stylistic. However, in the absence of independent evidence it is often difficult to recognize truly non-stylistic morphological variation, for potentially all kinds and levels of variation can be stylistic.

A great deal clearly depends upon the morphological – and therefore potentially the stylistic – description of attributes. The difficulties of decomposing a whole artifact into its component attributes are well recognized. Continuously varying attributes are particularly problematic. They are potentially infinitely divisible. For example, every morphological variation in a pictorial sign is potentially meaningful semantically (so-called "continuous correlation" [Bach 1970]) – so it would seem impossible to be sure of capturing all semantic nuances in a descriptive metric for the sign. However important to the art historian, strictly speaking these are all problems in the analysis of (attribute) morphology – logically prior to all derived stylistic *and* non-stylistic taxonomies.

Of more immediate consequence for the theory of style are the problems not of attribute but of artifact morphology. Searching through the group only for similar instances of attributes produces only a polythetic classification of attributes. However, the total composition of all attributes may be quite individual in each artifact. An appropriate terminology for this composition – for the "look" or "feel" of whole pieces, what Wollheim (1979: 137) calls the "coordinating rules" – has proved hard to find. Despite its elusiveness, art historians tend to focus on the whole artifact as such, as a cluster of attributes mutually correlated in a specific sequence or coordination.

Typical art historical preferences do not invalidate the fact that stylistic description proceeds equally legitimately at the level of unities, pairs, or other sub-artifactual clusters of attributes, of whole artifacts, or of clusters of artifacts (e.g., in buildings or rituals). The study of style is not ineluctably tied to the study of single "objects." In fact, although "the object of classification should be what Hennig [e.g., 1979: 7] calls the *holomorph*, all the characteristics of the individual throughout its life" (Simpson 1961: 71), in practice no art historian ever handles *all* of the attributes of an artifact in their full coordination. Operating stylistic descriptions are almost always sub-artifactual, building from certain attributes. Therefore in our definition of style the attribute is the analytic primary.

A group of artifacts

In our definition, stylistic descriptions apply to artifacts. The definition of an artifact (see Clarke [1983, chs. 4, 5]; Wollheim [1980]) is not entirely a problem for the theory of style. Although sufficient for most purposes, the usual definition of an artifact as a human-made physical object is theoretically too restrictive. At the extreme, an artifact is anything – object, process, etc. – any attribute of which was produced or assigned by human agency, including unexhibited symbolic or institutional attributes not actually manufactured by anyone wielding tools and working matter (see further Dickie 1974). This broadened definition allows us to include natural or "found" objects, often used in rituals, buildings, etc., physical processes, human persons or personalities, and so forth. In some circumstances, all of these entities can be said to have, to be in, or to be part of a "style," however minimal, broad, or uninteresting.

Although the preference easily reaches its limits, especially in the study of the contemporary scene or the very remote past, art historians tend to study heavily worked, deeply meaningful, and socially valuable artifacts – in a phrase, *highly stylized* artifacts or "works of art."

Needless to say, the theory of style must be able to accommodate anything we take to be a work of art (see Weitz 1956; Dickie 1974; Danto 1981), in which many attributes are manipulated at many levels in many ways. The material attributes are often wholly produced by human manufacture, constrained by the physical properties of the medium and technology. The symbolic and institutional attributes are extremely complex: a painting may depict complex objects, and even simple non-representational artifacts, like a Japanese tea-cup, may require elaborate interpretation or have a role in substantial social activities. The traditional fine and decorative arts – drawing, painting, sculpture, gem- and metal-work, etc. – provide some paradigmatic examples of artifacts of this kind (Kristeller 1951–52). Further transcendental descriptions of these artifacts – in terms of aesthetic quality, good, significant, or perfect form, beauty, and so forth – in practice do little work for art history and need not be considered here; "there is nothing inherent in the notion of style itself that encourages such distinctions being made" (Alpers 1977: 97).

Beyond the traditional "fine" arts, we can certainly find many further examples of "highly stylized" artifacts (such as machines or vehicles, weapons, and costume) studied at the moment by archaeologists, historians of science and technology, and others. Furthermore, considerations of style and therefore art-historical research need not be limited to "highly stylized" artifacts.

A somewhat stronger case can be made for art historians limiting themselves to artifacts – "highly stylized" or not – which possess symbolic attributes (Goodman 1972a, 1978), that is, function as denotations, depictions, expressions, or exemplifications. These concepts all seem to entail a theory of style, for symbols are such relationally (syntactically and referentially), and therefore a description of shared or similar attributes between instances must be available by definition. Goodman claims that stylistic attributes are "properties of the functioning of the work as a symbol" (1978: 35), which rules style out of any artifact we do not take to be symbolic.

Why style?

We may now ask what stylistic description in art history – both "taxonomic" *and* "generative" (Wollheim 1979; Sauerländer 1983: 260–65) – is supposed to do for us. "Why," Goodman asks, "should style matter more than some quality that might be discerned, with enough study, as characteristic of works in a random selection?" (1978: 39). The question admits either a simple answer or a complex and still controversial one.

Simply, style can be seen as the *the explanation for* the similarities between the attributes of artifacts. The attributes are similar because they have, are in, or are part of a single style. Therefore style matters simply because it has explanatory value. Statements based on this reasoning are frequent in art-historical and archaeological writing. However, by the terms of our definition, they are obviously tautological, for style simply *is* a description of the similarities among artifacts.

The truth of the matter is really more subtle. The tautology can be seen as a convenient shorthand for another, more difficult analysis, indicated in clauses (b) and (c) in our definition (p. 19, above). Style – the similarity among artifacts – is explained by the history of the artifacts. Therefore style matters as the *explanandum* for art history or archaeology; without style we have nothing to talk about, no problem to solve.

Reading from style to history

Since its modern inception in the work of Burckhardt, Riegl, Wölfflin, and others, art history has flirted with and often embraced the idea that the "history" explaining style is revealed or made available to us in and by style itself. In the frequent absence of any other information about artifacts apart from their stylistic descriptions, we might nonetheless find in them their histories – their authors, dates, values, and significances. "Style is the mirror which makes all the buildings, the statues, the images of the past accessible to aesthetic historicism, for its dreams and for its files" (Sauerländer 1983: 254).

Although reading from style to history and back again to style is ultimately a great circularity – in Sauerländer's stronger word, an "illusion" (1983) – it is important to consider the justification of the procedure. If we make certain

supplementary assumptions in addition to those adopted in stylistic description itself, both the *internal structure* of styles and their *external correlations* might in a sense be given directly in stylistic description. These structures and correlations are often thought to be all that is required to explain styles historically.

The diachronic reading: the internal structure of styles

A purely stylistic description of artifacts is an unwieldy affair unless and until it is structured by cross-cutting information, particularly about sequence and distribution. Ideally, sequence and distribution are established by independent archaeological evidence about the time and place of production of different artifacts in the group. Less ideally, sequence and distribution can also be established by hypothesis – by granting assumptions about variations in production over time and space not necessarily inherent in the theory of style itself. Unfortunately, art history has not paid much attention to developed theories of sequence (e.g., seriation) or distribution (e.g., deposition) in archaeology (but see Kubler 1962, 1979).

Armed with both archaeological and hypothetical information about sequence and distribution, many art historians and anthropologists have claimed to find regular temporal and spatial structures in styles. These structures were commonly conceived as connected series of slightly varying artifacts – lines of variation or evolution connecting two or more fixed temporal or spatial points, such as a line between a point of "origins" and a point of "fulfillment," or a line between a point at a "center" and a point at a "periphery." As art-historical analysis became more complete and elaborate in the first half of this century, recurrences or cycles of these simple structures were described, resulting in detailed accounts of the life-history of styles (see further Munro 1963; Ackerman 1963: 170–74, 177–81).[2] Any artifact could be positioned, described, and in a sense explained in terms of the life-historical structures of style: an artifact is archaic or classic, cosmopolitan or provincial, inventive and authoritative or degenerate and derived, and so forth. Although many statements of this kind incorporate actual archaeological dates or contexts, many of them are also partly or wholly stylistic.

For critical purposes, it is enough to observe that many of the life-histories of style were erected on a slight base of independent dates and contexts. They depended frequently upon dubious procedural prescriptions not inherent in the theory of style itself – for example, that it is best to begin the search for similarities to the attributes of an artifact with the very next artifacts (in either or any direction) in sequence or distribution. In fact, in the absence of archaeological evidence, sometimes artifacts were initially positioned next to each other in sequences or distributions on the basis of morphological similarity, making possible, by definition alone, a coherent stylistic description with a satisfyingly regular structure. Teleological notions – "the fine arts spend much of their course evolving toward their ideal or goal" (Kroeber 1957: 21), ultimately "attained" and then "exhausted" – at the extreme gave rise to almost mystical conceptions, like Riegl's *Kunstwollen* or "will-to-form" (Riegl 1985). In evolutionist or diffusionist enthusiasm for regular lines of temporal and spatial variation, especially when further and closely cross-cut by narrative biography and chronicle, much of the power and flexibility of polythetic classification was forfeited.

None of these difficulties at all proves that regular temporal or spatial structures cannot be found in styles or will not be confirmed archaeologically in some instances. That they exist is something we may find out about some styles. However, they are certainly not universally or essentially immanent. *The representation of matched or similar attributes in a population does not always change in any single linear direction but may oscillate or fluctuate in complex ways.* In fact, the theory of style makes no inherent predictions about the rate, pace, direction, or degree of change.[3] Erected *a priori* or by hypothesis alone, the life-historical structures of style do not reliably make available a history of style from within.

The synchronic reading: the external correlations of styles

Any artifact can be anchored to its historical context – its time and place of production, its maker, etc. – in a variety of ways. Ideally, we have independent archaeological or documentary evidence for these details; the artifact was unearthed in a sealed deposit, was described in a contemporary letter, etc. The procedures for critically evaluating this evidence are not part of the theory of style itself.

Somewhat less ideally, the non-stylistic morphology of an artifact may be the unique product and therefore the trace of its context. For example, a stone can be traced by archaeologists to a single quarry. Or again, a photograph is in part a representation of just those objects before the camera when the shutter closed. However, neither stylistic nor non-stylistic morphology is invariably the product of anything as specific as a particular historical instant or individual. The sputtering of my pen might be due to my illness in a given month, but it also might be due to built-in features of a pen-type in use for generations. Only independent experimentation will settle the point.

These possibilities are greatly complicated by the fact that *all* morphology is potentially stylistic by our definition. Therefore the traces of past contexts could be imitated (preserved, revised) in an artifact, as an element of its style. If I arrange objects before my camera in a certain way, I am at least in part working in the style of (say) Stieglitz, and the unique non-stylistic trace of my own context must be sought in different attributes. Morelli, Berenson, Beazley, and other great connoisseurs proceeded on the assumption that in an artifact it will always be possible to locate non-stylistic morphology directly due to the habit or preference of an individual producer. However, as any morphology might instead be either stylistic or non-individual, or both, the matter can only be pursued on an *ad hoc* empirical basis (see Hill 1977, with references, for experimental investigation of morphological variation).

Perhaps least ideally of all, context can be established by hypothetical correlation alone. A *stylistic* grouping is held to be co-extensive with some other grouping of *historical* data or with actual *historical* entities – with artists, workshops, "periods" or "phases" of cultural and social history. In our stylistic description, then, we can be given history – for we can read from style to the presence of an artist, a workshop, a social convention, instruction, or institution, a cultural preference, outlook, or way of life, and so on. If sustainable, the possibility of such a reading is the most important contribution of stylistic description, for it would show stylistic description, as Ackerman (1963: 164) and many other art historians hope, to be an "indispensable historical tool." However, although deeply entrenched in art history, reading from style to history in this way seems to falter badly on two counts.

Style co-extensive with what?

First, the mapping between stylistic and historical entities must actually be stronger than mere correlation, for correlation could be due to sheer chance and therefore cannot always be counted on to do the work we want. If the relation is not a mere chance correlation, then how should it be construed?

Art historians apparently often assume that style is the *expression* of an historical entity, such as an individual's idea or emotion (that is, the mind of the maker in a particular state) or a society's way of life or world-view (that is, the consensus or consciousness of the community in a particular state). Although style regarded as having co-extensive historical correlations may seem to require a theory of expression, theories of expression can be defended independently of a theory of style. In fact, for Wollheim (e.g., 1979: 133), Gombrich (1963), and others, style is a precondition of expressiveness. For our purposes, considered here solely as the alleged *cause* of style, expression is an uninformative concept. If expression by definition is made identical with all stylistic attributes, then we have not gained anything or established any causes at all. If not all stylistic attributes are expressive or expressional – for example, are representational or exemplificational instead (Goodman 1978: 32–33) – then the correlation between style and expression is not one-to-one; expression is *not* the (only) cause of style.

Moreover, in the absence of independent archaeological and historical evidence, an "expression" cannot be easily identified with any well-defined historical entities. Where and what are the ideas or emotions x, y, and z, the ways of life or world-views p, q, and r? Logically, further correlations have to be established on independent evidence between an entity-of-style-as-expression-of-idea-x and whatever historical entity it was that expressed that idea – one person at one point in his or her life? a group of persons in agreement? Since historical individuals and social groups potentially can express many ideas or emotions, stylistic description alone cannot lead us necessarily and invariably to find historical individuals or groups. But if in stylistic description we can only find "individuals"-expressing-ideas-x-y-or-z, then again we have not gained anything beyond our definition of style as expression.

It may be that we do have independent evidence for the ideas or emotions expressed in a style and for the entities – individuals, groups, cultures – carrying out the expression. We might have a letter by or an interview with an artist declaring his aesthetic or other aims; we might have sociological data informing us that everyone making artifacts within a well-bounded temporal and spatial region was a Christian and professed Christian values in thought and action. However, using this evidence in effecting correlations between a stylistic and an historical entity would be reading *from* history *to* style – a procedure that might just as well turn out to disconfirm as to confirm any correlations established the other way around.

To avoid some of the difficulties noted in the last three paragraphs, the correlations between stylistic and historical entities need not be interpreted as a relation of expression but rather as an *indexical* or *symptomatic* relation. According to this view, style is necessarily the index or symptom of the presence of an historical entity. This approach has been characteristic of some recent archaeology, which does not use the humanist's language of expression and intentions and avoids interpreting archaeological entities like artifact-types, style-areas, or culture-phases (see Clarke 1983) as ideas, emotions, or world-views. However, we have really gained nothing beyond our stylistic description itself if we do not specify precisely *what* historical entity *is* represented, in fact, by an artifact-type, style-area, or culture-phase. When such a specification is thought to be "given" in the stylistic classification, it is exposed to all of the trivialities and circularities noted already.

An indexical or symptomatic correlation does not have the advantages of a truly co-extensive, let alone of a causal, correlation. Indexically, the stylistic description does *point to* an historical entity, but does not *map* it and is certainly not necessarily caused by it. The real entity could be much larger and very different from the respects singled out by a stylistic description. The description sees the entity behaving in a particular way at a particular time, but knows nothing more about the whole of the entity in its other respects. Among other things, it risks partitioning the entity into falsely independent entities. These matters have been much debated by Binford (1972) and others in the Mousterian controversy and elsewhere.

In sum, the first problem with historical correlations established solely on the basis of or directly given by a stylistic description is simply the fact that we cannot know, without independent evidence, whether it has picked out a real historical entity, a fragment of an entity, or a conflation of entities. We may not care, of course, that we happen to be studying fragments or conflations – one artist's "mood" or "phase," the production of many artists sharing a plan (Muller 1977; Redman 1977) – *as long as we know that this is what they are*. A stylistic description alone cannot give us this knowledge.

Perhaps the problem can be minimized by employing several parallel or superimposed stylistic descriptions. As we have seen, stylistic description may proceed at any level or particularity. Therefore a description tuned to pick out an

individual's lifelong mannerisms overlaid with descriptions of more momentary or more stable attributes might provide a valid picture of a group of makers, each with some transient and some stable mannerisms, working over a period of time. Art-historical writing usually consists of such complex grids of descriptions. Nevertheless, the historical validity of the most complex grid still cannot be confirmed from within.

A pure non-historical stylistic description?

The second problem with the external historical correlations of style cuts much deeper. To lead us to valid historical correlations, in addition to technical and formal characterizations of artifacts, a stylistic description incorporates statements about "unexhibited" attributes, as discussed above. These are necessarily historical statements about the use and significance of artifacts in a particular context (like the Virgin-in-the-style-of-Raphael in 1500 or in 1989). Therefore to avoid fatal circularity or illegitimate correlations obtained by artificial stipulation, valid statements about these attributes must be obtained prior to and independently of the completed stylistic description.

This problem figures in much art-historical and archaeological analysis. For example, the connotation of a representation cannot be read off directly from the appearance of the figures, however precisely described. Pictorial meaning must be fixed through detailed study of representational and iconographic conventions. In his remarkable studies of iconographic "disjunctions," Panofsky (1944, 1960) stressed how stable classical forms often shifted significance profoundly in the long development from antiquity itself through the formative centuries of the Christian "late antique" into the Middle Ages and on to the Renaissance revivals. Kubler (1979) has offered a similar treatment for Pre-Columbian Mesoamerica. Their research does not necessarily show that we should reject descriptions of remarkably stable "classic styles" in the Hellenized West or the Central American heartlands. Stylistic description may be legitimate at many levels of historical particularity. Nevertheless, at the limit we will find formally similar artifacts produced by people entirely unrelated to or uninfluenced by one another and employing their own unique symbolic conventions and institutions (see Kubler 1985). From formal description alone we cannot differentiate disjunctions and diffusions from true discontinuity or dissimilarity; we must refer to context.

In addition to considering unexhibited symbolic or institutional attributes, knowledge of production methods, authorship, and other historical aspects of artifacts will be used to inflect a stylistic description. The description will be cross-cut by these independent monothetic classifications. For example, two works produced by an Inuit carver and Henry Moore respectively might look very similar (a valid statement in the inclusive concept of style (a); see p. 19), but they were probably made in altogether different ways, especially if we discover, as we might, that Henry Moore knew nothing about Inuit sculpture. Knowledge of production methods could lead us to assign the Inuit and the Moore work to different styles. Or again, a stylistic description might pick out a group of artifacts-in-the-style-of-Vermeer, although it turns out that Vermeer himself made only about 34 of these artifacts. Although strictly speaking monothetic and independent, individual or cultural authorship (or authenticity) seems such a necessary element for the historical correlation of style that in practice it is often treated as an unexhibited or even an exhibited stylistic attribute of artifacts.

In sum, the second problem with historical correlations established solely on the basis of, or directly given by, a stylistic description is simply the fact that a full stylistic description of potentially relevant attributes is not something independent of and prior to history, which leads into, makes available, or correlates with history. In brief, history has already entered into the stylistic description which is supposed to be "giving" history.

From style to history?

Putting together our results, these two problems show that the hope of reading from style to history is unintelligible. A stylistic description that does not employ historical statements about the attributes of artifacts cannot prove from within that it is validly correlated with any real historical entity, or any fragments or conflations thereof. But a stylistic description that does employ historical statements about the (often unexhibited) attributes of artifacts, although it may be validly correlated, is already assuming some prior knowledge of the history to which it will be correlated.

Most art historians would not ordinarily depend wholly on reading from style to history. In some respects, the procedure might be more common in archaeological disciplines where nothing is known about the past except what can be said about its artifacts. A full-scale art-historical analysis is often a bewildering, jerry-rigged maze of purely morphological characterizations, purely archaeological facts, interpretive statements, and stylistic descriptions, some of which, it is true, are not supposed to be revealing historical structures or correlations. Nevertheless, a survey of the whole domain of art history would probably show how few independent contexts and confirmations are used, and how frequently arguments invoke stylistic structures and correlations suffering from some or all of the difficulties noted here.

Reading from history to style

In construing the critical clauses (b) and (c) of our definition of style (see p. 19, above) so far we have seen simply that a stylistic description itself cannot reveal the history which explains style. As the *explanandum* of art history, no matter how sophisticated the integration of one level of "directly given" internal structure or plausible external correlation with another, style does not explain itself. We need to read *from* history *to* style – and this history is not style itself.

This "history" has been specified in a number of ways. Clause (c) (see p. 19, above) attempts to characterize it

specifically and positively; style in the art historian's sense is the result of the common descent of a group of artifacts from an artifact-production system. However, it is not immediately clear what an "artifact-production system" might be and how artifacts "descend" from it.

Modern art history employs two important accounts of artifact-production systems or, more briefly, of production. According to the first account, production is the use of a "language." According to the second, it is an activity or process of making. The central metaphors and arguments of both accounts have much to recommend them as well as obvious drawbacks.

Production as the use of a "language"

All current concepts of style have deep roots in the classical rhetoricians' treatment of style as a normative prescription for oratorical, epistolary, or other verbal practices aimed at desirable effects, like the persuasion of audiences or elaboration of philosophical arguments (see Bialostocki 1961; Gombrich 1968: 353–54; Sauerländer 1983). The various contemporary accounts of production as a "language" share with the ancient analysis the view that style involves choosing and following norms or rules for obtaining specific effects, of which the bare minimum is intelligibility or communication. This "language" requires a choice between two or more and up to an infinity of alternatives – it has informational value. Furthermore, it is a competence its users possess and employ in particular circumstances (Wollheim 1979: 138) – it has psychological or social reality. Insofar as artifacts are produced "linguistically" – as a rule-governed selection among alternatives – they have style.

At the simplest and most general level, the linguistic model requires only the elementary terms of information theory. In a language with three possible elements, $+$, $-$, and $!$, always to begin a message with $+$ and end it with $!$ is consistently to convey particular information (in the middle variables) or, in our metaphor, to use a particular style. Gombrich (e.g., 1963, 1968) has devoted several influential papers to working out the implications of this insight for art history and the analysis need not be repeated here. For our purposes, ignoring their actual intellectual histories, more sophisticated versions of the linguistic model may be regarded as building from this level.

In archaeology, Sackett's "isochrestic" model for style (e.g., 1982: 67–80; see also chapter 4, this volume) proposes that "style resides in the specific context-determined variants ('choices') assumed by functional form" (Sackett 1977: 371). The model requires that function could be fulfilled by any one of a set of alternative forms – that there are "isomorphic functional equivalents" (1977: 374). Therefore, the form actually found represents a "selection" from these alternatives. Furthermore, the model assumes that the selection must be determined in or by a well-defined context. By all our earlier arguments, the nature of the selection or style itself will not tell us directly what this context actually involved, its scale or particularity, and so forth. Conceivably, the "selection" was made by some individual or group acting in a certain way, for certain purposes, and with certain habits, knowledge, and values. However, this possibility cannot be confirmed *from within the stylistic description itself*.

Sackett associates two further and logically quite independent proposals with the isochrestic model itself: (1) apparently as a "highly specific and characteristic manner of doing something," namely, selecting among functional isomorphs, a style is "always peculiar to a specific time and place"; and (2) "the degree of similarity among the choices that are made in two historically related loci depends upon the intensity of social interaction shared by their occupants" (1977: 371).[4] In these senses, "form is an index to history," and by this reasoning, the isochrestic model of style, like any other, might be put to use in attempts to read from style to history.

We have already seen the difficulties of this kind of correlation. The claims of (1), above, are clearly invalid: people at a specific time and place may not make use of or determine a "peculiar" style, that is, a *single* characteristic manner of doing something which is *also* not to be observed at other times and places (either within society or among societies). To establish a one-to-one correlation, in theory we would need at least two further assumptions – namely, that the use of different alternatives at a given time and place (e.g., in a given activity) is mutually exclusive in some well-defined temporal, spatial, or other sense, and that "an object of its precise form and design is most unlikely to recur in any locus other than the one in which we have actually found it" (Sackett 1977: 370, but cf. 1982: 73). These two assumptions are much too unreliable to include among the necessary assumptions of theory of style.

Although, like (1) above, it might be confirmed *on independent evidence in some instances*, the necessity or logic of (2) is also open to question. A similarity-relation of whatever kind does not in and of itself necessarily reveal the cause of the relation between the two attributes. Furthermore, although the presence of a similarity-relation may (or may not) be evidence of the historical relatedness of artifacts, and therefore of their producers, its *absence* is *not* evidence of their *un*relatedness. A description of similarities alone not only might erect false histories of relations among artifacts but also might miss relations. *On independent evidence*, we might actually discover "intense social interaction" among the producers of artifacts. Even so, intense interaction could *also* lead to stylistically divergent production by very closely related producers. Therefore, and in sum, we need an *independent* characterization of interaction – as, for instance, of producers sharing a plan, quoting a model, imitating a master, revising an ancestor, rejecting a competitor, etc., also admitting such possibilities as reversing oneself or forging another. Although often contaminated by purely stylistic inference, such "ethnoarchaeological" analysis is the bread-and-butter of many art-historical studies of schools and workshops, academies, movements, and traditions of art, and so forth.[5]

Although the isochrestic model of style, like any other,

should not be put to use in reading from style to history without independent supports, for our purposes here its true usefulness is simply as a specification of the *nature of production*. The isochrestic model simply states that style is the process – however distributed or institutionalized – of selecting among functional isomorphs and employing the chosen variant(s) in a given context.

In theory, selection is "context-determined." No particular specification of an *actual historical context* is necessarily implied in a pure information-theoretic or isochrestic account of the "linguistic" production of style. The selection could be made by a machine responding to certain frequencies of external stimulation (e.g., output + if high, − if low, ! if middling). The "selection" could be due to a natural process in which one alternative state of the possible outcomes appears with a frequency greater than chance. Such possibilities lead to the difficulty – much underlined in recent archaeology – of differentiating in the absence of independent evidence among "style" produced by robots (a technology acting automatically and leaving certain by-products), by non-human creatures, or by human beings.

However, we can certainly include a specification of the context of selection by definition. In art history and the other humanities, selection among alternate states of a function or message is variously defined as a human being (1) using a code, (2) following a rule, (3) indulging a preference or fulfilling an intention, and so forth. Codes, rules, or intentions are things that a human being uses, follows, or fulfills only in certain contexts. Therefore, it is possible to assert definitionally that style is generated only by a system in those contexts or having those states.

(1) A semiotic account of visual and verbal production would be impossible to outline here. Peircean, Saussurean, structuralist, and other accounts have been extensively treated in the literature (Eco 1976; Eagleton 1983; Barthes 1983). In general, from a semiotic point of view a visual or verbal representation – using the term in its widest sense – is an individual message within a complex code. The code has particular units and imposes a structure upon the message; it consists of paradigmatic and syntagmatic levels of articulation. In verbal language, the units are the phonemes and the structure is the syntax of the language. Although the issue is controversial, in semiotic analysis of graphic displays the units are usually thought to be basic graphic means (like points, lines, and fields of color), and the structure the means of combining them to construct forms or figures and compose a design or scene. In theory, any particular message in the code can be located precisely on the paradigmatic and syntagmatic axes, making possible a precise – a uniquely defining – description for every message. Many topics – for example, syntactic hierarchy, intertextuality, and modality – can be considered in this framework.

(2) The tendentious notion of following a rule is as suggestive as the semiotic notion of using a code. Notions of style as "ruled originality or originality bound by rules" are at least as old as the eighteenth century (Sauerländer 1983:

255–57). From this point of view, we specify the rules of
manufacture, use, and interpretation that gave to the original
makers and users (and/or would give to the modern typologist)
all and only those artifacts brought together in a polythetic
classification. As an historical assertion, following the rule
produces artifacts in the style.

The algorithm itself can be written at any level of
particularity and complexity. Some writers claim to have
isolated the rule – of so-called "intellectual realism" (Luquet
1927) or "aspective" (Schäfer 1974) – which produces the
non-naturalistic, "conceptual" images of children, of many
pre-Greek (pre-perspective) societies, and so forth. This rule
has to be exceedingly general and specifies an extensive global
style. Within this style, the conventions of particular cultures
can be isolated. An ancient Egyptian draftsman apparently
followed a complex set of at least four interrelated "canonical"
rules of drawing, each with dependent sub-rules (Davis 1982,
1986a). Within Egyptian culture itself, we could write
algorithms – now of extraordinary complexity – which would
give the styles of individual workshops or craftsmen. Even in
the absence of independent historical evidence for the rules,
their encoding, and their transmission, the formal adequacy of
all these proposals in a sense can be tested directly. A suitably
programmed computer should be able to produce all and only
the artifacts brought together in a stylistic description.

(3) The humanist's traditional and eclectic talk about
having and fulfilling intentions probably still constitutes the
richest vocabulary for verbal and visual production (e.g,
Baxandall 1985). One intends or means to say what he says.
The limits and paradoxes of this claim – must one say what he
means? is what he means what he says? – are too well known
for review here (see Davis n.d.): however tendentious the
description, style is the result of meanings one intends, and in
selecting among alternates, one uses or chooses that which is
his meaning or intention.

Needless to say, reading *from* a stylistic description alone
to a code, rule, or intention may go badly wrong. The stylistic
description itself is grossly underdetermined. *Many* kinds of
codes, rules, or intentions could produce just, and only those,
artifacts brought together in a polythetic classification (see
Muller 1977: 33 for a formal statement). For our purposes here,
the true usefulness of these models is *only* as a specification of
the nature of production. Clearly, codes, rules, or intentions
are not easy historical entities to work with: they can be
anything from innate response-systems of the human organism
through highly social conventions and "languages" in the
everyday sense to the private states of individual personalities.
However, although independent evidence for these entities may
be hard to come by, clause (c) of our definition (see p. 19,
above) instructs us to search for it archaeologically; found, it is
the source and explanation of style.

Some suspicions must be voiced about all accounts of
production as the use of a "language," at whatever level. First,
no satisfying explanation of the origins of rule-governed
selection has ever been provided. Why should we have style at

all in this sense? If, for instance, there are functional, formal,
or semantic alternates among which choice is made by code,
rule, or intention, why should this procedure be any better or
more common in human culture than simply adopting the first
or only alternate to hand – or does this occur as well? As we
have seen, a stylistic description cannot tell us from within
whether variants were "selected" or just brought together
randomly or under complete constraint. Furthermore, even
when "selected," the information-value or information-content
of a style must fluctuate from artifact to artifact, for although
an initial selection would have full value, repetition and
variation will be redundant to some degree; at the limit, if a
producer has no choice in production whatsoever, strictly
speaking his work is completely lacking in information-value.
Implicitly or explicitly, the linguistic model asserts that style
communicates (see further Schapiro 1953: 304), and must go on
to assume or to provide a theory of the nature and evolution of
communication. Did *Australopithecus* have style because he
communicated, or did he communicate by style – or both (by
definition), or neither (in fact)? Bees and porpoises
communicate; do they have style? Such questions suggest that
style and communication may vary independently – so how,
then, should a concept of communication be built definitionally
into a general theory of style?

Second, a fully satisfying account of the "alternate" states
of a function or message also has yet to be provided. A stylistic
description encompasses only the variant state actually selected
and recovered archaeologically. Where, then, are the alternates?
Should we be able to find them archaeologically, or perhaps
picked out in another description? Although it may make sense
to assert that something could have been done differently, in
many cases this will merely be an argument from silence. In
fact, because a stylistic description cannot tell us from within
whether a selection was random, rule-governed, or completely
constrained, how do we know that things *could* have been done
differently?

Furthermore, the very notion of a formal, functional,
semantic, or other isomorph is logically problematic (as Sackett
recognizes [1977: 374]). Although form, function, and content
are not neatly separated (Goodman 1978), we have to say that
two forms could fulfill the same function or have the same
content, that two functions could have the same form, etc., in
order to envision selection among alternate states. This
notorious doctrine of synonymy is not easily defended (see
Goodman 1949, 1978; the suspicions of Schapiro 1953: 303; and
the defense by Gombrich 1968). For instance, the "continuous
correlation" (Bach 1970) of form and content in depiction
implies that if any formal detail of an image is altered its
meaning necessarily alters correlatively. In speaking, one
cannot really choose between two ways of saying the same
thing; rather, one chooses to say one of two different things.
Moreover, *any* aspect of an artifact – formal or functional,
exhibited or unexhibited – can be stylistic. We cannot have it
(for example) that function will *always* be invariant, with form
varying: cutting may be performed by shears or knives, but two

formally indiscernible knives might be stylistically differentiated in a polythetic classification by functional or semantic criteria – one used at the table, the other in warfare, or one connoting political authority, the other servitude. In sum, the "alternates" selected seem necessarily different or unequal – non-comparable in ways that prejudge the rationales and procedures for selecting among them (see further Wollheim 1979: 144–45).

None of these suspicions necessarily invalidates all accounts of style as the use of a "language." They remind us that specifying the artifact-production system – here, as a system in which selection among alternates has information-value and some kind of psychological and social reality – supports many interpretations and requires supplementary assumptions not inherent in the theory of style itself.

Production as an activity of making

An account of production as an activity of making is more general than an account of production as the same use of a language. It may therefore escape some of the difficulties of the linguistic models.

Making does not necessarily involve communication. In a description or explanation of making, there is no necessary place for a spectator, audience, or receiver (see Walton 1979: 50). Making does not necessarily imply that the artifact will have public inter-subjective meaning, that it will represent, express, or exemplify anything intelligible to anyone, including its maker, or that it will "signify" at all; nonetheless, the artifact has style. Making does not necessarily imply that the artifact will end up being used in any particular way if it is even used at all. Making does not necessarily imply that the producer selects among alternate possibilities; the making might be completely constrained, always limited to one procedure or sequence of procedures. Making generates style insofar as certain actions have certain exhibited or unexhibited effects. Repeating the actions will result in a repetition of the effects, within some tolerance of variation – resulting in the set of similarity-relations among artifacts picked out in a polythetic stylistic description. As an historical assertion, reading from history to style, the necessary condition of style is that the artifacts must have been made in the same way.

This very general account requires considerable fine-tuning, especially to meet some special cases in which archaeologists and art historians tend to be interested. For instance, if completely constrained making still results in products with style, then ants building a hill are working in a style. From a social scientist's or humanist's point of view, this implication may be counter-intuitive or unacceptable (e.g., Kroeber 1957: 150), but only if we feel we have to build into a theory of style various further assumptions about rule-governed selection, intention, communication, and so forth. From a biologist's point of view, this implication may be unexceptionable. Although she might not say that ant-hills have a style, nevertheless she may use ant-hills diagnostically or as one element in a polythetic taxonomy to differentiate one species of ant from another, to recognize changes in the responses of ants to their environment, etc. She will here be extracting all the classificatory and historical information a stylistic description provides. To rule out cases of this kind, but now confronting difficulties we have already reviewed, the qualified necessary condition of style is that artifacts must have been made in the same *but for the maker potentially variable* way.

The account also has the consequence that a Vermeer and an extremely successful forgery of it might belong to different styles, insofar as they were made in different ways. The consequence is unexceptionable. The Vermeer is in the style "Depicting-Dutch-landscapes-and-interiors-with-great-sincerity-using-mid-seventeenth-century-oils (etc.)"; the forgery is in the style "Copying-Old-Masters-with-considerable-cynicism-using-twentieth-century-paints (etc)." The forgery is polythetically similar to the Vermeer in some formal respects, but also to other modern forgeries. Here, we are merely recognizing once again that the stylistic attributes of artifacts may be exhibited or unexhibited, formal, functional, symbolic, or institutional, and so forth. Moreover, polythetic classification might always end up judging an original and a copy to be polythetically very similar in many relevant attributes, grouping them together stylistically – as when we are studying not forgeries but a student's copy of a master's drawing, an artist's homage to an ancestor, or other productions.

Although it must be one of the prime desiderata of archaeology and art history, a fully satisfying account of making itself has yet to be worked out (see further Davis n.d.). We must avoid relying on assumptions about making those artifacts we ordinarily believe to have style, for here style is our *explanandum*. Strictly speaking, our account of making, as of language, must be established independently of a theory of style.

At the limit, our concept of making must extend to natural substances left materially unaltered by human craft but constituted symbolically and institutionally. We want to include rocks brought into a Japanese garden (in the style of Buson) or a pile of felt assembled in a New York gallery (in the style of Robert Morris). Among other things, the "making" in such cases is simply transporting and exhibiting – not, in some instances, a negligible task. Even if materially worked by human hands and tools, alteration can be slight: early statuary might have derived from a tree-trunk gouged by a few rough blows of the axe. Representation itself might derive from the ambiguity, for the human perceptual system, of a completely happenstance clustering of marks and scratches on a surface: the "making" here can simply be the inaugural phenomenon of "seeing-as" (Davis 1986b). The ordinary (and for most purposes comprehensive) art-historical concept of making seems to require the partial or whole manufacture, transport, exhibition, symbolic interpretation, and institutional affiliation of a thing, but it is not clear that these are all and always necessary or sufficient criteria (see further Levinson 1979).

Interesting formulations have been put forward by

Wollheim, for whom the stylistic features of an artifact are just those dependent on the "processes of acting as a painter" (sculptor, builder, etc.) (1979: 134), and Walton, who suggests that in style "we 'see' in the work the action of producing it" (1979: 51) (see also Sircello 1972, Hermerén 1975: 21). "Acting as a painter" or the "action of producing" – making – must be highly variable by time and place. Much stylistic description in art history might be (and often is) taken as a rich historical description of variable ways of making artifacts. Needless to say, by all our earlier arguments, we cannot read securely from the stylistic description to the history of making: "acting as a painter" may not be so easily or at all correctly "seen in" the artifact.

Walton opens the Pandora's Box by reminding us that how an artifact *appears* to have been made may be sufficient for critical purposes, generating description in our inclusive sense of style, (a) (see p. 19, above). Under the inclusive definition, an observer writes up his "vivid impressions of the physical behavior of the artist as well as perhaps more ambiguous impressions of his motivations and personality" (Walton 1979: 54), generally construing the artifact as an "apparent intentional act" (p. 52). However, problematic cases are easily located. The forged Vermeer appears to have been made by a Dutch painter using mid-seventeenth-century oils. The metopes of the Parthenon appear to have been made so as to present the velvety white surface of crystalline marble. The marked bones from Cueva Morin appear to have been made by the cutting tools of a Neanderthal. Only independent evidence will tell us that the Vermeer was actually made by a modern criminal, that the metopes were once fully painted, or that the bones were gnawed by carnivores.

Our new evidence about authenticity, condition, or artifactuality itself could certainly lead us to see other attributes in the artifact, that is, to a substantial revision in the stylistic description. Nevertheless, this possibility does not establish that we will always eventually see the real history of making from an (endlessly revisable) stylistic description, but only that stylistic description could be underwritten by any number of coherent scenarios for "apparent" acts of making – none of which can be seen from the description itself to be an historical specification. "We need to be careful about in what sense the property of appearing to have been made in a certain manner is to be 'located' in the work in which it does so appear" (Walton 1979: 56).

Read in the other direction, from history to style, an archaeologically identifiable system of making artifacts (clause (c)) is the explanation for style (clause (a)) (see p. 19, above). Evidently this account includes but is not limited to a notion of making as the use of a "language"; making may or may not require selecting among alternate states. In an adequate account of making, some steps in the sequence might be regarded as completely constrained by the physical nature of the medium, the maker's knowledge and skill, and so forth, some steps as requiring rule-governed selection, and some steps as completely unconstrained. Making at any of these levels may be stylistic or non-stylistic, for polythetic classification may or may not be able to locate any repetitions in or similarities for some elements of production. However, insofar as making cannot be entirely unique, every time a new artifact is produced, any balance or permutation of these possibilities results in an artifact with style.

No reassuring conclusions

Little has been said so far about how an artifact-production system might be "archaeologically identifiable" (clause (c)) (see p. 19, above) without using inferences from stylistic description. Our theory of style states only that an archaeology of production – of language, of making – will be our context for, control upon, and explanation of style. "In the study of the arts, works – not institutions or people – are the primary data" (Ackerman 1963: 164): data they certainly are, but it is the archaeology of institutions and people which, in the logic of the theory of style, must be primary.

However, "independent evidence" for production – a notion relied upon heavily so far – is in a sense a contradiction in terms. Insofar as archaeology provides evidence of institutions or people at all – a chronicle or archive, a letter or interview, a manual or contract, a tool-kit or workshop – it cannot be evidence independent of style, for as we have seen all documents and artifacts of whatever kind can themselves be brought under a stylistic description. When we refer to seasonal technology to account for a taxonomy of Mousterian tools, or to Jackson Pollock's interviews to account for a reading of his paintings, we are simply underwriting one stylistic description (the taxonomy or reading) with another (the technology or document). For the moment, in a given analysis one description is "style," the other "history," but, as archaeological evidence, both are no more and no less than stylistic descriptions.

From this point of view, "history" is therefore a stylistic description specially privileged in a given archaeological analysis according to theoretical commitments beyond any possible reach of evidence. Any stylistic description can become "history," the privileged description, by theoretical stipulation. We could, by stipulation, explain the "style" of Mousterian seasonal technology by a taxonomy of Mousterian tools, or the "style" of Pollock's interviews by a reading of his paintings.

Our theory of style implies only that we must *choose* which description of archaeological evidence will be used in a given analysis as the privileged description, as the "history" by which all and sundry other stylistic descriptions will be explained, and that once we have made this choice, throughout the analysis we are completely constrained by it. However we specify our history – as technology, or as intention, or as institution, or as unconscious, etc. – we cannot read back to it by or attempt to find it through any other stylistic description. We must choose the description which we stipulate gives history to us, and read from there. For the moment, the historical description has become irreducible and incorrigible: it is the source, guarantor, and test of any styles it underwrites.

The theory of style says nothing one way or another about *which* stylistic description of whatever archaeological evidence should be privileged as "history" in a given analysis. That decision is taken and defended on other grounds.

Notes

1. I cannot undertake detailed discussion of other studies of style; this note must be my acknowledgement. I have learned from, and sometimes take issue with, Schapiro 1953, Munro 1956, Kroeber 1957, Ackerman 1963, Gombrich 1968, Sackett 1977, Wobst 1977, Goodman 1978, Kubler 1979, Walton 1979, Wollheim 1979, Robinson 1981, Sauerländer 1983. Appropriate references appear in the text but do not exhaust my debt to these studies. Philosophical aesthetics (especially Dickie 1974; Goodman 1972a; Wollheim 1980; Danto 1981) suggests, among other matters, the importance of the symbolic nature and institutional context of artifacts, of authenticity, of indiscernibility and similarity, and of the criteria of identity of works of art. Classic studies in the methodological foundations of art history (especially Riegl 1985; Wölfflin 1932; Panofsky 1939, 1960; Gombrich 1960, 1963; see also Podro 1981; Mitchell 1986) are constant if somewhat implicit points of reference. Formal studies of taxonomy and phylogenetic explanation (especially Hennig 1979; Simpson 1961; Sneath and Sokal 1973) provide exact analytic tools. Finally, I hope this paper will be read in relation to actual art histories or anthropologies of art which put to use, test, and sometimes abandon theories of style and worry about its history (especially Baxandall 1972, 1980; Clark 1973, 1985; Grabar 1973; Leroi-Gourhan 1965; Lévi-Strauss 1982; Lewis-Williams 1981; Robertson 1975).

2. An early opposition to these views was the archaeologist-historian-philosopher R. G. Collingwood's stress on historical periods, cycles, and patterns as artifacts of the observer (1929; 1946: 205–334). Although Richardson and Kroeber's (1940) study of fashion is still perhaps the best-known empirical examination of cycles (see also Sorokin 1937), Kroeber also voiced skepticism about the treatment of cyclical or other periodicity in art history (1957: 137–49).

3. The "constancy" of form so central to Schapiro's (1953) concept of style is not a necessary feature of style by our definition (see also Kubler 1979). Various interesting attempts have been made to demonstrate the "inherent unity and continuity of the development of art" (Levinson 1979: 246) – for instance, in studies of influence (review in Hermerén 1975), in emphasis on stylistic *traditions* or *fashions* (by our definition, special cases of style, adding further detailed specifications of the rate, pace, direction, degree, and regularity of change), or in relatively formal theories like Kubler's (1962) "rule of series." The theory of style certainly accommodates but does not inherently call for "continuity."

4. Compare Sackett 1982: 73. For the role of this claim in recent archaeology, see the reviews and criticisms by Hodder 1979.

5. Although almost any work of traditional and much revisionist art history could be cited, see the classic studies of Panofsky (1953), Richter (1970), and Schapiro (1979). Wiessner (1983, 1984) provides a review and provocative extension of work on style conducted by archaeologists and anthropologists, especially the problem of "deriving social information from style" (1984: 191); the relevant literature includes central studies by David and Hennig (1972), Wobst (1977), Conkey (1978), and Hodder (1982b).

Chapter 4

Style and ethnicity in archaeology: the case for isochrestism

James R. Sackett

In this chapter, the author sets out to clarify and to tie together in a single essay many of his earlier thoughts on the isochrestic perspective on style, which derives from the notion that there are equally viable options for attaining any given end in the making and/or use of material items. This isochrestic perspective, however, does not comprise a theory or even a model of stylistic behavior; rather, it focuses on what is a key question to the author: where in formal variation does style reside? Sackett's perspective involves some important distinctions and definitions that set his views apart from others; for example, he articulates how and why style and function are not distinct but dualistic in instrumental form.

In addressing some issues raised by his earlier formulations on isochrestic style, Sackett discusses here his notions of active and passive style, the problems he sees with iconological approaches, what the central issues of debate are between himself and Binford and Wiessner, and why isochrestism, as a perspective, provides a starting point in stylistic studies.

One of the livelier debates exercising archaeologists and their ethno-archaeological colleagues today is the relationship between style, ethnicity, and material culture. How does style in human craft products inform upon and mediate the shape, boundaries, and interrelations of ethnic groups? And how does it function to provide a kind of symbolic congruence to the material environment within them that helps structure the day-to-day lives of their members in ways that are deemed to be culturally appropriate? My own contribution to the debate consists of several articles written from the so-called *isochrestic*

perspective of style. The purpose of this essay is to assemble in one place the various ideas and arguments that have appeared in fairly piecemeal fashion in these writings, which were aimed more toward airing specific issues of the debate than toward providing a coherent picture of isochrestism in and of itself. Apart from providing an interesting counterpoint to the other chapters in this volume, the exercise should prove useful by characterizing the thrust of my position as a whole and by giving me the opportunity to expand and up-date it to conform to my current thinking.[1] I shall not hesitate to employ here certain examples and turns of phrase that I have used before. The cause is not that my muse is on strike, but rather that they seem particularly well suited to the purpose and have come to constitute a kind of idiom for pointing up the distinguishing features of the argument.

Two additional introductory comments are in order. First, this chapter constitutes a fairly loose and personal sally of the mind and it assumes no responsibility for systematically reviewing the literature. The comparative rarity of textual references should in no sense be misconstrued as a lack of appreciation of, or denial of indebtedness to, the contributions of my fellow workers. Most of the individual points I make have no doubt been made several times before by others. Whatever may be novel here largely arises not from the points themselves but rather from the specific fashion in which they are interwoven to form my argument. Second, although the reader will encounter a rather formidable array of special terms and labels, none should be taken too seriously; they are simply vehicles that help carry the argument and I feel no particular loyalty to any of them. This includes, by the way, "isochrestism" itself. Care is taken in what follows to state precisely what I do and do not mean by it, but it is an unwieldy term and, in any event, so much violence has already been done to it in the literature that we might well be rid of it (see S 1986b: 10).[2] What counts is the argument, and it may be time to give it a new name. Finally, like so many others, I feel uncomfortable in following the practice now common among anthropologists of equating "style" in such broad but still exacting fashion with ethnicity itself. Let us come up with a replacement, and restore to the word the happy ambiguity that once made it so flexible and effective a tool of discourse.

The isochrestic model

Isochrestism is a model for style in the general case, designed to be valid in all branches of archaeology and, indeed, material culture studies as a whole (see S 1977; S 1982: 67–80 for detailed expositions). It is grounded in the fundamental issues and never departs far from them, attempting to range over the entire landscape occupied by style rather than (like most models) to elaborate an edifice of theory on any single promontory of the terrain.

To begin at the very beginning, the archaeological record reflects people doing things, and it is our charge to ask the double-barrelled question: who were they and what were they up to? There is then a dualism inherent in our inquiry between actors and actions, groups and tasks, ethnicity and activity. It is customary to refer to artifactual patterning that reflects ethnicity as "stylistic" variation and to that reflecting activity as "functional" variation. Style may be expressed at several different levels of ethnic resolution, ranging from individual kin groups within individual settlements, such as a clan in a Four Corners pueblo, to great culture-historical complexes that occupy considerable blocks of space and time, such as the Anasazi cultural tradition of which that clan represents but one highly specific manifestation. Regardless of whether the degree of resolution we happen to work at is fine-grained enough to allow us to see it, we assume that a network of social relations underlies all ethnic units. The expression of function, on the other hand, is usually categorized according to the cultural domain in which it operates; it will suffice for our purposes to distinguish simply between the utilitarian domain of techno-economics and the non-utilitarian one of societal and ideational life. While our primary concern may lie with style rather than function, it will be seen that the pursuit of one of them in material culture necessarily calls for grappling simultaneously with the other.

We turn first to the nature of the link between style and ethnicity in formal products. Why do specific patterns in material culture characterize individual ethnic groups and reflect the nature and degree of their relations with other such groups? The reason is that there normally exists a spectrum of equivalent alternatives, of equally viable options, for attaining any given end in manufacturing and/or using material items.[3] I refer to these options as constituting *isochrestic* variation. The term is a neologism from the Greek which literally translates as "equivalent in use" and which connotes in essence that there is more than one way to skin a cat (see S 1982: 73).

Style enters the picture when we see that the artisans of any given fraternity (or sorority) are aware of only a few, and often choose but one, of the isochrestic options potentially available to them when performing any given task, and that the choices they make are largely dictated by the technological traditions within which they have been enculturated as members of the social groups that delineate their ethnicity. These choices tend to be quite specific and consistently expressed within a given group at a given time, although they are subject to revision as a result of changes in its patterns of social interaction (and concomitant exposure to alternative isochrestic options) with other groups. Isochrestic variation in material culture that is socially bounded in this manner is consequently diagnostic or idiomatic of ethnicity, and it is such variation that we perceive as style. The likelihood of unrelated groups making similar combinations of choices is as remote as the number of potential options is great. Hence each social group or unit of ethnicity tends to possess its own distinctive style, and the overall degree of stylistic similarity represented by two groups' material cultures taken as wholes can be regarded as a direct expression of their ethnic relatedness.

Now, the key question is: where in formal variation does style reside? In my view it is to be found wherever isochrestic options exist and factors allied to ethnicity dictate the choices made among them. And, since isochrestic choice is essentially ubiquitous in all culturally conditioned form in all of its aspects, so potentially is ethnically significant style. The point can be illustrated with reference to a decorated cooking pot found in the Anasazi pueblo that appeared a couple of paragraphs back. Its decoration for one thing is probably a rich source of style. For this constitutes what may be called *adjunct* form, that is, variation that is added on and supplemental to the utilitarian *instrumental* form involved in the pot's manufacture and functioning as an item in the techno-economic realm.[4] Decoration is of course particularly style-rich because it is largely free to vary outside of the mechanically contingent design constraints imposed by functional necessity upon instrumental form, and it consequently has the potential to offer an extremely broad range of options to choose from.

Nonetheless, the instrumental form that is built in, rather than added on, to the pot is also a great reservoir of style. For the pot's manufacture and the utilitarian ends it was designed to serve required its maker to choose (whether consciously or not) among a considerable variety of isochrestic alternatives with respect to clays, tempers, shapes, thicknesses, and techniques of construction and firing, some or possibly even all of which can be just as ethnically – and hence stylistically – significant as the decoration that may be applied to its surface. No single one of these elements may have offered as great a range of choice as the decoration, but choice was involved nonetheless. And, as a simple function of their number, the total stylistic potential of the pot's instrumental formal variation might rival that of the decoration itself.

Thus the isochrestic model postulates that style is essentially ubiquitous in formal variation, residing in both its instrumental and adjunct components. Despite the above illustration, isochrestism is not a model likely to attract the average ceramicist, who is prone to see style nearly exclusively in the play of decoration. This position may aptly, if not particularly felicitously, be termed *adjunctism*. Decoration has always exercised a kind of tyranny over the thinking of archaeologists about style, and sometimes to good effect. For example, a straightforward equation of style with adjunct form has underlain most of the achievements of the modern school of *ceramic sociology*. Its realization that decorative motifs in pottery can be viewed as a reflection of – and, hence, a key to – the social groupings that produced it has undoubtedly prompted some of the most sophisticated efforts yet to recognize ethnicity in the archaeological record (S 1977: 376–77; S 1982: 80–82). Yet even here a kind of closet isochrestism can often be discerned. For example, although he feels compelled to restrict the word "style" to decoration, Stephen Plog does not hesitate to read possible ethnic significance into such "technical" features as vessel wall thickness and physical composition of clays (1983: 134–35). And in his recent study of ethnicity and Kalinga pottery, William Longacre goes the full isochrestic distance, noting decoration as only one of a list of "stylistic features" that include such aspects of instrumental form as the thickness of the rim, wall, and base, and various contours and proportions built into vessel shape (1981: 62).

In any event, given the fact that the overwhelming bulk of material culture consists of utilitarian functional form bearing little or no decoration, an isochrestic model would seem to be indispensable if more than a small fraction of the stylistic potential of the archaeological record is to be realized. Without it the search for style would largely have to be abandoned by default in such broad and diverse areas of artifactual variation as stone tools, architecture, bone and antler implements, milling equipment, hearths and other such features, many metal items, industrial and domestic debris, as well of course as the instrumental form of decorated objects – in all of which style is something built in, not added on. Furthermore, as is illustrated so well by the range and variety of instrumental form in perishable material culture described by Pierre Lemmonier (1986) among the Anga of New Guinea, the arena in which stylistic variation can be sought and defined would be even more greatly restricted for ethnographers in the absence of an isochrestic perspective.

Let us turn now to two important implications of the above line of argument. The first is that style, being virtually omnipresent in all formal variation, must necessarily share that variation with function. In other words, style and function are not distinct, self-contained, mutually exclusive realms of form in themselves, but instead complementary dimensions or

aspects of variation that co-exist within the same form. Perhaps none of my colleagues would dispute this in the case of adjunct form, since it is customary to regard decoration as functioning in the ideational and societal domains. Style theorists generally emphasize its role as a means of symbolizing the presence of, and distinctions between, ethnic groups. Here then a decorative ensemble recognized as a specific style diagnostic of a specific ethnic group, different from the alternative styles that characterize other such groups, can be regarded simply as an instance of *function writ small*.

But some find it disconcerting to try conceptualizing style and function as complementary and dualistic aspects that also simultaneously reside in instrumental form. Nonetheless, alternative modes of spalling the bevelled front of an endscraper, of slipping a pot, of shaping a brick, of flanging a bronze axe, or of twining cordage can be just as stylistically diagnostic of ethnicity as alternative design elements on the bodies of ceramic vessels. They may be potentially less "style-rich" than decoration in the sense that they entail narrower ranges of isochrestic choice, but the difference remains one of degree and not kind. And again it may equally be said of them that they represent function writ small.

This dualism of style and function in instrumental form holds not only among attributes of objects, as in the above examples, but also at the higher levels of objects themselves and the assemblages into which objects in turn cluster. Thus a *ko* halberd no doubt functioned as a lethal instrument in the hand of a Shang or Chou Dynasty warrior, yet at the same time it can be regarded as but one Chinese "style" of a kind of weapon whose isochrestic variants are to be found in several different Bronze and Iron Age contexts in much of the Old World. In the same manner, a parrot-beaked flint burin is at once a chisel (function) and an object that is exclusively diagnostic of French Magdalenian VI industries (style). At the level of the assemblage, the collection of Linear B clay tablets recovered from Pylos obviously functioned as part of an inventorying system vital to the economic and military direction of a complex society, but the specific form and content of the tablets are nonetheless stylistically unique to Late Bronze Age Mycenaean culture. And, regardless of the fact that it functionally permeated all aspects of the lives of those who used it, the particular array of mounds, plazas, and courts seen at Tikal is but one of several styles that monumental ceremonial centers could assume in a Mesoamerican civilization.

In each of the above cases – whether attribute, object, or assemblage – style can be viewed as function writ small, that is, as the specific ethnically bounded isochrestic choice assumed by functional form. Although some archaeologists seem to find it perplexing (e.g., Binford 1986; see also note 6, below), the notion that objects can be viewed as making up a world of functional classes and their individual stylistic (albeit still functional) variants is built into our common sense. This is implicitly reflected in the binomial, specific-generic form of designation we habitually use to name things in all walks of life, e.g., Hoosier axe, Navajo blanket, Romanesque church, Samurai sword, Carolingian minuscule, Boston baked beans.

The second implication of the model requiring mention at this point is that the search for style ought not to be restricted to those formal properties of design in which material culture is conventionally defined for purposes of systematics and museum display. For isochrestic choice permeates artifactual variation in the broadest sense of the term, essentially existing wherever culturally conditioned activity materially manifests itself. In my own field of Stone Age archaeology, for example, apart from the stone tool typologies used in conventional systematics, the imprint of ethnicity should be suspected in the choice of one flint source as opposed to another, in the core reduction techniques used to produce tool blanks, and in alternative modes of backing bladelets and spalling burin facets. It should also be reflected in *themes* that cross-cut conventional typology altogether, such as the degree of standardization with which design notions are realized in tool manufacture, the seemingly arbitrary preference for more robust tool blanks rather than gracile ones, or the easy-going opportunistic manner in which the artisans of one assemblage have rejuvenated broken tools that in another assemblage would have been abandoned and replaced by new ones. It is often such "funny little somethings" intuitively perceived by the journeyman excavator that provide a distinctive family air to each of his occupations and allow him to recognize their presence in different sectors of his site long before he has sufficient stratigraphic exposure to confirm his guesses or sufficiently large tool samples to give their assemblages formal typological definition.

Lithic archaeologists are also quite aware of the fact that style may be seen as well in the broader patterns of behavior of stone tools that arise from ethnic variation in the technological contexts in which they served. To mention an obvious example, territorial differences among ethnic groups of prehistoric hunter-gatherers would presumably have entailed differences in resources that called for different economic and demographic strategies, which would be reflected automatically by site placement and organization, tool densities, and the manner in which artifact types spatially cluster into tool-kits over occupation surfaces. Finally, not to be overlooked are the stigmata of the use of stone tools on other materials that might be considered artifactual only in a secondary sense. This last point means that, in isochrestic perspective, a specific butchering technique may well convey as much ethnically significant information as the typology of the tools with which it was carried out. No doubt all of the above points could be made with more telling effect with reference to fields of archaeology – such as the Near Eastern Neolithic, and American Southwest, or the Canadian Arctic – whose artifactual evidences of techno-economics are richer, more various, and better understood than those at my disposal.

The behavioral background

It should be stressed that isochrestism as such does not entail a theory of stylistic behavior. The model restricts itself to the question of where style resides, which is quite a different issue. Furthermore, as should be obvious from what has gone before, an isochrestic point of view is in any case an etic, or "outside," one in which style is regarded primarily as an organizing concept imposed upon material culture by the researcher rather than an emic pattern he attempts to evoke from it. While I may refer to "stylistic variation" for purposes of exposition, I mean in fact "variation that exhibits stylistically significant patterning" – which is not quite the same thing. Hence, while the opening sentence of this essay states that style both informs upon and mediates ethnicity, an isochrestic approach in and of itself is largely preoccupied with discerning the former rather than elucidating the latter.

In this perspective, then, to argue that style is necessarily a dynamic element of culture in its own right suggests the logical fallacy of misplaced concreteness, that is, the reification into an active force of what is essentially an abstraction. And, in turn, to inquire into the nature of "stylistic behavior" would consequently seem to beg the very question it purports to attack. The point might be made by stretching it a bit to the realm of aesthetics. Everyone agrees that aesthetics permeates material culture, at least in the sense that we feel free to make aesthetic judgements with respect to any object, ranging from the proportions of the statue of David to the texture of bricks. But few indeed would feel comfortable attempting to define "aesthetic behavior." Precisely when was Michelangelo involved in aesthetic behavior and when not; and was the bricklayer who erected the wall whose surface so pleases me engaged in aesthetic behavior at all?

However, while I may assume an agnostic position with respect to stylistic behavior in and of itself, there is much to be said about the behavioral foundations of isochrestic choice that lie behind what we conceptualize as style. For one thing, what I refer to as isochrestic choice is no more than the expression in material culture of a kind of behavior that permeates all aspects of cultural life. That artisans tend to "choose" by conforming to and perpetuating the isochrestic options imposed upon them by the technological traditions within which they work is presumably no different from their conforming to and perpetuating the specific gestures, idioms of speech, ways of disciplining children, and magical practices appropriate to, and characteristic of, the social groupings in which such traditions are fostered. Thus isochrestic choice, whether conscious or not, is an integral component of cultural life itself, and it therefore seems not unreasonable to speak of "isochrestic behavior." Secondly, regardless of how obscure its root causes, the need for such choice is obvious, since living in human groups would simply be a chaotic if not altogether impossible business without it. As Alfred Kroeber reminds us, "for things to be done well they must be done definitely" (1948: 329). Order, skill, and facility in human relations and technology require the definitiveness and effectiveness that come from choosing specific lines of procedures from the broad arc of alternative options and then sticking to them. It is isochrestic behavior that, so to speak, standardizes a cultural system, furnishing it the congruence and efficiency without which it could not operate.

Of special concern to us here is the fact that the standardization such behavior lends to craft products creates a structured material environment that serves to regulate the social fabric itself. For it is at this point that we touch upon the symbolic role of style in material culture, the fact that it constitutes a kind of iconicism that functions to promote an ethnic group's self-identity and cohesiveness, to maintain its boundaries, and to arbitrate its interactions with other such groups. It is here then where we turn from the static etic domain of style as something that informs to the dynamic emic one of style as something that mediates, and it is also here that the question of stylistic behavior cannot be avoided. As it is usually formulated in the literature, the question becomes: how, when, and to what degree is style intentionally created and manipulated by artisans to achieve the above iconic ends?

It is sufficient for our purposes to recognize two different points of view (S 1986b). The first I have labelled *active* style. This view holds that the iconic properties of style constitute ethnic "messaging" generated by what is essentially self-conscious, deliberate, and premeditated behavior on the part of artisans, primarily with the intent of identifying and maintaining boundaries between social groups. (Not surprisingly, many students follow Martin Wobst's [1977] lead in referring to it as the "information exchange" theory of style.) Here, in other words, isochrestic behavior, the business of making choices among options, is essentially guided by symbolic behavior, the business of assigning meaning to these choices; the two in fact are wedded so closely as to become essentially one and the same behavior, which is often labelled "stylistic." The second point of view maintains that iconism in style is for the most part *passive*. This latter position by no means denies the existence of intentional signalling (i.e., active style) altogether. But it does assert that the overwhelming bulk of iconic information carried by objects is only latent, inherent in the isochrestic choices which lie behind their manufacture and which themselves are for the most part made unself-consciously. The manner and degree to which this latent iconicism is given functioning life depend upon the meanings subsequently assigned to the objects once they enter the matrix of cultural life – that is, only after they become subject to the symbol-mongering that seems to be built into human nature. In this view, in other words, isochrestic behavior and symbolic behavior remain distinct from each other in form and timing, and there seems to be no room for "stylistic behavior" at all unless it is simply employed in a metaphorical sense.[5]

Now, the active school has been most viable over the past two decades, apparently receiving much of its original impetus from provocative essays by Lewis Binford (e.g., 1962, 1965), and subsequently being elaborated by researchers with such otherwise varied outlooks and fields of expertise as Martin Wobst (1977), Margaret Conkey (1978a), Edwin Wilmsen (Wilmsen and Roberts 1978), and Polly Wiessner (1983), to name but a few. The notion that style constitutes a kind of

intentional iconic signalling is an attractive one, if for no other reason than that it provides students of material culture a bridging argument by means of which their data can be translated directly into statements about human behavior couched in functional terms that find sympathetic vibrations in much of anthropological thought. The allure of the notion is witnessed by the fact that many of its proponents claim to see no alternative to it other than theoretical chaos. Unless subjected to the discipline of their narrow definition, style itself is said to become an unworkable concept, "unmanageably multidimensional" (Wobst 1977: 317) and to be "relegated to the position of some largely inexplicable, randomly varying phenomenon" (Pollock 1983: 385).

Further, most proponents of this view tend to gravitate toward an even more embracing and rigid position, wherein active style is wedded to adjunctism in an alliance that I have sometimes referred to as the *iconological* approach to style (e.g., S 1982: 80). There are of course historic reasons for this alliance stemming from the tyranny that decoration has traditionally imposed upon style theory, a received opinion that has been reinforced in the recent past by the desire to give a "functional" explanation to the exciting results ceramic sociologists have obtained from pottery design motifs (e.g., Binford 1965).

Apart from its historic credentials, the iconological approach is in any case doubly attractive in that it simultaneously offers a seductively simple theoretical stand combined with methodological security (see S 1986b: 271–73). With regard to the first, equating style with adjunct form, which constitutes a distinct realm of variation divorced from utilitarian function, allows one to conclude that that which is stylistic is nothing else but stylistic. This in turn gives the empirical mandate for reifying style into an active cultural force and attributing it to "stylistic behavior" on the part of those who create it. And since adjunct form by definition functions in the societal and ideational domains, stylistic behavior becomes a matter of conscious ethnic signalling or symbolizing. The argument is indeed compelling, because it defines how one can explain style in what are presumably emic behavioral terms and because it dictates precisely where one should, and where one need not bother to, look for it (see Pollock 1983 for a recent, and particularly explicit, example of this line of reasoning). It is the latter point, of course, that provides the methodological "security" mentioned above (to which we shall return).

To be sure, the study of true formal iconography treated as a discrete entity in and of itself is an entirely legitimate and important enterprise, as Timothy Earle's contribution to this volume (chapter 8) well illustrates. But the iconological approach as defined above is something else, and in so far as it pretends to be valid for material culture in general, I reject it as a viable approach to style. In great part, of course, my opposition stems from its alliance with adjunctism. While I myself might not find it a congenial idiom, I would not object if the iconologues' references to "messaging" were simply a metaphor for arguing that the symbolism inherent in style entails purposeful behavior as such. For what we conceptualize as style is indeed the product of behavior of some kind and, as an anthropologist, I am happy to admit that all behavior may in one sense or another be regarded as purposeful. However, because it embraces adjunctism – a specific theoretical stand on the question of where style resides – the iconological argument must be viewed not as dialectical metaphor but as a model of empirical expectations. The two are altogether different. (Just as it is one thing for a psychoanalyst to talk about my "superego" but something quite different for a brain surgeon to claim he can show it to me.) And this is a model I reject because, in freeing one from any responsibility for coming to grips with the broad world of instrumental form, it fosters a highly impoverished, parochial view of the extent and play of style in material culture.

It also bears noting that, in postulating that adjunct form and style are one and the same thing, adjunctism is itself a tautology and promotes tautological thinking. This presumably accounts for the absence of solid empirical verification that is to be found in much of the research of the iconologues, who tend to proceed on *a priori* grounds alone, asserting as facts only what their theoretical stance has already led them to assume to be true.[6] It is for this reason that I have sometimes questioned whether they are not primarily employed simply in applying an anthropological veneer over what really amounts to ethnographic and archaeological question-begging (e.g., S 1985a: 159).

At the same time, I believe there is in any case a great deal to be said for the notion of passive style. My argument here is based upon points I have already touched upon: that the choices involved in isochrestic behavior create the raw material of style, that style which informs upon ethnicity is an etic perception of the observer, and that style which mediates ethnicity is an emic phenomenon involving the operation of symbolic behavior upon the products of isochrestic choice. The notion of passive style differs from active style, then, in that it regards making choices and assigning meaning to those choices as two distinct kinds of behavior rather than as one and the same behavior. Thus, to put it in the form of a simile, in the perspective of active style a unit of material culture may be likened to a recording of, say, Bach's "Goldberg Variations," while in the view of passive style it more likely brings to mind the image of a harpsichord on which one performer may indeed play Bach but another might render Handel or Scarlatti, or, indeed, nothing at all. In the latter view, then, the harpsichord may be prerequisite to a certain kind of music, but it does not itself produce it; rather, it manifests music in responding to something external to itself.

The point is an important one, and a concrete illustration may help to nail it home. Let us imagine an American tourist in Paris. He is directed to his hotel by a policeman, whose uniform and its accompanying insignia do indeed constitute active style. But consider what our tourist encounters once he enters his room: armoire instead of closet, shutters over the windows, door handles and window hardware of novel configurations, pillow the shape of a sausage running the full width of the bed, toilet (if not located on the stair landing) partitioned off from bathing area, and so forth. There is no reason to believe that these furnishings were deliberately designed to signal "you have crossed an ethnic border and are now in France," or "you are a foreigner," or even "we are different and perhaps not to be trusted," even though the tourist is sure to draw one or more of these ethnic conclusions. Instead they constitute passive style and are simply the product of French artisans doing things the way they have learned is the proper manner of doing them. This manner, by the way, contrary to its effect upon Americans, happens to create for French visitors to the hotel a familiar and congruent symbolic environment, and they read messages of quite a different nature, such as "you are on home ground, among people whose actions are predictable and trustworthy." (In terms of our above simile, the harpsichord remains the same but another composition is being played on it.) Style then can usually be passive but it nonetheless functions iconically because people automatically react symbolically without prodding. Thus it may be said that ethnic messages are far more often read than deliberately sent.

It must be stressed that, unlike my opposition to the adjunctism of iconological theory, my brief for passive style constitutes what should be referred to, for want of a better term, as "Sackettism" rather than isochrestism (see S 1986b: 274). For, while it may be logically consistent with the isochrestic model, it is not necessarily logically dictated by it. As I have taken care to stress, the model exclusively concerns itself with the question of where style resides; in and of itself it does not preclude one's assuming a more sympathetic position with respect to active style than my own happens to be. We shall in fact see an example of this in the next section.

Some criticisms and clarifications

Although occasionally referred to in passing (with varying degrees of enthusiasm and accuracy), isochrestism has to date received little detailed examination in the literature. There are two exceptions, both consisting of fairly substantial exchanges between myself and critics of the approach. These merit discussion here, not in order to continue the debates themselves but rather to clarify and expand upon certain important issues they have raised.

One, the strongest reaction that isochrestism has yet evoked, is a recent paper by Lewis Binford (1986), which was apparently written in response to the detailed criticism of his own, heavily iconological, interpretation of Middle and Upper Paleolithic assemblage variability that was incorporated in my 1982 paper on style and lithic archaeology. The substance of his response need not be repeated here, as I have dealt with it in a reply that was published simultaneously (S 1986a). Suffice it to say that it is vintage Binford, mixing New Archaeology dialectic, *ad hominem* argument, and misrepresentation of my views in about equal proportion, and conveyed in a debating style seemingly based upon the credo that truth will somehow emerge simply by bashing with a club whatever one happens to regard as error.

However, the central issue that exercises Binford does warrant comment, as it concerns a question that sometimes seems to trouble even those who approach isochrestism in an informed and open frame of mind. In brief, if isochrestism holds that style resides in all artifactual variation, does it not follow that all archaeological variability must be regarded as a direct reflection of ethnic variability? And, in turn, does not this lead to the error that traditional archaeologists frequently made of automatically regarding similarities and differences in the make-up of archaeological assemblages as unambiguous measures of their degree of ethnic relationship? The reader will presumably recognize here the kernel of the classic debate between François Bordes and Binford regarding Middle Paleolithic assemblage variability, wherein Bordes maintained that the Mousterian industrial types represent distinct cultural traditions and Binford argued that they represent alternative techno-economic complexes left by a single tradition (e.g., Bordes and de Sonneville Bordes 1970; Binford 1973). What was at stake here, in short, is the basic actor/action, ethnicity/activity, style/function distinction with which my argument begins. Not surprisingly, it was this debate that saw the embryo of isochrestism conceived (S 1973), and it is an issue that I have subsequently discussed at some length with respect both to style (e.g., S 1982) and to the evolution of method and theory in French Paleolithic archaeology (e.g., S 1983).

In any case, the key to resolving the question raised above is suggested by asking another, equally valid but altogether antithetical, one: if isochrestism also holds, as it does, that function resides in all artifactual form, does it not follow that all archaeological variability must on the contrary be regarded as a direct reflection of activity, and hence that differences in the make-up of archaeological assemblages are unambiguous measures not of ethnicity but of functional variation? It takes little reflection upon the paradoxical collision of these two questions to realize that neither is in fact legitimate. Instead, the question that *should* be asked takes an altogether different form: if both style and function are simultaneously present in artifactual form, how are we to tell when, and to what extent, the observed make-up of an assemblage reflects ethnicity and when, and to what extent, it reflects activity? The answer lies in the arenas of specificity and context. For style and function are obviously cross-cutting patterns, and whether artifactual variation presents itself in terms of its functional or stylistic aspect depends upon the level of resolution at which it is regarded and how the assemblage in which it appears is defined.

The point can be illustrated by the example of an able, if historically naive, crew of archaeologists excavating a World War I battlefield in northern France (see S 1982: 77). (The site may be a dismal one, but a better example does not exist of boundary-maintenance, an issue close to the heart of both

iconologues and most ethno-archaeological students of style.) The researchers would quickly learn to recognize those recurring features we know as dugouts, first-aid stations, and kitchens and in turn to discover that any one of them associated with trenches lying to the west of no man's land would bear close similarity to its counterpart to the east with respect to its physical layout, inventory of generically functional items like "rifles" and "helmets," and even the relative frequencies in which such items appeared. Yet, provided they succeeded in gaining even a slight acquaintance with isochrestic variation within the material of warfare of that epoch, they would have no difficulty appreciating the stylistic distinction between the Mauser and the Lebel and between the Frenchman's *casque* and the German's *Stahlhelm*. As a consequence, our archaeologists would recognize that certain dugouts shared stylistically important formal similarities with certain first aid stations and even kitchens on the western half of the site that were not shared with dugouts on the eastern half. And they would presumably quickly work their way toward the conclusion that is already intuitively obvious to the reader: that the dugouts, first-aid stations, and kitchens represent three functionally distinct kinds of activity that were pursued simultaneously and in pretty much the same fashion by opposing armies of distinct ethnic compositions.

But this is not to say that, when viewed in different contexts or different degrees of specificity, the same artifactual variation might not be regarded in quite different fashion. For example, a French officer immersed in tactical matters presumably viewed the dugouts, first-aid stations, and kitchens associated with his trenchline as components of an entirely functional system. On the other hand, from the perspective of a military historian, all three might simply constitute – regardless of which side of no man's land they happened to occupy – elements of the style in which West European nations conducted warfare in the early twentieth century (quite different, to be sure, from the style in which, say, the Japanese conducted it during the seventeenth century).

We turn now to a second and altogether different issue involving isochrestism, which emerged from an exchange between Polly Wiessner and myself concerning her work on style among arrows made by San of the Kalahari Desert (Wiessner 1983). I regard her article as an excellent piece of ethnographic reporting. But I have been critical of certain iconological overtones her argument assumed that in my view are neither justified on theoretical grounds nor warranted by the data themselves (S 1985a). Her reply (Wiessner 1985) has in turn clarified some of the issues I raised, posed some new ones, and in general stimulated me to re-examine my own argument – or at least the terms in which I couched it (S 1986b). In contrast to my confrontation with Binford, this was a true exchange from which I believe both participants have profited. My aim in what follows is not to repeat what has already been raised. This seems particularly suitable in view of the fact that Wiessner herself is furnishing a companion chapter to this volume (chapter 10) and will therefore have the opportunity to comment directly.

It would seem that our positions are in fact appreciably closer than her original article and my critique of it might suggest. For one thing, if I understand it correctly, her reply appears to adopt what is essentially an isochrestic position with respect to the question of where style resides. She has come to agree, in short, that style need not necessarily entail some sort of adjunct form and that it can in fact co-exist with function in instrumental form. Furthermore, she renounces active style at least in its extreme guise, that is, wherein it narrowly restricts style to "clear, purposeful, conscious messages aimed at a specific target population" (p. 162) She still views style as an "active tool in social strategies," but in broader terms that seem to entail unconscious as much as conscious behavior on the part of artisans and that range in specificity from purposeful signalling to mere insinuation. Although I am unsure as to where her position lies in terms of my own dichotomy between active and passive style (it might qualify as "tempered active"), it may indeed be appropriate to the kinds of behaviors she describes with respect to the manufacture and use of San arrows.

Nonetheless, I must admit to being troubled as well as puzzled by the theoretical content of Wiessner's argument. For one thing, postulating active style in the San case still seems to rest upon assertion rather than testable argument. One is left with the impression that her brand of active style can in reality only be defined on ethnographically pragmatic grounds, in short, as those elements of isochrestic variation that one's informants happen to identify as playing active social roles. In the case of her own research, this has certainly provided us with one of the best accounts in the literature of the interaction between material culture and ethnicity. But it has brought us no closer to a viable argument for active style in the general case nor provided any guidelines that might help an archaeologist recognize it in either artifacts or the kinds of patterns in which they present themselves in the ground.

The second reason I find her approach unclear is that it is defined in large part by way of contrast to a depiction of my own position that is far from accurate. To begin with, she views isochrestism as a model concerned with stylistic behavior rather than with the issue of where style resides – a misconception for which I myself must assume partial responsibility due to the terms in which I presented it in my critique (see S 1986b). This allows her to assert that isochrestism has no explicit theoretical basis – which, if one does mistake it for a behavioral model of style as such, would not be far from the truth. In turn, apparently taking her lead from my reference to Kroeber's notion of style as picking specific lines of procedure and then "sticking to them," she proceeds to re-define isochrestism. In short, it concerns only the highly conservative, essentially static core of technology that largely entails the routine duplication of standard types, that is acquired by rote learning and employed automatically, that fails to respond when exposed to new ideas (i.e., alternative isochrestic options), and that is consequently divorced from the dynamic social currents entailed in ethnic relationships. In brief, isochrestism may be responsible for some patterning in material culture, but it is not stylistic patterning at all!

Now, Wiessner's isochrestism is not my isochrestism, and I am by no means convinced that any technological core like that with which she confuses it even exists. The depiction of isochrestism in such terms has its heuristic value as a foil for debating purposes. For one need not be very specific in defining one's own notions of style if the theoretical issues are posed simply as a choice between them and an approach that really has nothing to do with style at all. However, I believe that her misreading of isochrestism stems less from the exigencies of debate than from a true difference in outlook. For our theoretical statements cannot help but be colored by our specific empirical experiences. Undoubtedly, my own descriptions of style and the stand I take with respect to its behavioral foundations are influenced by my being a prehistorian habituated to regarding material culture at a relatively coarse level of ethnic resolution in contexts where the artisans themselves are anonymous. My position may appear conservative indeed to a field ethnographer engrossed in studying craft production among living artisans who are engaged in highly fluid, essentially ephemeral, networks of social interaction within a narrowly constricted sphere of ethnicity. In brief, what may primarily separate Wiessner and me are conflicting idioms of thought stemming from the fact that I by trade deal primarily with the structure of material culture systems, whereas she by trade deals primarily with what is fashionable in craft production.

It is interesting to note as an appendix to the debate that Wiessner's comments have provoked me to begin chasing the hare of what I have recently referred to as "background" style but which might more aptly be labelled *vernacular* style. While in no sense the static technological core depicted above, it is indeed conservative enough to be informally defined as passive style with a vengeance. It would consist of

> the bedrock design notions artisans of any given group inherit and in turn perpetuate as the agents of that group's craft tradition, notions that are as deeply and unconsciously imbedded in their behavior as their motor habits, the dialects they speak, or the received opinions they hold with respect to questions of proper conduct or the supernatural. Inculcated as much by insinuation as by instruction, and therefore all the more unquestioned, these design notions thus constitute a kind of substratum to the group's style, the heavy sediment that lies at the bottom of its reservoir of stylistic production. They even might be viewed as a kind of stylistic genotype of which its actual material products can be viewed as contextually dependent phenotypic expressions.
>
> (S 1986b: 274–75)

Given the level of resolution at which prehistorians work, vernacular style may be responsible for a significant portion of the ethnically significant variation they are capable of perceiving. And the notion may be equally useful to the ethno-archaeologist precisely because it takes us, so to speak, both behind and beyond the merely fashionable.

It must be stressed with respect to this last point that vernacular style in itself in no way inhibits an artisan's receptivity to new ideas (i.e., alternative isochrestic options); but it should nonetheless strongly influence the precise manner in which these are executed and made congruent with the prevailing environment of their material culture. One tired of searching for anthropological examples will find in art history a rich source of illustrations of this process. A splendid instance of vernacular style in action is Van Gogh's 1887 painting "Japonaiserie: Trees in Bloom," which is a direct copy of Hiroshige's 1857 wood-block print "Plum Garden at Kameido." Although the two productions are essentially identical in subject matter and composition, the vernacular distinctiveness of the traditions in which the two artists worked is apparent to even the most casual observer.

Methodological issues

It is often observed that theoretical essays like the present one remain only scholarly diversions until they have been operationalized and pragmatically tested on a real body of empirical data. It is therefore worth noting that this is in fact being done in the case of my own research on ethnic patterning in Upper Paleolithic assemblage variability in the Périgord region of Southwestern France. This has entailed an extensive program of excavation in the so-called Neuvic group of open-air sites (Sackett and Gaussen 1976; S 1988), considerable preoccupation with the chronostratigraphic background of regional Stone Age industrial variation (Laville, Rigaud, and Sackett 1980), and the design of alternative approaches to conventional lithic classification entailing attributal systems and inferential statistics (S 1989; n.d.). In truth, isochrestism developed historically not as a theoretical exercise pursued in an empirical vacuum but rather as an attempt to generalize for my colleagues in other fields the notions and attitudes regarding artifactual variation that gradually evolved in my mind during the course of this research.

If one reads my articles in their order of publication something of the intellectual stratigraphy of this evolution as well as its empirical grounding in lithic archaeology are clearly revealed. It will be seen, for example, that my basic ideas were already established before I commanded more than a passing knowledge of the literature on style. This is why the term "isochrestism" itself only appears in my third essay (S 1982), nearly a decade after the first (S 1973). It was not until then that I realized that my model, instead of simply making explicit what most archaeologists knew intuitively, actually constituted a minority view that required both vigorous wrestling with the competition, so to speak, as well as a distinctive name if it were to receive serious attention. And that my empirical homebase lies in a fairly remote and recalcitrant segment of the archaeological record presumably accounts for the somewhat detached, broad, and mundane view of style and ethnicity

which some perceive as an integral if implicit feature of my writings and which, as I suggested above, may partly account for what could be a mutual failure of Wiessner and myself to quite grasp what the other is up to. Here is not the place to review the specific analytic machinery of my own research. Given the great range of alternative ways style can be expected to express itself among different segments of the archaeological record, each will presumably call for somewhat different methods that can only be designed by those who know the relevant data at first hand. In any event, our interest here should remain focused upon archaeology in the general case.

Now, isochrestism is in no strict sense a method, since to show where style resides is not the same thing as to reveal how to get at it. But it does have certain implications with respect to what constitutes good and bad methodology. These become evident simply by casting what has already been said in previous sections into the frame of systematics. This is appropriate both because systematics happens to be the idiom of thought archaeologists are most comfortable with and because it is classification that dictates which aspects of formal variation in the archaeological record are recognized as warranting coherent organization.

At the general level, simply by reminding them of the potential ubiquitousness of style in artifactual variation, an isochrestic perspective encourages conscientious researchers to review continually their classifications and to consider whether those aspects of variation being ordered are in fact the ones best suited for revealing stylistically meaningful patterning. In a sense, it prods them to ensure that the right components of the data are in proper working order for embarking upon stylistic inquiry, in much the same way qualified pilots run down their checklist before taking off. At a more specific level, an isochrestic perspective influences the manner in which those aspects of variation that have been chosen for analysis are defined and given organization. Particularly important here of course is to distinguish between what I have referred to as generic and specific categories and the relative degree of resolution they achieve. Our archaeologists in the parable of the World War I battlefield were sufficiently acute observers to appreciate distinctions like that between "rifle" in the generic sense and "Mauser" in a more specific one. Less able researchers would have been apt to confuse the two levels of classification or, likelier still, would have more or less consistently organized their artifacts on but one of them. Had it been the generic level, which is perhaps more often the case where our knowledge is less perfect, they would have succeeded in distinguishing dugouts, first-aid stations, and kitchens but – unless auxiliary evidence were brought to bear – they would have failed to distinguish the ethnic division that cross-cuts the three types of features. Indeed, if equipped with no more insight than archaeologists have the right to expect, they might well have found themselves wondering whether dugouts, first-aid stations, and kitchens might themselves manifest distinct occupations of the site by three different ethnic groupings!

This "fallacy of the generic" frequently marred traditional archaeology and is by no means always avoided successfully today. The issue is of course what lies at the heart of the controversy between Binford and myself. And it is frequently seen repeated in the modern ethno-archaeological literature on ethnicity and style. How often we read of neighboring groups who are described as constituting distinct ethnic entities but who nonetheless supposedly possess material cultures that are in most respects indistinguishable. It is tempting in such instances to inquire whether the observer really observed deeply enough. The point has recently been brought home by Pierre Lemmonier's superb descriptions, mentioned earlier, of material culture in neighboring Anga groups, among whom he has succeeded in discerning subtle differences from one group to the next in what might be considered the most banal of technological items. Either the Anga display a brand of isochrestic compulsiveness rare among human cultures or, as is more likely, the quality of Lemmonier's work exemplifies a point which he too modestly relegates to a footnote: "ethnic groups produce objects whose morphology or mechanical properties differ to the degree that the observer is precise" (1986: 182).

In this connection, two additional points need to be kept in mind. One is that the generic/specific distinction is of course a relative one, and the given class is to be thought of as but one in a series of nested boxes. What is regarded as a generic class (e.g., "rifle") in one instance may in another instance be viewed as but a specific member of a more comprehensive generic class (e.g., "firearm"). Secondly, the generic/specific distinction in itself bears no inherent logical relationship to the distinction between function and style. As I have labored to show in the previous pages, any class of objects is inherently dualistic in nature, and whether it assumes its functional or its stylistic mode depends upon the context in which it is viewed. To return again to our battlefield, while in the perspective of our archaeologists the specific category "Mauser" was an ethnic marker of the German side of the line (that is, style), it nonetheless served in the hands of German soldiers themselves as a highly effective killing weapon (function). This is precisely the same moral that was drawn earlier in this chapter with respect to the *ko* halberd wielded by Chinese Bronze Age warriors. In combination these last two points have a profound methodological consequence, one which should by now be obvious to the reader but which deserves explicit recognition. This is that style cannot be pursued in isolation from function, or vice versa. The two must necessarily be attacked simultaneously, and in dynamic juxtaposition, by procedures that allow us to observe how any given segment of formal variation alternatively assumes stylistic and functional significance as we view it at different levels of specificity and in different contexts.[7]

It follows from the above that what is called for is *manifold* classifications, in other words, a pluralistic approach to systematizing our artifactual variation. So far in this connection we have been discussing the fairly straightforward matter of hierarchical ordering, that is, grouping our data into ascending or descending scales of the generic/specific variety. This presumably calls for little more than refining and/or adding greater flexibility to our conventional systems of codifying attributes, artifact types, and assemblages. However, I suspect that of equal importance and considerably greater intellectual challenge will be the design of alternative classifications of what might be termed a *thematic* variety. These are systems which run against the grain of our conventional ways of categorizing things and which reveal ethnically significant patterning that cross-cuts and thematically unites what are ordinarily regarded as disparate elements.

It may be particularly here that what I have called "vernacular style" comes into play, the genotype that lies behind and gives congruence to the more obvious phenotypic expressions in material culture. Most of the patterning here still lies asleep in the den of those "funny little somethings" that all journeyman archaeologists sense but never get around to defining formally. As has been noted, two Upper Paleolithic stone tool assemblages even from the same site can share highly similar conventional typologies and patterns of type frequencies and yet exhibit indications that the artisans who made them observed quite different degrees of tolerance in expressing their design templates, held quite different notions regarding how and to what extent their tools should be rejuvenated before being discarded, and even practiced quite different motor habits. Another example of a cross-cutting thematic pattern has been observed by Longacre in his study of ceramic sociology in Kalinga ceramics. He reports that it is not so much the specific design elements they bear that point to ethnic distinctions among the pots as it is combinations of motifs and compositional features such as symmetry (1981: 63). It is tempting to inquire whether analogous compositional themes recur in other areas of their material culture and whether one might envisage writing a "grammar" of Kalinga artisanry comparable to the one Glassie (1975) perceives underlying folk housing in eighteenth-century Virginia. As Glassie's work suggests, the themes may well be ones that also channel and give congruence to isochrestic choices in non-material aspects of cultural life.

At this point we may have crossed the border into a territory that might be called *deep style*, that is, the realm of patterning that unifies and provides congruence to the vernacular styles that underlie isochrestic choice from one domain of cultural life to the next. At least it is my impression that this is what researchers who go by such labels as structuralists, semioticians, and symbolic anthropologists often seem to be talking about. Much of Ian Hodder's work seems to concern this realm (e.g., 1982b), as does that of Glassie (1975) and James Deetz (1977) on colonial American archaeology (see Leone 1982 for a most useful discussion). An exciting recent example along somewhat different lines is a study by Tedlock and Tedlock (1985) on "intertextualities" within and among such seemingly diverse aspects of Quiché Maya life as textiles, instrumental music, storytelling, and divination.

If I am a typical specimen of the type, it is probably safe to say that journeyman archaeologists are largely ignorant of such work.[8] They are perhaps also somewhat distrustful of it, as the game seems to have few rules; or, to put it more fairly, *a priori* argument and the individual researcher's insight seem to be given greater emphasis than replicability of results or empirically verifiable propositions. Nonetheless, it is provocative work indeed and presumably has much to offer in the way of potential theoretical hybridization with more prosaic, data-oriented approaches to style like the one advocated here. Indeed, if deep style penetrates the scholarly enterprise the way it does the more quotidian aspects of cultural life, it may be presumed that we already share much in common regardless of the degree to which we seemingly differ at the more obvious levels of terminology and analytic procedure!

Turning to another domain of methodology, some comments are in order respecting the kinds of variation that are chosen for our pursuit of style. I am no doubt regarded as something of an apologist for the stylistic value of instrumental form and even, as a consequence, for what might be termed the "banalization" of our search for style. To some extent this stems from my insistence upon the point that style is more often built in, than added on, to objects, an emphasis that inevitably turns one's attention toward the humbler, unadorned objects of day-to-day life. But for the most part my preoccupation with instrumental form simply stems from the recognition that it makes up the overwhelming bulk of material culture and that to ignore it is to dismiss the greatest source of stylistic potential available to us.

This is in no sense to deny that the potential for, or at least accessibility of, stylistic variation is greater in some kinds of material culture than in others. Nor is it to deny that the greatest of all is most often the realm of adjunct form, precisely because its options are largely unconstrained by the mechanical contingencies that fetter instrumental form. To be sure, decoration presents its own hazards to stylistic analysis in that it can be too easily copied by artisans and too easily codified by archaeologists. The first means that, as ceramic sociologists are well aware, postulating one-to-one equations between specific decorative elements and specific ethnic units can be a hazardous business. It is for this reason, of course, that Longacre's statements about cross-cutting compositional themes in Kalinga pottery are of particular interest. The second point means that classifications of decoration all too often tend to be quite schematic affairs that partition it among rather obvious classes of geometric forms and their recurring combinations. One might ask whether art historians, if they were to employ equally schematic systems for classifying and comparing, would succeed in distinguishing Hiroshige's wood-block print mentioned above from Van Gogh's copy of it.

In any event, my quarrel is not with adjunct form but with adjunctism, that is, the position that style resides solely in decoration. My theoretical objections need no further comment, but there remains one to be considered in the realm of method. This concerns the attempts too often made by iconologues to extend adjunctism to instrumental form by analogy. In brief, it is argued that if the search for style in undecorated objects is restricted to those areas of formal variation that at least entail considerable transformational change during the process of manufacture, the elaboration involved supposedly afforded the artisan an opportunity for intentional investment not unlike that seen in decoration itself (e.g., Wilmsen 1972; Rick 1980: 102). In my view this analogy between decoration and elaboration or artisanal investment has not led to sound empirical research (see S 1982: 99–104; 1985b: 280). And, in any case, it is a false analogy. Elaboration is by nature no more inherently invested with style in material culture than it is in music. The style of the flutist Jean-Pierre Rampal is evidenced as much in the purity of his tone as in his execution of complex technical passages, and in the same manner the few deft and graceful spalls that occupy the ventral face of a Raysse burin carry as much stylistic information as the removals repeated one-hundredfold upon a Solutrean laurel leaf point. At the same time, artisanal investment cannot be gauged simply in terms of an object itself, since it may very well have entailed a considerable expenditure of time and effort in such areas as raw material procurement and in manufacturing processes apart from those immediately involved in fashioning the final form that ends up in the museum case.

Coda

The questions currently being raised by stylistic research are considerably more interesting than any conclusions that have been reached. I at least am aware of no trustworthy pan-cultural patterns to which style conforms, and, indeed, I suspect that it – like ethnicity itself – may play by rules that differ significantly from one culture to the next. Matters are tangled by the fact that, because they necessarily observe ethnicity at such different levels of resolution, archaeologists and ethno-archaeologists tend to talk past one another, the first largely preoccupied with style that informs and the second with style that mediates. In any case, unless one is willing to restrict oneself to the parochial security of adjunctism, there are no ready-made formulae nor methodological short-cuts for isolating style. The methods will presumably be developed on a case-by-case basis, by researchers who are intimately acquainted with the empirical data of a given block of the archaeological or ethnographic records, who appreciate the dualistic, complementary roles of style and function in formal variation, and who are consequently prepared to wrestle with them simultaneously in dynamic juxtaposition. Their route to style will lie in realizing the potential inherent in all isochrestic variation, whether adjunct or instrumental, and much of it they will probably find in aspects of form that hitherto have largely been ignored in our conventional classifications and museum exhibits. For ethnicity lies as much in the manner in which a Chinese cook butchers a chicken as in a Mao jacket or a Ming vase.

Notes

1. This statement is incorrect, as this chapter was actually written in the Summer of 1986, and some significant changes have taken place since then in the shape, terms, and context of my thinking about style.

2. Given the frequency with which I cite myself in these pages, it should help unclutter the text as well as free the reader from constant bombardment by my name to employ an abbreviated form of referring to my own writings. Thus (S 1982) may be read as (Sackett 1982).

3. The concept of the spectrum of equally viable options is of course a tenet, not a truth, whose empirical proof or disproof must wait for the distant future. Suffice it to say that the answer does not lie in museum-case functionalism, that is, in analyzing objects in the piecemeal fashion in which they present themselves in ethnographic and archaeological collections. Instead it calls for studies that compare them with reference to the efficacy and cost-effectiveness they possessed when operating in their total cultural contexts (see S 1977: 373; S 1982: 73–74).

4. The distinction between adjunct and instrumental form, just like the utilitarian/non-utilitarian and techno-economic/societal/ideational distinctions, is admittedly heuristic, and all of them – both singly and in combination – beg some interesting theoretical questions (S 1977: 370ff; S 1982: 70–73). However, none of these directly affects the substance of my argument itself and they need not trouble us here. It should be noted for the record however that, apart from decoration, adjunct form includes such things as formal iconography, mathematical symbols, and so forth. In addition, the term "instrumental form" has been substituted for the journeyman archaeologist's "functional form" that appears in several of my earlier articles, whose techno-economic and utilitarian implications are lost on the non-specialist reader. I have borrowed it from Jacques Maquet (1979: 20–21) with only minor changes in nuance.

5. It may surprise the reader to find me adopting the term "isochrestic behavior" here after having disowned it in a recent essay (S 1986b: 9). What has happened is that I disavow its usage as an equivalent to "stylistic behavior," an error that I had made in a still earlier essay (S 1985a: 158). However, I recognize now that isochrestic behavior is indeed a reasonable concept, so long as one regards it as providing the raw materials of style and not style as such. What I am arguing in this section is that formal style in itself is not isochrestic behavior, but it is instead the meaning or significance assigned to the material results of isochrestic behavior, whether emically in its cultural context by the artisan and/or his contemporaries or etically by an archaeologist or ethnographer regarding that context as an outside observer.

6. Two particularly telling examples of this circularism are treated in detail in my 1982 article (see pp. 82–104 for the discussion and rather lengthy literature citations involved). One is Lewis Binford's denial of the existence of style among Mousterian industries on the grounds that style entails purposeful iconological signalling among self-conscious social groups and that such groups did not emerge until post-Mousterian times (e.g., Binford 1973). Although his arguments do bring artifactual data to bear on the issue, they largely comprise alternative ways of affirming his original thesis in terms of the data rather than rigorous attempts to put it to the empirical test. The second is a particularly clear-cut example of the analytic tautology fostered by adjunctism that is seen in Edwin Wilmsen's investigations of ethnicity in the lithic assemblages from the Lindenmeier site, employing a methodology that assumes style is iconological and that automatically excludes from consideration variation which does not meet the empirical expectations of this thesis (e.g., Wilmsen 1972). (The methodology itself is discussed below in this chapter, p. 42). Interestingly enough, he elsewhere treats the issues involved in quite sophisticated terms, basing his argument in part upon isochrestic variation among instrumental form (Wilmsen 1973).

   In fairness it must be observed that the theorist who has most profoundly influenced iconological thought, Martin Wobst (1977), is an exception to the generalization that elicited this note, since he does suggest ways in which its line of argument might be subjected to independent empirical testing. It is also noteworthy that some of his illustrations of the workings of active style involve examples of purely instrumental form.

7. It is, by the way, a failure to appreciate the thesis of this paragraph that has led scholars such as Randi Halland (1977) and Robert Dunnell (1978) to give a peculiarly misleading methodological twist to the fallacy of the generic. They argue that a single trait cannot possess both functional and stylistic significance, since the former implies adaptive consequences whereas the latter by definition entails that which must be adaptively neutral or arbitrary. As a result, functional traits cannot be used as ethnic markers since they must inevitably distribute over, rather than delimit, boundaries of neighbouring ethnic groups who follow similar lifeways. The flaw in this argument is, of course, one of scale, that is, a failure to distinguish between a class of isochrestic variation and the individual alternative expressions that class may take when it assumes concrete form. The latter, being equally viable options, may well have neutral value *with respect to each other*, but each nonetheless retains the adaptive significance attributed to its class when it is observed as a functioning element in its own cultural context (see Wendorf, Marks and Shiner, 1977: 24). David Meltzer makes this last point clearly during the course of an analysis that, oddly enough, fails to take it to heart (1981: 314).

8. Symptomatic is the fact that my discussion here begs the question of how deep style relates, if at all, to that realm of patterned symbolism structuralists tell us is common to all minds and hence universal. In other words, how and to what extent is my "deep style" in reality what Leone (1982: 754) refers to as "deep structure"? It is a question I have simply not yet explored and about which I consequently have no infomed opinion. However, I should imagine that – regardless of whatever views I may come to hold with respect to the tenets of structuralism – dealing with the issue will presumably call for untangling the frequently confused notions of style and symbolism, and in turn arguing that symbols will still receive different stylistic expressions from one ethnic context to another even though they may be pan-cultural.

Chapter 5

Style as historical quality

Ian Hodder

This chapter presents what style is and is not. By trying to move beyond the traditional view that style is largely a spatial construct, the author discusses the notion that style involves simultaneously the objective event; the spatial and temporal pattern; the subjective interpretation, including a judgement of quality; and the power embedded in the first two aspects, which need to be created. Since all interpretation has elements of ambiguity, a multiplicity of meanings is involved in all style and stylistic analysis. As a way of critiquing previous stylistic analyses, Hodder reviews the archaeological analysis of stylistic similarities from the Neolithic of Europe and the Near East. This illustration attempts to demonstrate how style has multiple and contradictory meanings that exist only in the style of social contexts.

I wish to begin my discussion of style by considering what in my view style is not.

First, although style has a number of social functions, it does not consist of those functions. It cannot be contrasted, therefore, with utilitarian functions. Rather, both the social and utilitarian functions of an object have style, and the same can be said of the ideological functions. It is the social functions which have played a predominant role in recent discussions of style (for example, Wobst 1977; Wiessner 1984; Hodder 1982b) and these approaches, including "ceramic sociology", have been justly criticised by Sackett (1985a). Certainly style does transmit information, including group membership, and it allows self-evaluation in relation to groups (Wiessner 1984), but it cannot be reduced to these social functions.

Second, style is not a summation of cultural attributes. It is not a polythetic set of similar but varying attributes. David Clarke (1968) used the notion of a polythetic set to define cultures, assemblages and types which do have summative properties. Part of the summation involves style. Cultures, assemblages and types have style, which therefore remains a distinct property in need of definition.

Third, style is not a set of rules for action. Dictionary definitions of style often refer to a way, manner, mode of writing, walking, being. Certainly there has been a tendency in archaeology to focus on structure and compositional rules of design configuration as a component of style (e.g. Washburn 1983). But these rules only form part of style, inseparable from its content. Thus at one level a pot may have the decoration content "lozenge". At another level the lozenge itself is constructed with compositional rules, while rules also locate the lozenge in relation to other motifs on a pot surface.

Fourth, style is not the summation of objective content (e.g., motif) and rules – a polythetic set of similar attributes and structures. In other words, by conjoining the above second and third inadequate definitions, we do not end up with an adequate account. Any two objects are at the same time both objectively similar and objectively different. For example, a ceramic pot and a metal cauldron are both similar (they are both objects rather than emotions, for example) and different (they are made of different materials). The fourth definition of style does not allow us to identify the objective similarities that are to be summed in order to produce a style.

Fifth, style is not the choice made between functional equivalents (Sackett 1985a). It is in any case difficult to imagine different objects which are in a strict sense functionally equivalent. But the major limitation of the "isochrestic" view is that, while style involves choice, choice has style. There is a way, manner, mode in which we make choices. Once again, therefore, there remains a distinct property of style which is not dealt with in the "isochrestic" definition.

What style is

I wish to start with the colloquial view that style is "a way of doing", where "doing" includes the activities of thinking, feeling, being. This definition raises the issue of whether style is particular and hence historically diagnostic, or general. The definition encompasses particular ways of doing, as well as universal, non-cultural processes. Everything has a function, and equally everything is done in some manner. Thus a species of tree has a "style" of branch growth and leaf pattern. Many animals bare their teeth when angry, and all healthy, adult humans walk upright. These various "styles" of doing are in part genetically encoded. They are general and non-cultural.

As well as being genetically determined, some style (when defined as a way of doing) is functionally determined. Some cultural attributes may be entirely determined by function, in that no other solution would achieve the same end. Thus it could be argued that the cutting down of a tree or the killing of an animal from a distance requires sharp, hard edges or points. The provision of a sharp edge on an axe is to some degree functionally determined, but it is also part of the style of objects classed as "axe". Any "way of doing" or style may be largely determined by function.

On the other hand, most archaeologists use the word style to refer to particular historical ways of doing. Yet here again they emphasise generalities: style is a repeated way of doing in a particular cultural-historical context. This emphasis on repetition implies that an individual, unique event cannot have style. Yet even an individual act has to be done in a certain way. The general definition of style as "a way of doing" thus forces us to consider the relationship between the particular and the general.

In a western commercial world highly attuned to the production of style, it is possible to observe, almost on a daily basis, particular novel events. At the moment when a Boy George or a Johnny Rotten creates a unique "way of doing", can we say that he has created a new style? Of course, many others have tried, and failed, to invent styles that become repeated and popular. Boy George and Johnny Rotten were more successful precisely because, in their novelty, they played on pre-existing, general themes such as the sexuality of ambiguous male/female categorisations or the violence of swastikas and heavy boots. I shall return to the social context of such events. For the moment, it is important to recognise that

the original events are both particular and general. They are both similar and different to previous acts.

Boy George and Johnny Rotten create styles that get repeated because they make references in their clothes and ways of living to more general themes that play on dominant social and cultural issues in a way which is found interesting by other people. In other words, they have successfully linked an individual event to a general "way of doing". But that linkage is highly subjective and evaluative. Many people do not call Boy George and Johnny Rotten stylish. Their actions and clothes can be read in numerous ways, to mean many different things. They can be placed in many different styles depending on what aspects of their music or dress are stressed.

Style is therefore a relational property, but it is not an entirely objective relation. Rather it is an interpretive property of all events. Style is defined here as: "the referral of an individual event to a general way of doing".

Various implications of this definition can now be discussed. To begin with, the definition asserts that an individual event cannot have a style of its own. The style only exists in reference to other events. Style is the pattern we make around a particular event, recalling and creating similarities and differences. Style only exists in these repetitions and contrasts.

An ambiguity seems to exist in this definition of style. Is style observed or acted? On the one hand, any event can be interpreted in the light of other events. Here we are taking the point of view of the onlooker or self-analyst. Style is the subjective interpretation. On the other hand, in the action of creating a pot, style exists in the material similarities and differences created in comparison to other pots. Style is in the objective event.

This and related dichotomies between subjective and objective, materialist and idealist, or interpretive and positivist, have long dogged archaeology but can be transcended. In discussions of style, it can be recognised that actor and observer are both involved in event and interpretation simultaneously. Both the acts of doing and observing have style. On the one hand style involves interpretation as event, and on the other hand, event as interpretation.

By "interpretation as event" I mean that every statement, however interpretive, is itself an event with effects on the world. An interpretation cannot be reduced to that which is being interpreted. It is never possible to close the gap between signifiers, or between signifiers and signifieds. Any interpretation changes the context in which it is made. It has a real "objective" existence as event. By "event as interpretation" I mean that every act in the world is also an interpretation of that world. By making verbal or material comparisons between forms, by the use of comment, metaphor and analogy, any event involves a subjective understanding and a creative component.

An adequate discussion of style will incorporate the dialectic relationship between event and interpretation. To return to the style of leaves, trees and other genetically or functionally determined relationships, it is suggested here that such relationships only involve one aspect of style – interpretation as event. We form plants and animals into our categories and we recognise similarities and differences in leaf pattern or hoof pattern. Yet there is no event as interpretation involved in the construction of those similarities and differences.

The notion that style involves simultaneous "objective" event (in the construction of real similarities and differences) and interpretation (in the meaningful creation of similarities and differences) can be approached in a different way, through the distinction made by archaeologists between space and time. As described in archaeology, style is largely a spatial construct. Although normally bounded in time it represents a pattern that is frozen within a group of temporal phases. This view of style is an example of the widely found archaeological belief that a "present" can always be identified in which "now" things happen. Thus style involves spatial relations in a "now" or "then" time frame. It involves arrangements of decoration on pots, patterns of house construction, burial configurations and the like. It is only when time passes from phase a to phase b that the styles (spatial relationships) change.

An alternative conception denies the separation of space and time (Tilley 1982). Most events occur or are observed in sequence. The spatial patterns are produced through time. But as soon as an event occurs it changes the context for the event which is to follow. If no role is given to interpretation in the sequence of events, the resulting spatial pattern can be seen to have a fixed meaning within its temporal phase. But if the dialectic between event and interpretation is allowed, a different picture emerges. Any interpretation depends on the position, on the context, of the interpreter. Since interpretations are also events, they change the context for interpretation. The interpretation of an event is itself an event to be interpreted in an endless sequence.

There is therefore, in all interpretation, a necessary ambiguity and indeterminacy which results from the temporal distancing of events. A multiplicity of meanings is in the very nature of things. If style is the referral of the individual event to a general class it involves both event and interpretation (in the referral). The individual event is itself an interpretation making reference to other events, but as soon as it occurs it is "in the past", part of the resources for interpretive stylistic activity. The definition of style that I have suggested has an inbuilt dynamic – there can never be an end point, a stop to the event/referral dialectic.

Nevertheless style does appear to create a fixed present, an unchanging "now". It privileges the spatial over the temporal, appearing to halt time. Archaeologists have tended to make the assumption that phases in which certain styles predominate can be identified. And they may be right in that they are picking up a common characteristic of social life, that style is one of the mechanisms used to "fix" meanings. In order to limit the inherent and continual running on of meaning interpretations we (whether as social actors or as ethnographers creating the practical solution of an "ethnographic present") halt time and create a "present", situated ambiguously in the continuity between past and future. It may be the case that, in order for social life to continue, and in order to counteract event as interpretation, actors try to emphasise interpretation as event, objectifying the subjectivity of event and placing it in a constructed and spatially segregated "now".

From this it is clear that style as defined here involves social strategies. The referral of an individual event to a general way of doing includes the creation of social rules, norms of behaviour and economic practices. To control style is to control ways of acting and it is thus to have power. Style is involved in the social strategies of creating relationships and ideologies by the fixing of meanings according to established criteria. It includes the power to control spatial structures and the movements of people within them, and it includes the ability to halt time or control its passing.

In summary, style has three equivalent components. First it is objective structure and content. The "way of doing" incorporates spatial and temporal pattern and sequence, from the arrangement of rooms in a building to the organisation of designs on a pot. And it incorporates content, such as the function of the rooms and the motifs used in the decoration.

Second, it is interpretive and evaluative, involving an assessment of similarity and difference, but also involving a judgement of quality. The very term "stylish" rarely seems to be a matter of doggedly following a set of rules, although rules are, according to the first point made above, part of style. Rather, being stylish often involves "playing with" rules in competent and appropriate ways. Thus it involves linking general rules with a specific context, referring the individual event to a general "way of doing". The evaluation of the referral involves aesthetic, emotional and sensual perspectives.

Third, style is power. As already noted, varied social functions of style have been recognised by archaeologists over recent decades. The definition given to style in this paper emphasises that style is active and creative in that the relationships within style do not simply "exist", but have to be "created". To create style is to create an illusion of fixed and objective relationships. Style embeds event in interpretation but fixes that interpretation as event. It provides the potential for the control of meaning and thus for power. Style links a particular social context to a general way of doing, and thus acts upon that context.

Styles and wholes

I wish now to examine a particular aspect of the definition of style given above. To what extent, in referring an individual event to a general way of doing, do we create "wholes", totalities? The notion of "a style" appears to indicate that "wholeness" may be illusory. By definition style is dynamic and multivalent. How, then, is "the whole" constructed?

Certainly the relational aspect of style implies that wider generalities are produced. For example, many Western women today wear stiletto heels. Not all women do, and no women wear them all the time. Yet, because of the contrast with men, who only wear stilettos when dressing up as women, stilettos are a feminine style. Indeed they help to create the gender category "women" within a broader "whole". Stilettos are thin, fragile and delicate and these qualities are part of the general conception of "women" in Western society. In a pub in England women will often be served drinks in glasses with long thin stems. Men are served with heavy, thick glasses with flat bases. The stemmed drinking glasses may not refer directly to stiletto heels, but they do refer to a "style" which is a general way of female doing and which incorporates a range of evaluative qualities (including in this case sexuality) and social strategies.

The stiletto heels/stemmed glasses example of style appears to suggest that a general principle or essence exists underlying style. In this case the essence or "whole" might be considered to be "women as fragile and delicate". And yet stiletto heels can be used in other contexts as hammers to knock in nails, and parallels can be drawn to long sharp fingernails, claws, hard pointed objects, and aggression. The hard click of stiletto heels on a tiled floor may be part of their sexual evaluation, but they could also be said to have qualities opposed to the fragile and the delicate, from pointed claw to the click of male, military boots. The "whole" begins to dissolve into a series of conflicting interpretations depending on a wide range of particular contextual factors. Is the person walking across the floor in stiletto heels a man or a woman; how else is the person dressed; what is the type of room; who is the observer? Depending on the answers to these and other questions, the stiletto heels will be linked into different styles with different evaluations and with different social effects. There is, at least, more than one essence.

Perhaps the error is made by us as analysts, however. Perhaps we should not expect coherence within a whole. In fact the stiletto heels seem almost to rejoice in the ambiguity of meaning which they engender. Perhaps they form an attractive (to many), long-lived style because they play on certain dominant areas of concern in Western society. In referring an individual event to a general way of doing, style is not only designed to find answers and create an apparent coherence where none can exist. It is also designed to focus attention on that general way of doing as problematic and unresolved and hence as the focus of desire.

Styles do often appear as coherent systems, guiding actions. One could talk of a Protestant style of life, a Christian style, a Conservative-Thatcherian approach to the world. There is a style of Impressionist painting, but also a style for playing a game of cricket, and for being a naughty school boy. But whenever we look at these general coherent systems in detail we find hidden contradictions. To provide further illustration of this point I will use two recent events in which the archaeological community has been involved – the banning of South African and Namibian participants from the World Archaeological Congress in Southampton in 1986 (Shaw 1986), and the request by some American Indian groups for the reburial of their remains (Quick 1986).

An important aspect of the style of life of Western societies today is the notion of "freedom of speech". This essential belief organises many of our political, social and economic actions. It appears as an ambiguous rule, embracing "the whole" that is a democratic state. When translated into academia, this way of doing becomes "freedom of interchange within the academic community", regardless of colour, creed, gender, nationality. But the relationship between such a general principle and a particular context is always difficult and interpretive. In abstract, the internal contradictions within the principle remain hidden. It is the practice of contextual events which confronts us with a conflict. In practice, the question of whether South Africa should be banned from a world archaeological congress forces us to choose between freedom of speech for black South Africans (since the ban is aimed against apartheid) and between freedom of speech for archaeologists (since lifting the ban is aimed to ensure academic interchange). In addition, removal of such a ban would mean that archaeologists from many Third World and Eastern Bloc countries would not have been able to attend the Southampton Congress, since their governments would not allow them to attend with South Africans. The ban thus requires us to choose between freedom of academic interchange between Western and largely white South African archaeologists, and freedom of academic interchange between Western and Third World and Eastern Bloc archaeologists. The "freedom of speech" style of life remains a whole, coherent essence until it is confronted with events. Faced with events, the style is revealed for what it is – an interpretation which seeks to deal with, paper over, contradictions.

While one style may be internally contradictory, attempts are made to create a coherence in those areas of social life which are problematic. It is also in these areas that style is used to "work over" the contradictions, bringing them to light. But there may be many styles within one society that are contradictory but which do not normally come into conflict. For example, an aspect of the style of Western science is that scientists should collect and preserve information for future generations and for the sake of knowledge. Normally, this view does not come into conflict with the style of the way in which American whites deal with American Indians which is now influenced by the idea that American Indian groups should be allowed to follow their own traditions. In fact, there is an inherent contradiction between these two styles of life which we do not notice on a day-to-day basis, and so we do not try to resolve the conflict. It is events which bring the contradiction into focus, as when American Indians ask for the return of their remains (collected by white Americans as part of their scientific enterprise) in order to re-bury them (according to their own traditions). Some resolution is needed, and in the face of a series of such events a new style of academia and of American Indian relations may be produced.

In the above two examples, the general way of doing to which events are referred is revealed as ambiguous, contradictory and interpretive. Certain contexts force these contradictions to be resolved within a new general way of doing. But the abstract and general resolution, seen from another angle, distant as it is from the context in which it is contrived, always has its contradictions within it. The "whole" remains partly mythical.

The archaeological analysis of style

Archaeologists are already well trained in the identification of the objective structure and content of style. The categorisation of artifacts into styles has long been a central focus of archaeological research. It is in the analysis of stylistic similarities and differences that archaeologists approach the general way of doing to which an individual attribute refers.

However, such archaeological analysis has been inadequate in two main ways. (i) Archaeologists have tended to shy away from the interpretive element in style, pretending to mask their activities within empirical description or objective theory testing. Interpretation has been separated from the identification of similarity and difference within typology. However, in the present-day example used above there are many straight fragile things to which one could compare stiletto heels. The typology comparison in the link to stemmed glasses is made within an interpretive insight into the nature of femininity in Western societies. Equally, in archaeological analyses of past material culture, interpretive generalities need to be made explicit at all levels from typological identification to the recognition of prehistoric art styles. At all levels, the problem is: "how can the individual, contextual event be linked to a general way of doing?"

It could be argued, for example, that the Neolithic of Europe and the Near East is characterised by a general essence, or "spirit" that pervades the data, giving it an overall style (Cauvin 1972, 1978). No two objects or events in this area or period are identical, but there is a general way of doing which goes beyond the presence of pottery, domestication and settled villages. One finds, for example, that there is often evidence of excarnation (removal of flesh prior to burial of bones) and further treatment of the body after the removal of the flesh. From the human skulls with fleshy features of the face modelled in clay from Jericho (Cauvin 1972), to the evidence of excarnation at Catal Hüyük (Mellaart 1967), to the re-sorting of bones in the megalithic and earthen tombs and camps of northwest Europe (Shanks and Tilley 1982; Mercer 1980; Whittle 1985), a recurring theme emerges.

There is much variability in the specifics of this. For example, amongst the megalithic burial monuments of north and west Europe (Hodder 1984a) the numbers of bodies interred show considerable variation, and the precise treatment of the body involves both separation of bodies from skulls (Shanks and Tilley 1982) after the decay of flesh within the tomb, and the removal of flesh prior to inclusion within the tomb. Nevertheless, recurring features of these activities have commonly drawn archaeologists to suggest a general "communal" or "collective" ethic. The main aspects of the argument for the burial monuments of north and west Europe

are that the tombs themselves would have involved collective labour, that many bodies are placed inside the tomb, that the bones are often mixed or re-sorted prior to burial. In addition, amongst groups (such as the TRB – Whittle 1985: 204) that produced elaborate and varied decorated pottery which could have been identified with individuals, the pottery is left outside the tomb, in the same way that the individual flesh is removed prior to burial. In some tombs few or no objects are placed with the bodies.

In southeast Europe, from the late sixth millennium BC, there are different patterns, but here there is evidence, over a long period of time, for the same emphasis on masks and facial representation seen in the modelled face at Jericho (Tringham 1971; Whittle 1985; 68). It is not necessary to argue for direct links between Jericho and the Vinca face-lids, or the masks placed on symbolic bodies in the Varna cemetery (Renfrew 1978). Rather, there seems to be a general and widespread concern with masking the physical form using societal-wide conventions such as the types of face mask found in Southeast Europe. It can be suggested that excarnation and masking are linked in their concern to hide the bodily individuality of the flesh. Such a statement is an interpretive insight that links together varied events into an apparently coherent style. Excarnation, masks and the modelling of skulls occur at different times and places throughout the Neolithic of Europe and the Near East. At first sight they seem unrelated, in the same way that any link between stilettos and stemmed glasses is not immediately apparent. The coherence, the style, is only created as part of an interpretive insight. In the Neolithic case, the interpretive key is suggested to be a concern with the relationship between the social (the communal) and the individual.

There is more to this general Neolithic style of Europe and the Near East. Bodily representation, in the form of figurines, is common. The bodies are often unclothed and they are often of women. Indeed the representation of women and the symbolic elaboration and decoration of domestic houses and domestic pottery is widely found. Evidence for a link between women, houses and domestic pottery is common (Hodder 1984a). For example, models from southeast Europe show women working at domestic tasks in huts, and breasts and depictions of women occur frequently on pots which are often elaborately decorated. Figurines show women holding pots, and decoration similar to that occurring on pots is found on fragments of house wall decoration (Childe 1949). At Catal Hüyük, where there is some of our richest evidence for symbolic relationships, there is good evidence for a link between women, the domestic context and death (Mellaart 1967; Hodder 1987). For example, female breasts are modelled on house walls but hide within them the skulls of vultures which are elsewhere associated in the house wall painting with scenes of death and excarnation (the removal of human flesh by carrion-feeding vultures). Mellaart interprets much of the symbolism within the Catal Hüyük houses as being concerned with a link between female reproduction, death and the wild. A relationship between the domestic context and death is also seen in southeast Europe at Lepenski Vir, where burial occurs beneath the houses and is referred to within the houses by the placing of a carved stone head immediately above the skull of the deceased (Srejovic 1972).

The overall evidence for an emphasis on the female body, domestic elaboration of huts and pots can be linked to the general style discussed above, by a further interpretive insight. It is women who can be seen as giving life to individuals at birth and their contribution can be seen to be towards the individual family unit. Women thus create the community in the creation of flesh, and in the creation and caring for the individual bodies that make up that community. But they also create the flesh that dies and the individual transience that threatens to erode the continuity of the social totality.

The late Neolithic of Europe, characterised by the Corded Ware and Bell Beaker culture in the late third millennium BC, has a new and widespread style (Whittle 1985: 241). Individual inhumation under round barrows and without excarnation is found. This new style of burial, in which each individual is placed in the grave with a set of distinctive objects including weapons, pots and bodily ornament, is often seen as a move from the communal ethic to an individualising style. The major change is from excarnation to inhumation, from the removal of flesh to the retention of flesh. At the same time, individuals are buried with items which clearly demarcate their gender and status.

I have introduced the late Neolithic material to point to the contrast with the earlier situation described, because it is in the opposition that the earlier style can be more clearly identified. What I have argued is that, as in the present-day examples given above, style involves interpreting the world in terms of general principles which work over central areas of social concern. But since interpretation is also event it has an effect on the world interpreted.

(ii) The effects of stylistic interpretation are social and it is the notion of style as social action that is the second aspect of archaeological analyses that has been inadequately developed. Certainly, as already noted, many archaeological discussions of style have concentrated on social functions. Yet such discussions have tended to assume that style encodes messages which hold unambiguous information within cultural "wholes". How can we, as archaeologists, break away from such assumptions and focus on the dialectic between interpretation (in relation to a general "whole") and particular event?

In the archaeological example sketched above, to hypothesise such contradictions is to give style an active role in creating and containing society. Throughout the earlier and middle Neolithic, larger social units became increasingly well defined, either as agglomerated or defended settlements, or as regional style clusters (Dohrn-Ihmig 1973; Sherratt 1981, 1982), or as seen in megalithic tombs symbolising local communities (Renfrew 1976). As social wholes for the first time became larger, more complex and of longer duration as part of the adoption and intensification of agriculture (Bender 1978;

Woodburn 1980), it can be suggested that a contradiction developed between the bodily individuality of the flesh and the larger and more durable social roles that individuals both created and fit into. A conflict developed between the bodily self of the individual and the social self within the political unit. The authority and power invested in social roles would continually be shown, in confrontation with daily events, to be in contradiction with the ephemeral, the mortal, the transitory, and the individual. The occurrence of megalithic tombs of the ancestors in Neolithic western European cultures emphasises the attempt to link the present to the past, to legitimise the present arbitrary social order by reference to the ancestors, and hence to control time. A concern to hide or mask bodily flesh similarly acts to fix the individual within an established non-bodily social order.

The style of excarnation and facial masking thus creates an apparent whole. It appears to fix the self within the social, and it denies the passing temporality of a hesitant and flawed bodily individuality. At the same time, however, burial rituals such as excarnation can be interpreted in many contradictory ways in relation to contextual events. Indeed, the removal of flesh from human bodies may remove their individuality, but at the same time it reifies the distinction, the contradiction, between the individual and the social, the temporary and the permanent. The Neolithic style described above interprets events in relation to a broader whole. Many different ways are found, from Jericho skulls to megalithic burial in western Europe, of dealing with the same suite of problems. Power is created and re-created in the provision of a general interpretation of events and in the fixing of interpretation in event. But the problems do not go away. They are worked over as individual events are linked to general interpretations. The contradictions remain.

A specific example of this general pattern may help to clarify the relationship between theory and evidence that underlies the above generalisations. As already noted, the larger, more clearly defined social units that emerge in the course of the early and middle Neolithic in Europe are expressed in different ways. For example, they appear either as agglomerated or defended settlements, or as megalithic communal tombs. In fact, communal tombs are often associated with dispersed rather than agglomerated settlement. This pattern has been noted especially in France (Scarre 1983), where megalithic tombs appear in regional sequences (as in the Paris Basin or west-central France) at the moment when agglomerated settlement disappears, or they appear in marginal areas (as in the south of France) away from zones that do support contemporary stone-walled settlements. The rituals in the tombs can thus be seen as "working over" the problems of creating a unified social whole that is itself fragmented in many of the practices of daily life. Indeed the dramatic events at the tomb would have played their part in creating the social totality.

Another set of internal contradictions that the available archaeological evidence allows us to see concerns the positions of women and the domestic context. As already described, Neolithic symbolic elaboration often focusses on and links women, houses, birth and death. The evidence is best where the surviving symbolism is richest, as at Catal Hüyük (Mellaart 1967; Hodder 1987). But traces of the same style occur widely. Women and the domestic context in which new community members are cared for both create the social whole and the individual flesh which threatens to destroy it. I have argued (Hodder 1987) that in the Neolithic women were seen as both the creators and destroyers of social life, as both creative and dangerous. It could further be suggested that, since evidence from cemeteries such as Nitra (Sherratt 1982) implies that older men often fulfilled dominant social roles, the link between women and the domestic family unit set up a conflict between women as producers and reproducers of the individual family entity and wider social and political constructs dominated by men.

The distinctive Neolithic style of female figurines, elaborate domestic pottery, elaborate houses and burial rituals thus created an apparent whole, a general interpretation that both created contradictions (between the individual and the social, between birth and death, between women and men, etc.) and dealt with them (by fixing the temporary and subjective in the durable and objective as part of the dialectic between interpretation and event). The general whole to which individual events were related by the construction and use of this Neolithic style established women as both central to social life (in its continuity and reproduction) and peripheral to it (because women could be linked to discontinuity in the birth and death of temporary flesh). And yet the inherent contradictions emergent within such a scheme would have provided a possible basis for the negotiation of the female and the individual against the male and the social. The nature of the style shows us the locus of social debate precisely because it could not resolve contradictions, but only provide the medium for them to be played out.

I have argued that archaeological analyses of style would benefit, first, from a rejection of an "objective", quantitative and descriptive approach. It is inadequate to close our archaeological eyes to the recognised subjectivity in the definition of traits (within typology) and in the drawing of similarities and differences. Whether archaeologists are examining modern material culture (such as stiletto heels and stemmed drinking glasses) or prehistoric burial practices, the identification of style can be linked to self-conscious attempts made by the archaeologist to suggest interpretive insights which provide the general way of doing (or thinking or being) to which an individual event was and is meaningfully and socially referred in the past and in the present. Second, it is no longer necessary for archaeologists to assume that "a" style has "a" meaning. The whole to which an individual event refers is always an abstraction removed from events. It has always to be "read" in relation to events. Style is really process masquerading as thing. The creation of style may attempt to "fix" meanings in space and time. But in the interpretive

process there is a necessary ambiguity resulting from the inability of the actor to catch up with event, to halt the dialectic between interpretation and event, and to break the unity of these opposites. The task for archaeologists is to identify the contradictions and ambiguities in which the play of style rejoices. Style has meaning in the process of referral. Style thus has multiple, contradictory meanings that do not exist in the style, but only in the style as used in social contexts. Style does not have "a" meaning, but is part of the process of creating meanings.

The style of archaeological writing

There are many ways in which we can choose to write. The objective event of placing words on a page is a creative choice between alternative modes of expression. Thus I could have chosen to write this paper in a more personal style, or as if writing a detective novel, putting together the clues of the past, or as if writing poetry. I could have presented the whole paper in iambic pentameters or in the style of a poet like William Carlos Williams. I could have started:

> I wish
>   to think of style not
>   as it is
> but as it is not,
>   to count the ways
>   in which I disagree.
> (etc.)

I did indeed choose to start this paper in a particular style – rather abrupt and combative.

On the whole, however, this paper has had an historically conventional style used by most archaeologists, in which arguments are stated in a formal, dry and distanced manner. The problem is presented, the background stated, the theory proposed, the evidence examined and the conclusions drawn. To consider, as a contrast, novels and poetry is to note that archaeologists have chosen a particular discourse in which to express themselves. Archaeological site reports show this particularly clearly in their standardisation and formality.

Like all material production, the style of archaeological writing is both event and interpretation. As event it sets up objective similarities with scientific discourse and the balanced writing of neutral reports, and it sets up objective differences with novel-writing and the subjective. Keeping theory and data related but rigidly separate is a hallmark of this historical style of writing, and those who feel unhappy with or unconvinced by my account of European prehistory will point out that I have not properly tested theory against data and that I have indulged in too much story-writing. Another hallmark of the scientific style is that it is designed to provide a comforting circularity between aims and conclusions which gives the impression of an always successful completion of a coherent and independent endeavour. Note in this paper, for example, the repetition of the earlier interpretation–event theme in the above "conclusion" to the prehistoric analysis, as if the theme's relevance had been proved by that analysis. Note too its recurrence in this section, as if it is a universal principle of widespread validity.

It is not difficult to argue that archaeological writing as stylistic event is socially manipulative and politically strategic (Hodder 1984b). The links between archaeology and science have considerable historical depth. They result from intentional choices, made within an historical frame, about the style to which archaeology (as event) should be referred. Archaeological writing is thus also interpretation. When it is argued that "archaeological writing is scientific", a style, an apparent whole is created. The objective events are subjective interpretations of the world in which we live. Yet in many ways archaeology is not equivalent to a natural science. We cannot really conduct repeated experiments or hold variables constant, for example. A hidden dilemma within the archaeological embrace of a scientific positivism has been noted by Wylie (1982). Indeed, it could be argued that ultimately it has been the use of a scientific style of discourse that has revealed archaeology as non-scientific. By trying to cover and paper over the cracks and tensions, the differences have in fact become starkly visible. Equally, if I had written this chapter as a poem, the differences with poetry would have been both masked (in the similarity of the end-product to poetry) and revealed (since the poem would have shown that I am not a poet and that my aims are not fully poetic). In referring an individual piece of work to a more general way of writing, a "whole" is created, and at the same time revealed to contain ambiguities and contradictions. This double process results from the irreducible differences between the items being compared, and from the distance between signifiers and between signifier and signified. We could try to create an independent archaeological discourse unrelated to other styles of writing. But in the end we would have the same problem: is there a general basis for the similarities in the new archaeological "whole", or should there be different styles of writing for discussing death and burial as opposed to settlement and exchange, and should the style of writing be different for the discussion of each historical group, somehow wedded to the stylistic identity of that group? However one answers such questions, strategic, historically situated interpretations of the world in which we live are made. Archaeological writing is here social and interpretive.

If the style of archaeological writing is both event and interpretation, and if it thus involves choices about objective effects in the world, it is necessary for archaeologists to explore the limits of their discourse and to examine whether different styles of writing might be more or less appropriate for different types of data and for different interpretations of those data. For every type of archaeological interpretation there will be a good, a bad and an ugly mode of discourse. For example, if it is argued that the nub of cultural and symbolic behaviour is the play of contradictions and ambiguities rather than the passing on of information, a scientific discourse aimed at limiting subjectivity and ambiguity may be inappropriate. As an analogy, it is difficult fully to describe music in words, and even more difficult to encapsulate all its varied emotional and other effects in a dry scientific discourse. So too, while some aspects of material culture discourse may be revealed using a scientific language, the discussion of material styles as involving event and interpretation, object and subject, needs also to consider other ways in which to write the past in the present.

By way of not concluding

Style contains a duality of event and interpretation, object and subject. It is both an objective way of doing (the second and third definitions of style said to be inadequate at the beginning of this chapter), and it is the subjective and historically evaluated referral of an individual event to an interpreted general way of doing.

Put another way, and to begin to explore the ambiguities and contradictions in my own account, there is an inherent dynamism in style. All actions are interpretive in that they are stylistic. In other words, any action has to be done in some manner or other, and in making that choice, the actor continues a particular style. That stylistic choice is "read" by others – it is interpreted in relation to one of several general "wholes". But it is also an event with concrete effects in the world. Indeed, it adds to that world and in so doing alters it. Any action thus changes the context in which it, and any further stylistic reference to it, is interpreted. Meaning is always "running on", unstoppable because of the dualities of event and interpretation, particular and general, object and subject.

All actions (including words and thoughts) refer to other actions in order to have meaning. But there is always a distance between the reference and that which is referred to – between the signifier and the signified. There are always contradiction and difference which lie within sameness. Style is involved in this process of creating an apparent sameness (by referring the particular to the general). But the general can never adequately account for the particular. A rigid style in which items did have set meanings would be fragile and temporary, continually being eroded by its internal contradictions. Most long-lasting styles are, therefore, highly ambiguous and multivalent, encompassing and contributing to the reality of contradictory meanings. These are the types of style visible to archaeologists. In beginning to examine style, archaeologists need not only to develop theories about the stylistic process, but also to find a way of writing archaeology that leads to a fuller understanding of the styles with which we deal.

Chapter 6

**Investigating style: an exploratory
analysis of some Plains burials**

William K. Macdonald

*In this chapter Macdonald develops a basis for a more active and
specific analysis of style through the identification of two sources
of stylistic variability. Seeing style as a communicative, multi-
referential, and situational dependent entity, he defines* panache, *a
stylistic expression of separateness at the individual level, and*
protocol, *a set of social processes that support group identity and
membership. With these he sets out a form of multi-level analysis
and, using regression equations, defines these two elements of
style formally. To demonstrate how this analysis of stylistic
variability informs the archaeologist about the different processes
involved in the use of style, Macdonald presents mortuary data
from two American Plains groups, the Pawnee and the Arikara.
With these data, he shows that individual style and group identity
operated differently within these two groups, thus illustrating how
information about social processes may be gained from the
archaeological record.*

Introduction

Archaeologists generally agree that style is a particularly
complex, multidimensional and socially determined set of
phenomena; they generally disagree on how to construct
relevant and robust interpretations of style. There is even less
agreement on the definitional aspects of the phenomenon itself
(e.g., Whallon 1968; Wobst 1977; S. Plog 1980; Wiessner 1983,
1985; Sackett 1985a). However, archaeologists are all interested
in ways of investigating the variability that is encompassed by
the term "style," however they choose to define it, and in
attempting to assign social meaning to that variation.

My goal in this paper is to outline a conceptual basis for
investigations into variability, in this particular instance stylistic
variability. I wish to provide the beginnings of a toolkit for the
examination of stylistic variation in archaeological data. My
intent, however, is not the presentation of *the* method for
correctly analyzing something called style: a toolkit is a
conceptual rather than technical construct.

If it is granted that all human behavior is culturally and
socially mediated, an immediate emphasis is placed on the
social circumstances that tend to produce observable variation
in that behavior. That is, social context defines the limits and
modal constraints on the appropriateness of social behaviors;
human social behavior is situational and context dependent.
Since patterns of social behavior vary among particular
situations, then it follows that style will also vary among social
situations. The problem is to specify models of style that are
appropriate to particular social contexts.

Further, if it is granted that the phenomena we usually
call style play a role in the definition of the social contexts of
which they are a part, an immediate emphasis is placed on the
communicative component of stylistic variation (Wilmsen 1972,
Wobst 1977). The analytical position taken here is that, unless
demonstrated otherwise, style is in some way communicative as
well as situation dependent. This view of style implies that
variation expressed in material items is multireferential in that a
single morphological form of an artifact can potentially provide

a variety of messages depending on the social contexts of its use. Multireferentiality similarly defines style as a phenomenon likely to be heavily invested with *multiple levels* of symbolic coding.

Like most social phenomena, style minimally operates at the level of the individual, at a group level and on a regional, intergroup level. That is, we can conceive of individuals who work to stand out from their peers in terms of style, what the dictionary calls "panache." More formally, "panache" refers to those social processes and related behaviors that are aimed at an atomistic emphasis on the individual as a separate, independent, and unique element. This form of self-definition and self-expression should lead to an increase in the degree of stylistic variability in any group of individuals.

Social competition among a set of individuals, and consequent individual social differentiation, is one among a number of processes that might be expected to lead to an emphasis on panache in syle. The material results of such efforts at individuation would be expected to result in a high degree of assertive variation (Wiessner 1983). Note that panache refers to a set of behaviors and the processes that produce them while assertive style refers to the material consequences of panache.

"Individual" in an archaeological context does not, however, necessarily refer only to a single person. Material remains from a single burial may be associated with one person, but it may sometimes be convenient or necessary to consider the remains from a single dwelling or household as an element level variable. An *element* describes a level of data in the most dis-aggregated state possible with reference to a particular problem.

In a given analytical situation, it is necessary to argue justifiably that a variable being examined is referable to the specific *level* of social process under investigation. Such arguments should be a major component of any statement that seeks to establish the relevance of a variable to a particular analytical problem. Further, it is necessary in any archaeological analysis to substantiate the use of a variable that is not directly attributable to a single individual as elemental. It is both conceivable and likely that social processes may operate in opposing directions at different levels. Failure to disentangle these levels will most often mask the sort of significant relationships that we seek to investigate in our data.

More commonly in archaeology, we analyze style as a composite or group process whereby one batch of elements (e.g., individuals, households, sites) distinguishes itself from another batch according to some set of culturally defined and situation dependent rules, i.e., by means of a set of processes that the dictionary defines as "protocols." More formally, "protocol" refers to a set of social processes that is aimed at the promotion of group identity and membership at the expense of the individual. Such processes are typically institutional in scale and may or may not conflict with individual level social processes. In functional terms, protocols define expectations concerning behavior in order to facilitate social interactions; protocols are context specific and situation dependent.

Protocols may be present in either a vertical or a horizontal dimension, that is, as status protocols or as the etiquettes of social identification, and can be expected to result in emblemic style (Wiessner 1983). Again, note that I wish to distinguish between the social processes that generate variability and the particular morphological properties of the resulting variation. Just as panache produces assertive style, protocols produce style that is emblemic.

Face-to-face interactions and categorical relations shared among individuals as participants in social groups might be expected to produce a centripetal tendency in stylistic variability. That is, people in direct, daily contact often tend to behave in similar ways as members of a single social group. Rather than the contrastive social processes, such as competition and differentiation, implied by panache, protocol focuses on contagious social processes such as emulation and affiliation. These initial categories can be summarized as in Figure 6.1.

Protocol variables are *composite* rather than elemental. In this sense, "composite" refers to some justifiable aggregation of element level variables: spatially discrete clusters of burials, village site subdivisions, or entire sites may, depending on the problem at hand, provide relevant composite variables. It is necessary to keep in mind that the aggregation of data entails a loss of information or, perhaps more accurately, provides information on a qualitatively distinct order of phenomena. The arithmetic mean, for example, refers to a composite and aggregate property of data and does not yield information on variation among the individual elements from which it is computed. Simple as it may seem, the mean is not always a straightforward summary of element variation.

Composite variables may be nested or overlapping. Aggregation can be continued to higher orders of abstraction: burials, households, village subdivisions, villages, clusters of villages, all sites in a river valley, all sites in a region, etc. Stylistic variation is potentially observable at, and referable to, each and all of these levels. There is, however, no logical hierarchy implied in the aggregation of data; with the exception of the element level, it is not necessary that a variable be enclosed by any other.

For example, membership in a formal organization entity (e.g., a lineage) may often imply simultaneous membership in a

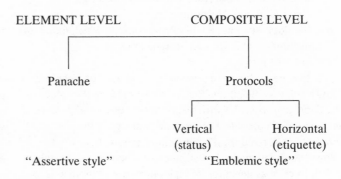

Fig. 6.1: The dimensions of stylistic variability

larger, more encompassing entity (e.g., a clan). In such cases the two composite variables (lineage and clan) may be logically nested. However, membership in either formal organizational entity does not necessarily imply categorization by sex. Neither lineage membership nor sex necessarily encompasses the other in a vertical hierarchy of orders; they are overlapping composites. The selection of level of observation and the ordering of those levels is necessarily theory driven and problem dependent since it is entailed by the nature of the research question under investigation. However, it is important to remember that analysis at composite levels of aggregation cannot proceed without some consideration of the distribution of maximally disaggregated, elemental data since composite variables are always a summary of element variation.

In abstract and formal terms, the above argument suggests that any stylistic variable, even in its simplest expression (e.g., frequency counts, similarity measures), is generated by a complex function of individual and multiple group processes. This can be expressed in more abstract terms as follows:

$$\text{style} = \text{constant} + \text{element} + \text{composite}_{1\ldots n} + \text{error} \tag{1}$$

That is, in any stylistic variable, we would expect that some portion of variation will be potentially explicable at the element level and other portions of that variation potentially attributable to various composite levels. In addition, some segment of variation may be the result of constant factors (e.g., technological constraints on manufacture) and some variation may be the result of random error factors in either production or measurement. An exhaustive account of the variation in any stylistic variable necessarily includes *all* of these levels of causal mechanism. Note that the terms on the right-hand side of equation (1) are assumed to be causal, or at least logically prior, to the measure of stylistic variation. As some readers may recognize, equation (1) is similar in form to the basic linear regression formula:

$$Y = \alpha + \beta_1(X_1) + \beta_2(X_2) + \ldots \beta_n(X_n) + \varepsilon \tag{2}$$

where,

- $Y =$ a dependent variable, in this case some measure of stylistic variation;
- $\alpha =$ the Y-intercept, the point on the vertical axis when the horizontal (X) axis is set to 0, which provides a convenient constant term;
- $\beta =$ the slope of a line, a multiplying constant which indicates increments of X for each increment of Y;
- $\varepsilon =$ an error term.

In general, linear regression refers to a set of techniques that calculates a linear equation that best predicts the values of the dependent (i.e., Y) variable. Note that the α and β values in equation (2) provide a convenient summary of the information derived from a regression analysis. Because it allows the simultaneous investigation of a number of variables, it is of interest as much for its exploratory (i.e., "predictive") role as for its confirmatory (i.e., "hypothesis testing") role.

Methods of analysis

The analogy that I am making here to regression is not coincidental since I will use those techniques below in an exploration of a variety of forms of stylistic variation. In addition to the appropriateness of the techniques to the task at hand, there are several reasons for selecting regression as an exploratory approach to the investigation of stylistic variation.

Regression represents a set of techniques that is commonly taught in introductory statistics courses. This is not because it is an easy or low-level set of methods, but rather because it is well established and often used. Because regression is taught at the introductory level, it is likely to be more widely known than some statistical alternatives (e.g., analysis of covariance or canonical correlation).

Anthropologists have made a relatively frequent use of regression (Chibnick 1985 provides a partial bibliography) and thus it represents a set of techniques that is likely to be relatively well known. Because regression techniques have been so widely used, the statistical behavior of the techniques is well known as a powerful and robust set of procedures (Cohen and Cohen 1975). This is not true of many of the statistical methods that are often used in archaeology (e.g., cluster analyses).

While I believe that regression is appropriate to the framework of analysis presented here, it is certainly not the only method, nor is regression without drawbacks. For example, in this paper I use *linear* regression but there is no necessary reason to expect that anthropological data will be distributed in a linear fashion. There are non-linear extensions of regression, but these are computationally tedious and beyond the scope of this paper.

Further, regression is based on a strict assumption of one-way causality: that is, it is assumed that the explanatory (X) variable causes the variation in variable to be explained (the Y variable) with no allowance made for feedback between them (e.g., Blalock 1972: 363). With anthropological data this assumption is frequently overly restrictive. In such cases, where causation is ambiguous or multi-directional, it is necessary to analyze a set of data through the use of simultaneous equations. In an exploratory approach, the assumption of causation is often relaxed to a form of logical priority rather than strict causality (e.g., Lewis-Beck 1980).

Both analysis of variance (ANOVA) and analysis of covariance (ANCOVA) have been suggested as general alternatives to the procedures outlined here. Most notable of these suggestions is that of Blau in a study of public welfare agencies based on nominalized variables (1960). The major drawback to these approaches is that specific explanatory effects are not directly related to particular variables, or to the particular values of those variables, as is the case with regression. It is the identification of specific level effects with specific variables and values that is of greatest interest here.

The literature on what is often called "multi-level analysis" (of which this paper is an example) is both large and varied in econometrics, political science, and sociology (a small sampling of such analyses includes: Alwin 1976; Alexander and

McDill 1976; Hannan, Freeman and Meyer 1976; Campbell and Alexander 1965; Doreian and Hummon 1976). Only recently has attention been called to the problem in anthropology (DeWalt and Pelto 1985) under the rubric of the micro/macro problem.

Finally, it should be pointed out that, while regression is generally thought of as a tool for confirmation, my emphasis here is on data exploration and data construction.

In any analysis, it is necessary to insure that the explanatory variables that we choose are relevant to the level of phenomena that we seek to explain. The more directly related and appropriate that our explanatory variables are, the more useful and robust they will be in any explanatory account. These common-sense observations imply an analytical emphasis on data construction rather than, as is often the case in archaeology, data reduction (Tukey 1969). In many archaeological examples, most obviously those using factor analyses, cluster analyses, and multidimensional scaling, a major effort is made to take a large number of raw data variables and reduce them to a smaller set of underlying variables. The attempt in such analyses is to extract those properties of the data that are relevant to a problem at hand. Often, however, a large portion of the data available *and the information contained in it* are left unexamined. In an exploratory approach, on the other hand, one begins with a relatively small and carefully selected set of variables and examines both the relevant portion, and the seemingly not relevant, in an attempt to maximize the amount of information that can be extracted from the minimum amount of data.

Summary

In sum, given the assumptions about human stylistic behavior outlined above, it seems reasonable to expect that rarely will any stylistic variable of interest be attributable to only a single level of social process. It is more likely that panache and multiple protocols will be present in any variable given the multi-referential nature of style. It is conceivable and often likely that mutually opposing social processes with varying social reference points will operate simultaneously on a single category of material item. That is, we would expect artifacts to be the complex material outcome of intricate and dynamic social processes.

In all, the above statements predict that style will be an extremely complex, complicated, and symbolically loaded form of material communication. Given this degree of expected complexity, it is perhaps not surprising that little has been advanced in the way of means to explore the ramifications of this complexity, although there has certainly been a great deal of argumentation concerning the appropriateness of the various models of style proposed in the literature. Simply put, we do not have the tools that we need in order to investigate the complexity of the phenomena that we call style.

Initially in these analyses, we must look for ways to attribute the complex variation embedded in stylistic variables into unique portions of causal or logically prior variables. That

is, it is appropriate to ask: what portion of this stylistic variation is explicable with reference to panache and what portion to protocols? It is only in this way that we can begin a more fruitful investigation into the multireferential layering of stylistic variation.

An archaeological example

The discussion presented above may be of some interest in clarifying the problems that may be encountered in attempting to disentangle variation in style. But as much as we sometimes like to think we are not, at heart all archaeologists are empirical. Some of us are empiricist and a few of us are theoretical, but most of us derive little satisfaction from a method or an artificial example. No method or analytical framework is of much interest until it has been brought to bear on an actual set of archaeological data.

Unfortunately, there are extremely few cases of stylistic data that have been published in sufficient detail to be appropriate to the level of analysis outlined above; this is not to imply that stylistic data *cannot* be cast in a form appropriate to the framework outlined here. As a result, I will use a set of mortuary data and speak of the "style" of a mortuary program. In this section, then, I will present an abbreviated analytical account of some "real" archaeological data using the framework developed above.

In a very real sense the notions of "panache" and "protocol" are as directly germane to mortuary data as they are to *style*. What is usually termed a mortuary program is a reference to protocol behavior; the variation that is labelled idiosyncratic, and thus often discarded, is panache. Further, terms such as "achieved" and "ascribed," often used in the analysis of mortuary remains, can easily fit as specific subdivisions under the more common language terms panache and protocol. Style permeates all social behavior and should not, in my view, be relegated to formal variation in material remains.

Note again that the mortuary analyses presented here are exploratory. I wish simply to point to the utility of a framework for analysis. I have nonetheless included significance levels resulting from F tests, primarily as an indication of the robustness of the procedures. In my view, tests of statistical significance are at best problematic in the analysis of archaeological data (see Thomas 1976, 1978; Cowgill 1977).

The data to be analyzed are largely drawn from a recent monograph on the analysis of mortuary variability using data from the American Plains (O'Shea 1984). Since the data are exhaustively described and analyzed in that work, only a brief description of the relevant variables will be presented here. Readers interested in further archaeological or ethnographic detail concerning the data used here (or, indeed, in mortuary analysis generally) are urged to consult the excellent book by O'Shea (1984) and the relevant reports cited therein.

Only three of the six sites analyzed by O'Shea are used here. Additionally, due to a relatively small number of sexed skeletons, two of the sites were combined for the present analysis. The first of these is the Linwood site (25 BU 1) which dates to the period 1777–1809 and which is subdivided into three spatially distinct areas containing 27, 13 and 14 burials respectively (O'Shea 1984: 55–56, 112). This site has been suggested to represent a village of the Chaui band of the Post-contact Pawnee. The second site, also representing an occupation of the Chaui Pawnee, is the Clarks site (25 PK 1) which dates to the period 1820–45 (O'Shea 1984: 56). The mortuary remains are segregated into 5 spatially discrete areas but only 4 of these (Burial Hill 4, 5, 6 and 7) are utilized in the present analysis due to sample sizes.

The total number of burials used in the "population" level analyses below is 111 for the two Pawnee sites; these burials span a time period from about 1770–1845, or about 75 years. For the analysis by sex, however, only 28 burials could be included (9 females and 19 males). For the analysis by age categories, 61 of the burials could be included.

The second case to be examined is the Leavenworth site (39 CO 9) which dates to the period from about 1800–32 (O'Shea 1984: 59; Bass, Evans and Jantz, 1971: 20; Wedel 1955). As noted by O'Shea, "the burial zone, which was located on the bluff tops behind the village area, was composed of five distinct areas" (1984: 19), that are used here as a primary grouping criterion. The occupants of the Leavenworth site were historic Arikara. One hundred and twenty-eight burials from Leavenworth were used in the "population" level analysis. Data on sex was available for 28 males and 19 females; 120 burials had data on age.

For the present analysis, the element level variable will refer to an individual grave; in this case the element and an individual are effectively the same since multiple burials are not included. Spatial subdivisions will be used as the initial composite$_1$ level variable. It is of some importance to note that the presence of cemeteries and spatial subdivisions within a cemetery have been argued to have relevance to social groupings of the people that interred their dead there (e.g., Goldstein 1980). Such areas thus provide a justifiable basis for the construction of composite$_1$ variables. In addition, in the analyses presented below, sex will also be used to discriminate categories as a descriptive composite variable; both males and females are present in each composite level sample.

It is often noted in mortuary analyses that both sex and age are important criteria for the discrimination of variation in mortuary programs. It is less often pointed out that sex and age are not often unrelated to group membership: in the present case, for example, both the Pawnee (archaeologically represented by the Linwood and Clarks sites) and the Arikara (who occupied the Leavenworth site) were ethnographically characterized as matrifocal (i.e., matrilineal and matrilocal) (O'Shea 1984: 72, 76 citing Murdock 1949, Weltfish 1965, and Grinnell 1891 for the Pawnee and Lowie 1916, Deetz 1965 and Brackenridge 1962 for the Arikara). That is, sex determined one's initial membership in a descent group.

The ethnographic accounts suggest that the strength of such corporate groups varied between the Pawnee and Arikara, although the latter were only relatively recently splintered from the former. In general the strength of matrifocal groups was considerably less among the Arikara as compared to the Pawnee (Brackenridge 1962: Deetz 1965: 27). The ethnographic record does not provide information on several points, however. For example, it is unclear whether a man was buried in the cemetery of his natal group or of the group of his wife. It is thus unclear the extent to which protocols of group affiliation played a role in mortuary behavior.

That is, it is unknown whether burial was carried out with primary reference to one's social group of affiliation rather than with reference to one's natal group (although strength of ties to one's natal descent group is highly variable cross-culturally). Thus, the relationship between an individual's sex and variation in mortuary remains is of some inherent interest but it must be first determined the extent to which males and females within a cemetery were subject to the same protocols. To what extent, in other words, was some form of social group important in determining the variation in distribution of burial materials within a grave from males as distinct from females?

In most mortuary analyses, including O'Shea's, variation according to sex is simply identified and summarized with a general statement to the effect that males and females may have been treated differently (e.g., O'Shea 1984: 159, 219, 247). But, as noted above, it is varying relationships between sex as a categorical variable and components of mortuary ritual that are of interest in defining what may be called gender protocols. As a result, sex will be used in the analyses below as an overlapping composite$_2$ variable, in particular since spatial subdivisions seem logically connected to social groupings that contain both males and females.

Similarly, age categories may be used to provided a fuller account of mortuary materials when considered in the context of social groupings. To what extent was some form of social grouping important in determining variation in the distribution of burial materials within a grave at various points in an individual's life cycle? In the sections to follow, I will address these questions first for the Pawnee sites and then for the Leavenworth site. The results will then be compared between the two ethnic groups.

The diversity of grave inclusions is an often-considered and important variable of interest in any examination of mortuary remains. The basic question addressed by this variable concerns variation in the relative distribution of goods found in graves. This variation may in part be accounted for by an individual's access to goods and in part by the social appropriateness of inclusions of certain categories of goods relative to that individual's social position.

It is clear, of course, that an individual is *being* interred and individuals are not interring themselves: the materials found in a grave are placed there consciously and purposefully by others and not by the deceased. Some of the observed variation thus may be directly referable to the individual and some may be appropriate to the individual's position within a group of one sort or another. In other words, we would expect there to be some component of panache and some component of protocol in any mortuary situation. An examination of the diversity of goods within a grave is one variable of interest in considering these components.

The measurement of diversity is a complex matter and a large number of measures have been suggested and reviewed (e.g., Kintigh n.d.). Due in part to the nature of the variables as recorded by O'Shea, a measure of grave good diversity will be constructed from category counts, which is in effect a measure of variation in the distributional evenness of grave inclusions. Here I will use a measure of diversity that is appropriate to data recorded as counts:

$$\text{Diversity} = (\Gamma_{[\text{observed}]}) / (1 - \Gamma_{]\text{maximum}]}) \qquad (3)$$

where Γ is defined as $\Sigma x^2 / (\Sigma x)^2$ over a given number of categories, k. Γ observed is the value for a given grave while $\Gamma_{]\text{maximum}]}$ is the maximum value of evenness that can be obtained for a given k. In the analyses presented here, the number of categories is always 5 (i.e., $\Gamma_{[\text{maximum}]}$ is always .80).

The categories are drawn from O'Shea's discussion of artifacts removed from the sites in which specific items are collapsed into relatively coarse functional categories (O'Shea 1984: Table 4.2). O'Shea's list of six categories is here collapsed to five since the distinction between "trade-derived body ornaments" and "trade-derived clothing ornaments" appears minor. The five categories used in the present analysis are:

Category	Rank
Native implements	1
Native ornaments	2
Trade implements	3
Trade ornaments	4
Sociotechnic objects	5

The number to the right of each category is a crude index of "value" used in the construction of a second variable (see Winters 1969; Braun 1977). I will refer to this variable as Wealth and it is meant to be an index of socioeconomic status. To calculate this variable, the number of items in a category is multiplied by the ordinal rank of that category and the results summed for each grave:

$$\text{Wealth} = \Sigma(n_k \, {}^* \text{value}_k) \qquad (4)$$

Note that, although both variables are constructed from category counts, the two are not automatically or mechanically related. This can be seen in Table 6.1., which merely demonstrates the calculation procedures for four hypothetical graves.

This table simply shows that Value is not necessarily related directly to Diversity; note, for example, that for both graves 1 and 3 Value is 30 and Diversity is 1.0 and 0.0 respectively. For graves 2 and 4 Diversity is 0.0 while Value is 50 and 10 respectively.

While there is no mechanically necessary reason for these variables to be related, we might expect that socioeconomic status, as indexed by Wealth, would be a major factor in

Table 6.1

| | RANK | | | | | Σ | Value | Σ^2 $1-(\Sigma)^2$ | Γ |
	1	2	3	4	5				
Grave 1	2	2	2	2	2	10	30	0.80	1.00
Grave 2	0	0	0	0	10	10	50	0.00	0.00
Grave 3	0	0	10	0	0	10	30	0.00	0.00
Grave 4	10	0	0	0	0	10	10	0.00	0.00

Note: $\Gamma_{[\text{maximum}]}$ for $k = 5$ is 0.80.

accounting for the Diversity of goods in an individual's grave. Wealth may index either some measure of an individual's accumulated status or it may alternatively signal the relative economic status of the social group with which they are affiliated (i.e., the group that buries an individual). The arithmetic mean of Diversity and Wealth by spatial subdivision are used as composite₁ variables.

The relatively limited but specific goal of this analysis may be framed as an investigation into the relationship between the distribution of categories in a grave and the relative value of goods represented in a grave. Put another way, of the observed variation in Diversity, what portion is determined by the Wealth that is attributable to various empirically definable levels of social process? More generally, the investigation is into the way in which socioeconomic status may impact differentially on one important aspect of mortuary behavior. This relationship may in turn signal a more ramifying set of social processes. Note that the goal is not to *identify* differences but to specify and account for varying relationships.

Initial examination of the variables for all three sites suggests that Diversity is distributed in an approximately Normal fashion. As might be expected for the distribution of a limited finite resource, however, Wealth is distributed in a fashion that approximates a LogNormal form. Because regression generally requires that a distribution be symmetrical (although not Normal), Wealth was transformed to an approximately Normal shape by taking the natural logarithm of each value. Means were then calculated for each spatial subdivision within a site and an interaction variable calculated as the product of Wealth and the mean of Wealth.

Initial regressions were carried out and correlations among the explanatory variables calculated. As expected, there is a high degree of multicolinearity observable among the explanatory variables and thus they were transformed as described above. The final regressions were calculated for the two Pawnee sites combined and the Leavenworth site; they were then analyzed by sex and age category.

The Pawnee sites

O'Shea points out that, on the basis of his analysis of Pawnee sites that he examined, "elementary differences, such as age and gender distinctions, were observed . . . Yet none of the more general features of horizontal organization, such as

Table 6.2.   Pawnee sites, population level (n = 111)

	Element	Composite$_1$	Interaction
Percent explained	33.1%	2.9%	0.4%
Adjusted r^2	0.325	0.020	0.794
Significance	0.000	0.197	0.000

corporate group membership, descent orientation, moiety affiliation, or society membership, could firmly be demonstrated from the mortuary samples . . ." (1984: 159).

By general features of horizontal organization, O'Shea clearly means social groupings at a composite rather than element level. This is, in the language employed here, a statement that the contribution of the composite$_1$ and composite interaction variables should be about 0 is consistent with O'Shea's interpretation. Beyond the observation that males and females were apparently treated differently, sex is largely unexplored in O'Shea's consideration of social groupings. That is, one can distinguish between males and females on the basis of grave inclusions but the significance of this observation is left unexamined.

At the Clarks site, O'Shea notes that "aside from differentiation of adults from subadults . . . and of males and females . . . only one horizontal social distinction was observed. This distinction, probably reflecting corporate group or lineage membership, was expressed through the use of distinct areas for burial" (1984: 152–55). This distinction is also recognized at Linwood and Leavenworth, but aside from the *recognition* of this distinction, its relationship to social variables is left unexplored.

Combined results for the two sites in terms of percent of variance accounted for are presented in Table 6.2:
Table 6.2 suggests that there is little indication of group (composite$_1$) socioeconomic impact on the diversity of materials found in a grave, an interpretation that overall tends to support O'Shea's statements concerning the Pawnee. There is a slight suggestion of composite$_1$ contribution but it is statistically insignificant. However, as noted above, sex may have a great deal to do with group membership and it is of some interest, therefore, to examine the same relationships with the data disaggregated by sex. Table 6.3 presents the results of such an analysis.

What is immediately striking in this table is the observation that, when separated by sex, the composite$_1$ variable accounts for more than 50% of the explained variation in Diversity for both males and females. This suggests that the combined "population" values were acting to mask variation that is a result of an individual's sex. It also suggests that in fact the social groupings indicated by spatial divisions played an important role in determining the distribution of inclusions within an individual's grave. The interaction variables indicate that one's status or the relative status of one's social group also

Table 6.3.   Pawnee sites: by sex

a. Females (n = 9)

	Element	Composite$_1$	Interaction
Percent explained	81.1%	54.0%	50.5%
Adjusted r^2	0.783	0.475	0.435
Significance	0.003	0.066	0.085

b. Males (n = 19)

	Element	Composite$_1$	Interaction
Percent explained	44.6%	51.2%	40.1%
Adjusted r^2	0.414	0.483	0.366
Significance	0.007	0.002	0.013

had an important effect in determining burial inclusions. While it is not possible to suggest the direction of the determination of interaction, it is reasonable to suggest that the value of the composite$_1$ variable is more important. Finally, note that an individual woman's status is extremely important in determining Diversity of grave inclusions.

The disaggregation by sex suggests that further disentangling can be accomplished by examining these same relationships through the life cycle of individuals as may be inferred from age distinctions. Table 6.4 presents the results of such an analysis for the Pawnee sites. (Unfortunately, sample sizes preclude differentiating age categories by sex for the adults.)

Although the critical adolescent category is missing, these results suggest that characteristics of individual status are most important for infants – presumably as a function of their parents' status. But this importance drops at least until age 12 or so. Individual characteristics of status then generally increase to age 30 when they begin to decrease again until old age. The significance of group membership follows a trajectory to that of the element variable; clearly, however, group membership is most important to adults.

Table 6.4.   Pawnee sites by age group

	Element	Composite$_1$	Interaction	n
Age category:				
0–2	75.8*	13.8	23.8*	22
3–12	34.4*	6.6	31.8*	15
13–17	n/d	n/d	n/d	0
18–30	42.6*	24.2	7.9	12
31–40	20.7	39.3	21.5	8
41–50+	90.1*	91.0*	90.4*	4
* Significance > .10				

Table 6.5. Leavenworth site population level (n = 128)

	Element	Composite₁	Interaction
Percent explained	39.3%	10.4%	10.3%
Adjusted r^2	0.388	0.097	0.096
Significance	0.000	0.001	0.001

The Leavenworth site

It is of some interest to compare these preliminary results to those obtained from the Arikara data recovered from the Leavenworth site. Table 6.5 presents the results of a "population" level examination of the Arikara data. In this table it can be seen that group membership, as indicated by the composite₁ variable, initially appears to play a more important role in determining the distribution of grave goods that was the case for the Pawnee at the aggregated population level. Again, disaggregation by sex is of some interest. Table 6.6 presents these results.

In this case, aggregation does not seem to have masked the relationships that exist when categories of sex are considered separately. For both males and females, group affiliation seems to make a relatively minor contribution to the diversity of goods in a grave. Indeed, the composite₁ value for males is almost twice that for females, although neither is particularly significant.

The results of analysis by age category are presented in Table 6.7. Except for the 3–12-year-old and 31–40-year-old categories, the protocols of group affiliation play a relatively important role in determining diversity of grave goods for all age groups. In comparison to the Pawnee, the composite₁ values are remarkably stable through the life cycle of an individual. The element level values, on the other hand, show some similarity to the Pawnee with the exception of the decreasing importance from age 30 onward.

Table 6.6. Leavenworth site: by sex

a. Females (n = 19)

	Element	Composite₁	Interaction
Percent explained	31.1%	9.6%	9.8%
Adjusted r^2	0.270	0.043	0.045
Significance	0.042	0.423	0.414

b. Males (n = 28)

	Element	Composite₁	Interaction
Percent explained	42.8%	5.9%	1.4%
Adjusted r^2	0.407	0.023	0.000
Significance	0.001	0.455	0.833

Table 6.7. Leavenworth site: by age group

	Element	Composite₁	Interaction	n
Age category:				
0–2	46.6*	20.5*	19.8*	42
3–12	37.6*	11.7	10.8	21
13–17	21.2	20.9	8.4	8
18–30	54.5*	20.7	5.4	20
31–40	32.3*	7.7	5.6	20
41–50+	31.0	16.6	8.4	9

* Significance > .10

Summary

The analyses presented above are a brief sketch of the sort of investigation into stylistic variability that I am advocating. I suggest that this framework for analyses allows a closer and more interesting examination of variation in social behavior at differing levels of social process than is presently carried out in archaeology.

I have refrained from making close comparisons between the results presented here and a variety of ethnographic and ethnohistoric information. As most people familiar with the Plains area will recognize, there is a close correspondence between the interpretations that can be drawn from the above analyses and the ethnohistoric and ethnographic records. For example, the Pawnee composite₁ values, when considered by sex, are much higher than those for the Arikara, an observation that is in accord with ethnographic observations noted above concerning the lower importance of corporate groups among the Arikara. For the Leavenworth site, disentangling the data by sex leads to the suggestion of decreased importance of the composite₁ variable. Note that the adjusted r^2 values at the population level, which measure the relative efficiency of Wealth in accounting for Diversity, are much higher for the Pawnee than are indicated at the Leavenworth site. This may indicate that socioeconomic status is of less consequence in determining grave inclusions among the Arikara than among the Pawnee and points to a search for a more efficient explanatory variable.

The results of the archaeological analyses presented here are in general congruent with the statements of ethnographers and ethnohistorians but is is important to recognize that this congruence does not provide *confirmation* for the archaeological analyses. (Nor, on the other hand, does the archaeological analysis confirm the ethnographic record.)

In most respects, it is not possible to justify observed archaeological statements with reference to ethnography. For example, variation in the relative importance or strength of group socioeconomic relationships among either the Pawnee or Arikara cannot be assessed with the available ethnographic information. In the last analysis, any archaeological interpretations must stand on their own.

As pointed out above, the analyses presented here are exploratory. Note that the suggestion made above concerning the varying importance of groups (i.e., the composite$_1$ variable) does not specify the nature of those groups. I have not archaeologically demonstrated the presence of matrilines, patrilines, secret societies, warrior societies, moieties, clans or any other "features of horizontal organization" that have been ethnographically documented for these Plains groups.

Rather, I have pointed out that variation in diversity of grave goods is in part accounted for by variation in socioeconomic status at a number of social levels within these societies. I suggest that some of these characteristics of "groupness" may be seen as *protocols* that are socially significant to individuals depending on their age and sex. I also suggest that, as tentative as this statement may be, it is a different form of statement than is normally made on the basis of archaeological analyses of mortuary remains. What I have attempted to do is assess the varying social significance of panache and protocol behaviors among the Pawnee and Arikara for two relatively short periods in their histories.

The point to be derived from these statements, however, has less to do with the relationship between ethnography and archaeology than it has to do with archaeological analyses generally: *if we fail to distinguish and disentangle complex levels of social process, we will fail in our analyses of style or anything else.* The framework outlined in this chapter is an attempt to allow the analysis of the social complexity that we can and should expect in our data.

Conclusions

In this paper I have not discussed "style" in the traditional manner of attribute distributions, artifact morphology, design construction and the like. Rather, I have attempted to broaden the notion of style away from purely archaeologically based conceptions involving formal variation in material culture to include the varying processes that anthropologists may expect to occur at different levels of social context. I have attempted to do this by outlining a conceptual framework for investigating variation. It is my impression that most analyses of style are *ad hoc* and unsystematic. Although often plausible, stylistic analyses too often lack sufficient rigor to hold up under careful scrutiny. At best, such analyses offer only superficial observations on material culture.

The goal of archaeological research is only initially an understanding of variation in material culture. It may be that this paper is not in fact as much about style *per se* as it is about ways in which archaeologists can begin to appreciate and analyze the variability that is inherent in any set of data that is the result of complex human cultural behavior.

Failure to consider the implications of cross level inference means accepting a high probability of false inference. Even if one is interested in social processes only *within* a composite context, it is necessary to consider the effects that element level behaviors may have on that context. Or, at the very least, it is necessary to eliminate the element variation by careful and appropriate selection of variables that are not sensitive to variation at that level.

Protocol and panache provide convenient analytical distinctions for social processes that we assume are appropriate to different levels of behavior familiar to anthropologists. I also suggest that the distinction between protocol and panache is embedded in larger issues of group and individual social process. Style is in this respect simply a metaphor by which we address questions concerning the generation of variation in the archaeological record.

Chapter 7

Sociopolitical implications of stylistic variation in the American Southwest

Stephen Plog

The use of stylistic variation in traditional archaeological research has been to date sites, to reconstruct village social organization, and to measure trade and interaction between communities. This form of analysis has been one of the primary uses of stylistic analysis in archaeology. This chapter reviews and questions the underlying but often implicit assumptions that exist within this type of analysis.

The author addresses the issue of the use of stylistic variation of design change, attribute association, and decorative characteristics for dating, using the illustration of prehistoric groups in the Southwestern United States. This area's cultural reconstruction has been derived primarily from analyses of stylistic variation in painted ceramic vessels. Plog proposes the need for serious revisions in the understanding of Southwestern culture change, associated with rethinking the ways in which theoretical interpretations of style and methods of stylistic variation have been applied. This entails a broader scope of the meaning of style, including symbolic and iconological variation.

Debate over issues in the analysis and explanation of stylistic variation has been a constant and major component of the archaeological literature, although that debate has varied both in its focus and in its intensity throughout the history of the discipline. This emphasis on style has been the result of the derivation of very basic aspects of spatial (cultural) and temporal frameworks from aspects of stylistic variation (i.e., formal variation that is less determined by utilitarian factors [Sackett 1985a]; thus, I use "stylistic variation" in its most general sense, rather than the specific sense defined by Wiessner [1985]). Many of the initial definitions of culture areas, for example, emphasize differences in artifact styles, as do later attempts to define residence patterns or measure levels of social interaction (e.g., Deetz 1965; Hill 1970; Longacre 1970). Studies of, or debates about, style in relationship to aspects of chronology are equally prevalent, however. Such debates are central to key issues in typology (e.g., Spaulding 1953; Ford 1952) and in seriation (e.g., Deetz and Dethlefsen 1965). Despite the emphasis on style in such studies, the basic question of why style varies was often addressed implicitly. As a result, clear and concise formulations of theories of stylistic variation were infrequent.

In contrast to many of these early studies, the most recent period of heightened interest in style differs in emphasis. Perhaps initiated by the publication of some major statements in the late 70s and early 80s (e.g., Wobst 1977; Hodder 1977, 1979, 1982b; Conkey 1980), much research has focused on developing and testing theories of style. While the interaction of style and various parameters of social relationships continues to be an important focal point of this research, the relationship of style, typology, and chronology building is addressed infrequently. Overall these recent studies have increased our understanding of the range of possible explanations of stylistic variation and offer clearer and more detailed formulations of alternative theories.

The exchange between Sackett (1985a) and Wiessner

(1985), for example, has provided distinctions among isochrestic, stylistic, and iconological theories of style and identifies issues that must be resolved to achieve a more complete formulation of those theories. Those distinctions will be followed in this chapter, although I will use the phrase "symbolic variation" as a substitute for Wiessner's category of stylistic variation because of the more general connotations the latter phrase has for most readers. Following Wiessner (1985: 160–61), the three theories or aspects of style can be defined as follows:

(a) *isochrestic variation*: variation resulting from behavior that is "acquired by rote learning and imitation and is employed automatically."

(b) *symbolic variation*: variation that has a "behavioral basis in the fundamental human cognitive process of personal and social identification through stylistic and social comparison. In this process, people compare their ways of making and decorating artifacts with those of others and then imitate, differentiate, ignore, or in some way comment on how aspects of the maker or bearer relate to their own social and personal identities." Thus, symbolic variation "presents information about similarities and differences that can help reproduce, alter, disrupt, or create social relationships."

(c) *iconological variation*: a more specific case of symbolic variation in which "stylistic statements conform to certain spoken ones, containing clear, purposeful, conscious messages aimed at a specific target population."

Although Sackett tends to equate symbolic and iconological theories, I agree with Wiessner (1985: 161) that Sackett's formulation of iconological style describes a highly formalized form of communication that encompasses only a limited range of possible symbolic behaviors. Moreover, as I will argue below, the material expectations of stylistic patterns that are iconological may differ from other forms of symbolic communication.

One noteworthy aspect of the exchange between Wiessner and Sackett is that they emphasize that these alternative theories are not mutually exclusive; each may explain aspects of stylistic variation on different materials and at different time periods. It has rarely been the case, however, that stylistic variation in a given area has been interpreted from such a multivariate perspective. In addition, given recent reemphasis on the interaction of style and various social relationships, the implications of these alternative theoretical perspectives for basic aspects of archaeological methods need to be addressed. Some of the expectations that Wiessner (1985: 163) outlines to distinguish isochrestic from stylistic variation, for example, have important implications for key components of methods of chronology construction used in many areas. In this paper, I want to examine some of these issues and their implications for our understanding of social relationships, chronology construction, and explanations of culture change in the American Southwest. It should be emphasized that basic to this analysis is the assumption that variation in the decorative

characteristics present on Southwestern ceramics may require consideration of all of the theories described by Sackett and Wiessner. That is, it is likely that the determinants of stylistic variation evolve and become more complex as social systems likewise evolve in complexity, although one theory may be more relevant than another in explaining decorative variation on different types of artifacts or on artifacts from different time periods.

Style and the prehistoric American Southwest

As in many areas of the world, analysis of stylistic variation, particularly designs painted on ceramic vessels, has been one of the primary means through which the prehistory of the American Southwest has been described and explanations of that prehistory tested. Initially, designs served as critical dating indices; despite the development of dating techniques in archaeology and the diversity of design studies that have been conducted that emphasis has continued. At least 99% of the sites in the area are dated on the basis of ceramic types, not the much more accurate tree-ring dates for which the area is well known. Those types are largely defined by particular design attributes. Similarly, efforts to understand various aspects of Puebloan organization also emphasize stylistic characteristics. Early definitions of culture areas and later attempts to characterize within-village social organization, to estimate levels of interaction between communities, or to measure changes in regional social networks all have been based to a large degree on various characteristics of decorative patterns.

The different types of stylistic analyses have generally led to similar conclusions about the prehistory of the region. Although I would in no way suggest that Southwestern archaeologists tend to agree with each other any more than archaeologists working in other parts of the world, I think it is fair to say that most differences in interpretation nevertheless have been expressed consistently within a relatively standard interpretive framework. Most cultural-historical reconstructions suggest that social groups were largely egalitarian, subsisting during the last 1000 to 1500 years primarily on an agricultural economy supplemented by hunting and gathering. Cultural groups are regarded as stable and conservative and their organization is usually modeled as a system regulated by homeostatic mechanisms that produced stable, successful adaptations for long time periods. The Pecos Classification, for example, that was developed to describe major periods of culture change, includes phases that are as long as 200 years, and even temporal frameworks developed from very detailed studies of small areas generally are based on phases 75 to 100 years in length. Change significant enough to suggest major alterations in adaptations is viewed as infrequent and, more importantly, only in a few unique instances of severe environmental change is that change regarded to have been serious enough that the stability of the adaptation was interrupted. Finally, despite the purportedly regional focus of ecological approaches advocated within the last few decades, most interpretations of the prehistory of the region at least implicitly suggest that the natural and social environment in which groups interacted was small spatially. Individual valleys no more than 20 to 25 square miles, or even smaller, in area are regarded as having been occupied by cultural groups that were economically, socially, and politically autonomous, though not necessarily completely isolated. Moreover, significant population movements within the region were infrequent.

Although disagreements with some aspects of this summary of standard interpretations have undoubtedly always existed, I submit that it is a fair characterization of the opinions of the vast majority of archaeologists who have worked or still work in the area. Only recently have there begun to be significant departures from this standard viewpoint on some issues. In a few instances, for example, some have hypothesized that groups in a few areas were not egalitarian. Nevertheless, arguments for any significant amount of social differentiation are largely limited to such seemingly unique areas as Chaco Canyon where towns with populations of a few thousand individuals existed during some time periods, along with road systems, irrigated fields, and evidence for long-distance exchange. While on the other hand I would not suggest that such arguments will be, or should be, extended to most other areas of the Southwest, on the other hand I think we are at a point where our standard interpretations of the Southwest are beginning to undergo serious revisions and we must reevaluate the fundamental basis of cultural reconstruction in all regions.

Problems with standard models of Southwestern prehistory are a product of several factors, including an overemphasis on ethnographic analogy. Too much weight has been placed on ethnographic descriptions of Pueblo groups in the nineteenth and twentieth centuries in developing models of prehistoric groups, as Upham (1982) and several others have recently argued. While many such factors could be discussed, most relevant to this volume is the role that theories of stylistic variation, and methods of studying that variation, have played in producing those standard models. What I will suggest in the remainder of this chapter is that the need for serious revisions in our understanding of culture change in the Southwest is to a large extent the result of serious problems with the ways that style has been used in archaeological research in the Southwest. Although those problems involve issues both in theoretical interpretations of style and in methods of describing stylistic variation, I will primarily concentrate on the latter. That focus should not be taken as an indication that I regard theoretical issues as less important or as unrelated to methods of stylistic analysis, however, and I hope to make that clear as the discussion progresses. Similarly, although there are issues concerning both the use of style as a dating index and the relationship of stylistic variation to aspects of social organization, I will initially concentrate on the former topic. While stylistic variation is paramount in recent proposals concerning sociopolitical relationships, those relationships cannot be understood or explained adequately until we have information on their trajectories through time (Plog and Hantman 1986a).

Style and chronology construction in the American Southwest

The most fundamental use of style in Southwestern archaeology, or in the archaeology of any area, is to date sites. Archaeologists working in the Southwest region are guided by one of the most comprehensive and detailed ceramic typologies, one that began to be developed almost 50 years ago (Colton and Hargrave 1937). In the northern Arizona area that I will discuss later in this paper, for example, the various types of Tusayan White Ware (Colton and Hargrave 1937: Colton 1955) have been modified very little and are used almost exclusively for ceramic dating. Although technological characteristics are a part of those type descriptions, stylistic variation is paramount. Studies have shown that over 75 per cent of the differences between types are based on decorative characteristics alone (Martin and Plog 1973: 252).

The pottery types are, in terms of the stylistic characteristics, polythetic. Assignment of a given artifact to a given type is based on the presence of one or more elements of a diagnostic set of design characteristics. Kana-a Black-on-white, a type common in the northern part of the Southwest from approximately AD 775 to 950 (Pueblo I) (Breternitz 1966: 79), is characterized by several design attributes: thin lines, appended ticks ("fringe" that is more rectangular than circular), zigzag lines, acute triangles that often have small flags or scrolls appended, and overlapping lines. Once a collection of ceramics has been sorted into the various types, the actual assignment of a site to a particular phase has been somewhat subjective. The assignment is based on the unquantified degree of similarity of the relative frequencies of all types at a site to ideal ceramic complexes or ceramic groups that have been shown by tree-ring dates to be characteristic of different temporal phases.

Theoretical expectations

Given that all but a handful of sites are dated by ceramics, our knowledge of patterns of sociopolitical relationships, subsistence change, or any other aspects of culture change in the region is overwhelmingly shaped by traditional chronological methods. There are several issues that can be raised about those methods, however, and one of the most important concerns the extent of covariation among elements of the polythetic set of design attributes that characterize types. Although combinations of the designs that define a given type certainly have been shown to occur on some whole vessels, other illustrations suggest little covariation between attributes and extreme variation among vessels belonging to the same type. The implicit assumption of type definitions, that there is strong covariation among all characteristic attributes throughout the life of a type, has never been tested statistically for any ceramic type from the northern Southwest. Moreover, the vast majority of ceramic material that is typed in order to date sites are small sherds usually characterized by only one or two of the diagnostic attributes. Thus, artifacts that are classified as members of the same type potentially can be extremely different and, if the implicit assumption noted above is not correct, potentially can obscure rather than improve the accuracy of dating efforts.

In addition, recent discussions of patterns of stylistic variation that should be expected given alternative theories of style suggest that strong covariation of attributes (and therefore types) should not necessarily be a consistent component of the archaeological record. Wiessner (1985: 163) has suggested that "artifacts resulting from isochrestic choices would vary around one standard mean type, with range of variation depending on functional requirements, materials, standards set by society, etc." Also, "isochrestic procedures should . . . remain relatively stable except in the face of internal or imposed technological change" and "will not necessarily be altered by shifting patterns of social interaction" (Wiessner 1985: 163). Thus, when one attempts to define artifact types on the basis of characteristics determined by isochrestic variation, we would expect those types to be relatively clearcut because of (a) a strong association of attributes as choices vary around a standard and (b) the stability of the standard over time.

In contrast, ceramic decorative characteristics that are symbolic "should be an updated, current, and dynamic commentary on social relations, and in many cases the processes of differentiation and emulation will cause 'fashion swings'" (Wiessner 1985: 162). Thus, "stylistic alternatives used and patterns of stylistic variation over space would be expected to be numerous depending on the nature of relationships in which style participates, cultural context, history and conditions, such as density of artifacts (Wiessner 1984), competition (Hodder 1979), and so on" (Wiessner 1985: 163). As a result, decorative patterns produced by symbolic behavior should be less stable and also less likely to exhibit the consistent patterns of attribute association that are expected to characterize types.

These proposals thus imply that the tight ceramic typologies that have been developed for many regions, including the American Southwest, could be more valid during some time periods than in others. If this is the case, the fundamental role that such types have played in our reconstruction of culture change in the region may have led to serious errors in our understanding of that change. The validity of those types (and the implications that such studies have for theories of stylistic variation) is then an issue that must now be considered.

The case study

Research by Michelle Hegmon (1986), Jeff Hantman and myself (Hantman 1983; Hantman and Plog 1982; S. Plog 1986a; Plog and Hantman 1986a, 1986b) has focused on several aspects of stylistic variation on northern Black Mesa in the Kayenta Anasazi region of northeastern Arizona (see Figure 7.1). In particular, we have studied the period from approximately AD 800 to 1150, an era characterized by at least one major epoch of population increase, though with little change in the average size of the individual small settlements occupied by a few nuclear or extended families, and a major abandonment episode in the first part of the 1100s. Several pottery types, characterized by similarly named decorative styles, have been identified for this period (see figure 7.2). At the beginning of the sequence, Kana-a Black-on-white, the type described above, was most abundant. Subsequently, it was replaced by Black Mesa Black-on-white, a type that Breternitz (1966: 70) notes was most common from AD 1000 to 1130, but appears largely to be restricted to the years between AD 1000 to 1075 within the study area. Finally, the end of the sequence we have examined is defined by the coeval development for the first time of two different black-on-white types, Sosi Black-on-white and Dogoszhi Black-on-white. Research over the last sixty years (Roberts 1931: 133-34; Colton 1939: 59; Beals, Brainerd and Smith 1945: 99; Danson 1957: 90–92; Wasley 1959: 292) has suggested that the geographical distributions of the design styles that define these ceramic types indicate that very broad spatial distributions of early styles (e.g., the Kana-a style) were replaced by more restricted, regional distributions of decorative characteristics (e.g., the Black Mesa, Sosi and Dogoszhi styles) after about AD 900–1000. Initial interpretations of these changing patterns of stylistic distributions largely followed from an implicit theory of style that Sackett and Wiessner have now formalized as isochrestic theory. Changes in stylistic distributions were therefore regarded as indicative of changes in areas inhabited by different cultures.

More recently, some aspects of decorative variation on ceramics have been regarded as symbolic (e.g., S. Plog 1980; Hantman and Plog 1982; Hantman 1983; Toll 1985) or iconographic (e.g., Hantman 1980: 217; Upham 1982; Neitzel 1985). Neitzel (1985), for example, has argued on the basis of ceramic distributions within Chaco Canyon in northwestern New Mexico that the Dogoszhi design style may be a religious or social icon. Hantman (1980: 217) earlier made a similar proposal for the Black Mesa study area tens of kilometers west of Chaco Canyon and an area where population density and village size were much lower than in Chaco. Some aspects of the changing *spatial* patterns in the distribution of ceramic designs in the northern Southwest also could indicate the increasing symbolic importance of decorative patterns as social networks decreased in area but became more dense and formalized internally (S. Plog 1980; Braun and Plog 1982). This interpretation originally was derived from Wobst's (1977) information exchange theory of stylistic variation, a theory that now appears to be incorrect in some respects, particularly in regard to expectations derived from an emphasis on the efficiency of stylistic messaging and the types of materials therefore likely to communicate social information (Graves 1982; Hodder 1982b; S. Plog 1983; Wiessner 1984, 1985). Nevertheless, there are strong similarities between the stylistic patterns that Wobst argues would occur under conditions where symbolic variation would be unlikely and the expectations that Wiessner (1985) derives from the theory of isochrestic variation. Similarly, Wiessner's (1985) discussion of possible symbolic functions of stylistic variation incorporates some aspects of Wobst's information exchange arguments. Thus, given Wiessner's formulation of the possible symbolic role of decorative variation, spatial patterns in design distributions in the northern Southwest could still be interpreted as changes in decorative variation that evolved as stylistic variation began to serve an increasingly symbolic role after about AD 900–1000.

With the exception of a few recent studies such as Neitzel's (1985) examination of Chacoan pottery and Hantman's (1983) analysis of stylistic distributions in east-central Arizona and west-central New Mexico, these interpretations of stylistic variation have received minimal empirical testing because of a lack of precise data on stylistic distributions and associations. They can now be further scrutinized, however, using data from recent research by Jeff Hantman and myself (Plog and Hantman 1986a, 1986b) on stylistic variation and traditional Southwestern dating methods. That research has been conducted primarily using data from the northern Black Mesa study area where archaeological research over a fifteen year period has allowed the discovery of over two thousand sites within a hundred-square-mile area and the excavation of over one hundred of those sites. Because of the sizable excavation effort, more tree-ring dates are available

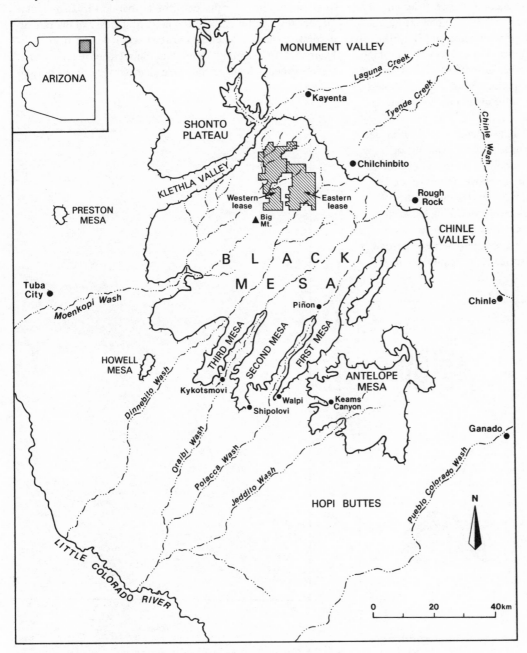

Fig. 7.1 The Black Mesa study area in the Kayenta Anasazi region of north-eastern Arizona (reprinted from *Spatial Organization and Exchange: Archaeological Survey on Northern Black Mesa*, edited by S. Plog [Carbondale: Southern Illinois University Press, 1986], with permission of Southern Illinois University Press).

from that area than from any other small region of the Southwest – and the existence of those dates has allowed us to examine the impact of patterns of stylistic variation and alternative dating methods on our understanding of culture change in the region.

Our research involved the examination of patterns of temporal variation in several individual attributes that were defined using a hierarchical attribute classification system (see Plog and Hantman 1986b). Fifteen of the attributes recorded (e.g., design composition) consisted of nominal categories, while the sixteenth, line width, was measured on an ordinal scale. Because of our focus on temporal change in designs, the particular attributes considered were those emphasized in the ceramic type definitions developed by Colton and Hargrave (1937; Colton 1955) for types made between AD 750 and 1150. While we have questioned whether such ceramic types can be used to date sites to short time periods, we do not question the fact that such types, and most of the attributes that define them, do change through time.

At issue here, however, is the extent to which these data can be used to test proposals concerning the symbolic or iconographic importance of decorative patterns. Given the arguments of Wiessner summarized above, three types of available information are most relevant: (1) the stability of decorative patterns, (2) the degree of association between decorative attributes that characterize individual stylistic traditions, and (3) the degree of association between particular decorative characteristics and structures or features related to

particular social groups or religious activities. Each of these categories will now be considered.

Rates of design change

Given Wiessner's proposals, it would be expected that the rates of change in the frequency of various design attributes would increase after about AD 900–1000 if decorative variation was increasingly symbolic, as opposed to isochrestic, variation. Although temporal change in some attributes of Black Mesa ceramics appears random, variation in others is highly patterned (Plog and Hantman 1986b), as shown in Figure 7.3. More importantly, for those attributes that do vary in a regular manner through time, there is a marked increase in the rate of decorative change sometime between AD 1000 and 1050. Figure 7.3, for example, shows that the relative frequency of lines between 4.2 and 5.0mm wide changed very slowly during

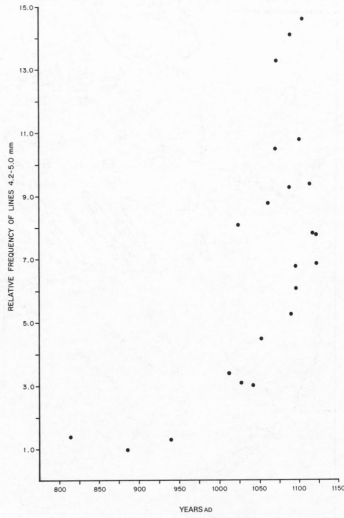

Fig. 7.3 Patterned nature of change in the relative frequency of lines between 4.2 and 5.0 mm in width (reprinted from S. Plog, ed., *Spatial Organization and Exchange*, with permission of Southern Illinois University Press).

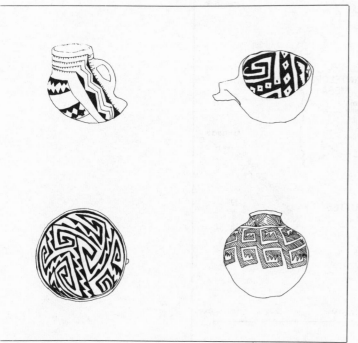

Fig. 7.2 Examples of decorative styles on pottery from the American Southwest: upper left – Kana-a style; upper right – Black Mesa style; lower left – Sosi style; lower right – Dogoszhi style.

the 200-year period from AD 800 to 1000, but increased rapidly during the succeeding 150 years. Overall, attribute frequencies were stable prior to AD 1000 and unstable after that date.

Part of the increased rate of design change likely can be explained by population change within the study area. Graves' (1981) recent analysis of the Kalinga ceramic assemblage collected by Longacre suggested that, of all the factors affecting design variation within one Kalinga settlement, birth cohort was the factor most consistently expressed – and those particular characteristics most likely to change were attributes at lower levels in the design hierarchy. It was primarily the latter type of attributes that Hantman and I have examined on Black Mesa ceramics. Because of the impact of birth cohort, Graves suggested (1981:288) that "rapid population loss or gain within or across a community might result in marked design changes." Given that the period of concern in the Southwest has been characterized as one of population growth, a claim discussed in more detail below, such growth could, through the impact of design transmission between birth cohorts, cause rapid design change.

The increasingly high rate of design change in the study area is much more continuous than rates of population change, however. The latter generally are high during the eleventh century, but also are discontinuous with some periods of little population change, and others of minor or major increases and decreases. Thus, while population change and birth cohort may explain some of the increased rate of design change in the study area, it also is likely that greater rates of change result from the greater instability in designs that would be expected if decorative patterns were increasingly symbolic.

Patterns of attribute association

The degree of attribute association also changed significantly. This can be shown most clearly by examining association patterns among design attributes that characterize the various black-on-white types noted above. Correlation matrices for attributes that are regarded as diagnostic of each type (see Colton and Hargrave 1937; Colton 1955; Beals, Brainerd and Smith 1945; Wasley 1959) and that were measured during the Black Mesa ceramic analysis were calculated using attribute frequencies from twenty-nine Black Mesa sites with tree-ring dates and are presented in Tables 7.1–7.4. In selecting the attributes to be examined for each type, an effort was made to focus primarily on attributes that were only characteristic of a single type, as opposed to some attributes discussed in type definitions that actually are listed for more than one type.

Although the coefficients were calculated using total attribute frequencies for individual sites, rather than by examining the association of attributes on individual sherds, the analysis should still be valid given the nature of most occupations in the study area. On the basis of tree-ring dates, Hantman (1983) has shown that sites had a mean occupation span of between twelve and twenty-two years. Given that these occupation spans are much shorter than the estimated

Table 7.1. Correlation coefficients between attributes diagnostic of Kana-a Black-on-white

	(1)	(2)	(3)	(4)	(5)	(6)	(7)	(8)
(1) Solid composition								
(2) Lines 0–.79 mm	0.57							
(3) Lines .8–1.29 mm	0.66	0.78						
(4) Zigzag lines	0.25	0.24	0.42					
(5) Parallel lines	0.51	0.64	0.84	0.35				
(6) Overlapping lines	0.67	0.63	0.70	0.70	0.64			
(7) Acute triangles	0.11	0.30	0.22	0.46	0.24	0.31		
(8) Ticks	0.62	0.80	0.95	0.25	0.78	0.65	0.15	
(9) Flags	0.42	0.81	0.60	0.09	0.47	0.27	0.45	0.54

Table 7.2. Correlation coefficients between attributes diagnostic of Black Mesa Black-on-white

	(1)	(2)	(3)	(4)	(5)
(1) Lines 3.2–4.19 mm					
(2) Lines 4.2–4.99 mm	0.71				
(3) Curved lines	−0.01	0.48			
(4) Series of triangles	0.25	0.18	0.07		
(5) Appended dots	−0.18	−0.20	0.25	0.42	
(6) Terraces	0.28	0.18	0.14	0.61	0.39

Table 7.3. Correlation coefficients between attributes diagnostic of Sosi Black-on-white

	(1)	(2)	(3)	(4)
(1) Lines 5.0–5.9 mm				
(2) Lines 6.0–8.9 mm	0.45			
(3) Opposed triangles	0.43	0.32		
(4) Internal dots	0.39	0.45	0.32	
(5) Terraces	0.13	0.09	0.09	−0.05

Table 7.4. Correlation coefficients between attributes diagnostic of Dogoszhi Black-on-white

	(1)	(2)	(3)	(4)
(1) Hatched composition				
(2) Straight hatching	0.99			
(3) Diagonal hatching	0.97	0.99		
(4) Curved forms	0.94	0.96	0.97	
(5) Lines wider than 19 mm	0.64	0.61	0.60	0.57

duration of the ceramic types, high coefficients would still be expected if there is strong covariation between the diagnostic characteristics of particular ceramic types.

The observed patterns of covariation between the attributes used to define the various types are, however, very different. Correlations between diagnostic characteristics of Kana-a Black-on-white (Table 7.1) and Dogoszhi Black-on-white (Table 7.4) are much higher than for Black Mesa Black-on-white (Table 7.2) or Sosi Black-on-white (Table 7.3). Coefficients for the former types average 0.50 and 0.82, respectively, while those for the latter types are 0.24 and 0.27, respectively. In addition, many of the attribute correlations for Black Mesa Black-on-white and Sosi Black-on-white are not statistically significant at the 0.10 level and some are negative. Although it might be argued that most of the coefficients for Dogoszhi Black-on-white should be high because most of the diagnostic attributes are characteristics of hatching, this is not the case. Correlations among hatched composition and other possible characteristics of hatched designs that are *not* regarded as diagnostic are low. Correlations between hatched composition and wavy hatching or perpendicular hatching, for example, are −0.01 and 0.34, respectively.

With the exception of the coefficients for Dogoszhi Black-on-white, the patterns of covariation among attributes indicate that not only were decorative traditions less stable after AD 1000 but the degree of association among attributes also declined sharply. This pattern was originally noted by Beals, Brainerd, and Smith in 1945 (p. 99), but then apparently forgotten as types became reified and stylistic variation was treated as a univariate phenomenon: "The design of the Pueblo II black-on-white pottery of this area presents a much more complicated problem than that of any other period. It lacks the close-knit quality of earlier and later times." This reduction in covariation among attributes is again consistent with the proposal that variation in decorative characteristics was increasingly symbolic, rather than isochrestic, variation after AD 1000. Patterns of covariation among attributes of Dogoszhi Black-on-white deviate from this pattern, however. This exception will be discussed in greater detail below when the contexts of various decorative characteristics are examined.

The context of decorative characteristics

Art styles that appear primarily in sacred contexts and are symbolic of religious or ideological concepts, or styles that are associated with higher status individuals have long been recognized in other parts of the world. Only in the last few years has such an iconographic role been discussed in regard to ceramic designs in the American Southwest, as noted above (p. 64). As a result, there have been few attempts to examine the contexts in which various decorative traditions occur either within sites or among sites of different types. One of those attempts, however, has focused on the Dogoszhi Black-on-white pottery. On the basis of the distributions of such pottery within Chaco Canyon, Neitzel (1985) suggested that Dogoszhi style may play an iconographic role, possibly as a marker of higher social status. If this hypothesis is correct, it could explain the higher level of covariation shown above between diagnostic attributes of Dogoszhi Black-on-white. It was noted earlier that stylistic variation that symbolizes social

relationships may exhibit little covariation among attributes because of the dynamic nature of those relationships. As style begins to become iconographic, however, and "stylistic statements conform to certain spoken ones, containing clear, purposeful, conscious messages aimed at a specific target population" (Wiessner 1985: 161), we would expect such styles to be characterized by the redundancy that is a necessary component of languages (e.g., Wollheim 1968: 52). In addition, the level of stylistic stability might correspond better with the more stable nature of larger social systems than with more dynamic patterns of individual or small-group social interaction or production. These proposals may explain the much greater stability of decorative traditions in such areas as Mesoamerica when compared to most design styles of the Southwest (S. Plog 1976: 271–72).

It is thus possible that some decorative styles in the northern Southwest in general may have increasingly symbolized the establishment of relationships or alliances across relatively broad regions of the northern Southwest, possibly as one mechanism of establishing social ties that would allow the pooling of risk as population increased, mobility declined, and local social networks became more compact (Hantman 1983; Toll 1985; S. Plog 1986a). In particular, the Dogoszhi style may be associated with segments of the Chaco regional system (Neitzel 1985), a network that some have argued encompassed a large part of the northern Southwest, including the study area, in the late eleventh and twelfth centuries (LeBlanc 1986). If this proposal is correct, given the association in the study area between exchange and alliance on the one hand and ceremonial structures on the other (S. Plog 1986c), we might expect to find higher frequencies of the Dogoszhi style in ceremonial contexts.

An examination of the context of Dogoszhi-style pottery within individual sites is not possible with available data, but intersite variation can be examined. Table 7.5 presents the proportions of some of the diagnostic design attributes on the black-on-white pottery discussed above that have been found at habitation sites with and without ceremonial structures (kivas). Unfortunately, because of small numbers of sites for other time periods, the comparison must be limited to sites with mean occupation dates between either AD 1051 and 1075 or 1076 and 1100. No statistically significant differences (i.e., $p < .10$) are present between the two categories of sites for any of the attributes characteristic of Sosi Black-on-white. Hatched designs, however, the primary diagnostic attribute of Dogoszhi-style pottery, are almost twice as common on sites with ceremonial structures during the AD 1076–1100 period, a difference that is statistically significant. This difference, along with the decrease in frequency of the style from AD 1051–1075 to AD 1076–1100 on sites lacking kivas, a drop suggesting that the use of such ceramics may have become more restricted, and the high levels of covariation among attributes of Dogoszhi-style pottery, are all consistent with the proposal that variation in the Dogoszhi style may have been iconographic.

Table 7.5. Statistical tests of equivalence between the frequency of decorative characteristics on black-on-white pottery from the study area

Characteristic	Time period	Proportional frequency (%)		*t*
		Site with kivas	Site without kivas	
Hatching	1051–1075	16.45	16.86	−0.09
	1076–1100	14.98	8.66	2.87*
Opposed triangle	1051–1075	2.38	1.44	0.74
	1076–1100	0.85	1.55	−0.61
Internal dots	1051–1075	0.53	1.33	−1.26
	1076–1100	0.40	0.00	1.60
Medium-width lines	1051–1075	25.75	21.12	1.01
	1076–1100	31.41	29.95	−0.27

* $p < 0.1$

Implications of the patterns

Variation in rates of stylistic change, in the degree of covariation between design attributes diagnostic of various ceramic types, and in the contexts of those attributes in the northern Southwest all indicate that stylistic variation is more complex than traditionally has been recognized. Those traditional treatments have assumed largely that variation in stylistic patterns is *isochrestic* variation. Evidence presented above, however, suggests that, particularly after AD 900 to 1000, at least some aspects of design styles are also *symbolic* (in the manner defined above) and some may be *iconographic*. An understanding of decorative variation on ceramics from the region thus requires consideration of the full range of stylistic theories suggested by Sackett (1985a) and Wiessner (1985). Given the fundamental role of stylistic variation and ceramic types in deriving reconstructions of culture history in the region, the implications of this conclusion are broad. I will therefore focus on two primary concerns, chronology and the scale of social systems.

As noted above (p. 62), traditional chronological methods based on type frequencies have allowed sites in the northern Southwest to be dated to phases seventy-five to a hundred years in length. Given the lack of covariation among attributes that have been regarded as diagnostic of these types, however, it is likely that heavy reliance on the type concept, the rapid nature of design change after AD 1000, and the problems that have previously been identified with the traditional methods of characterizing culture change using phases (F. Plog 1975; S. Plog 1986b) have produced enough dating errors to obscure patterns of culture change. In addition, the emphasis on polythetic types does not allow the highly patterned nature of change in specific design attributes to be exploited to achieve greater dating accuracy. That is, it would be expected that there would be a greater possibility of obtaining precise dating of sites if we based our study on the analysis of individual design attributes, rather than the constellations of attributes that define ceramic types.

Recent research by Jeff Hantman and myself (Plog and Hantman 1986a, 1986b) has supported this proposal. Multiple regression analysis was employed to measure the degree to which the tree-ring dates from twenty-two sites could be predicted from the attribute frequencies. We found that (using only three attributes in the regression equation) the dates could be predicted with considerable accuracy. The equation generated was statistically significant at the 0.01 level, with an R^2 value of 0.94, and a standard error of the estimate of ±19.1 years, a value that reduces the amount of error with type frequencies by 57 per cent. One of the advantages of this approach is that the regression equation can be used not only to place sites without independent dates in chronological order but also to calculate estimates of the actual occupation date of each site. That is, it is a type of *absolute seriation* as recently discussed by Braun (1985). Traditional relative seriation techniques provide an ordering of sites but do not provide estimates of occupation dates. In combination with phase-based population estimations, relative seriation techniques also can smooth curves, obscure short-term population fluctuations and lead to inaccurate estimates of demographic parameters.

The increased dating precision obtained from the regression method described above has led to several revisions in reconstructions of change trajectories in the region. Previous descriptions of population growth and decline in the northern Southwest usually suggest smooth and continuous rates of change as would be expected from the above arguments. In addition, these reconstructions are characterized by long periods of population expansion, usually explained as the results of stable, successful adaptations and favorable climatic conditions that led to indigenous growth; and by infrequent but significant population losses that are argued to have coincided with environmental change (e.g., Dean *et al.* 1985). Reconstructions of demographic parameters using the regression method described above, however, results in a substantially different perspective on population fluctuations in the area (S. Plog 1986b). Change was abrupt with few periods of stability, the abandonment or near abandonment of areas was common (see Figure 7.4), rates of increase were not constant and suggest significant population movements within regions, and periods of growth and decline correlate poorly with environmental fluctuations. These revised descriptions of change in population levels, as well as change in other variables (S. Plog 1986a), provide little support for the simplistic studies that explain culture change in the northern Southwest largely as a response to environmental fluctuations.

Such evidence is one reason why I have argued that we must pay more attention to social, economic, and political relationships, and the above results suggest that studies of stylistic variation will be critical in such research. My previous discussions of aspects of those relationships focused on changes in social networks as inferred from exchange patterns and

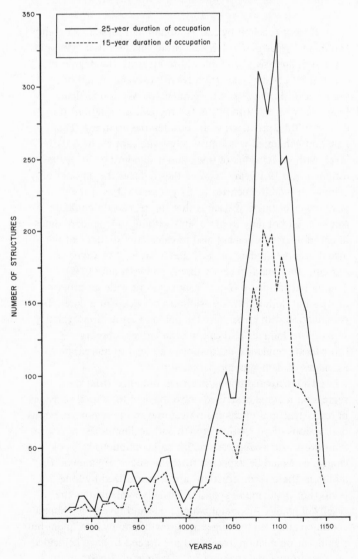

Fig. 7.4 Estimates of relative change in population levels in the study area (reprinted from S. Plog, ed., *Spatial Organization and Exchange*, with permission of Southern Illinois University Press).

stylistic distributions (S. Plog 1980; Braun and Plog 1982). Information on the exchange of both lithic raw materials and of some ceramic types suggested that exchange networks contracted between AD 1000 and 1125; the relative frequency of distant materials decreased while the relative frequency of materials from nearby areas increased. Similarly, as noted above (p. 64), the distribution of many stylistic characteristics also became more restricted as regional stylistic traditions evolved.

Braun and I (Braun and Plog 1982) have argued that those changes indicate the evolution of more tightly integrated local networks to minimize productive risk and pool resources (Wiessner 1982b; Cashdan 1985) as overall population levels tended to rise, mobility declined, and agricultural intensification increased. Hantman (1983) has offered a similar interpretation, proposing that when resource distributions and population densities allow, there are advantages for groups to maintain boundaries as a means of increasing the effectiveness of information processing and sharing, as well as a means to coordinate a group's efforts.

More recent analyses are largely consistent with these conclusions, although, as with the demographic data, more variation in some aspects of social relationships is apparent with the more precise dating achieved using the regression analysis of design attributes. At least until AD 1100, the spatial extent of exchange spheres for chipped stone raw materials contracted through time; long distance trade became less common and proportionally more material was imported from nearby areas. Similar changes also appear to have characterized networks through which ceramic vessels were exchanged. In addition, there was a gradual drop through time in the diversity of raw materials brought to Black Mesa from outside the study area (S. Plog 1986c). Finally, when the magnitude of exchange is corrected for population levels to derive an index of exchange intensity, more variation in this exchange parameter is evident. There appears to have been two primary peaks in the exchange of both certain ceramic wares (Figure 7.5) and of lithic raw materials (Figure 7.6) from about AD 950 to 1000 and 1075 to 1125, separated by a period of significantly lower exchange activity from AD 1000 to 1050. During the second period of high exchange intensity, there also is some evidence suggesting that exchange was centralized at some settlements. Sites with more than ten structures along with kivas and masonry storage rooms have twice as many nonlocally manufactured red or orange wares per structure as smaller sites with kivas and masonry rooms. They also have four times as many of the same wares as sites that lack kivas (S. Plog 1986c). Periods of high exchange intensity correspond closely with eras of population increase, settlement change, and reduced mobility, factors that initially increased productive risks and selected for social mechanisms for adjusting to those risks.

Changing patterns of social relationships also are suggested by other aspects of decorative patterns of black-on-white pottery. Stylistic change during the AD 850 to 1150 period is characterized by some trends that match the exchange data and others that are different. According to

Hegmon's (1986) analysis of white ware ceramics from Black Mesa, the degree of variation in stylistic attributes tends to increase during the period and she has proposed that the increasing levels of stylistic diversity within such regions as Black Mesa are a result of an increase in stylistic symboling associated with the alteration of social networks. That proposal is consistent with the evidence for much higher population densities through most of the period, significant immigration into the region, and evidence for some centralized control of trade in red and orange ware ceramics, as well as the evidence presented above that suggests that design variation after about AD 1000 was more symbolic than isochrestic.

The lack of a one-to-one correspondence between fluctuations in levels of stylistic diversity and fluctuations in population density, settlement locations, or levels of exchange intensity, however, suggests that stylistic diversity also is affected by and is affecting social networks which encompass areas larger than the Black Mesa study area. That lack of correspondence occurs despite evidence that the production of ceramics was becoming more localized and the number of villages producing ceramics was increasing. The increasing level of stylistic diversity in the study area thus may be the result of the establishment of different types of social ties across relatively broad regions as the amount of social interaction through long-distance trade decreased (Hantman 1983), as noted above (p. 70). Consistent with this argument is the strongly inverse relationship between stylistic diversity and the diversity of

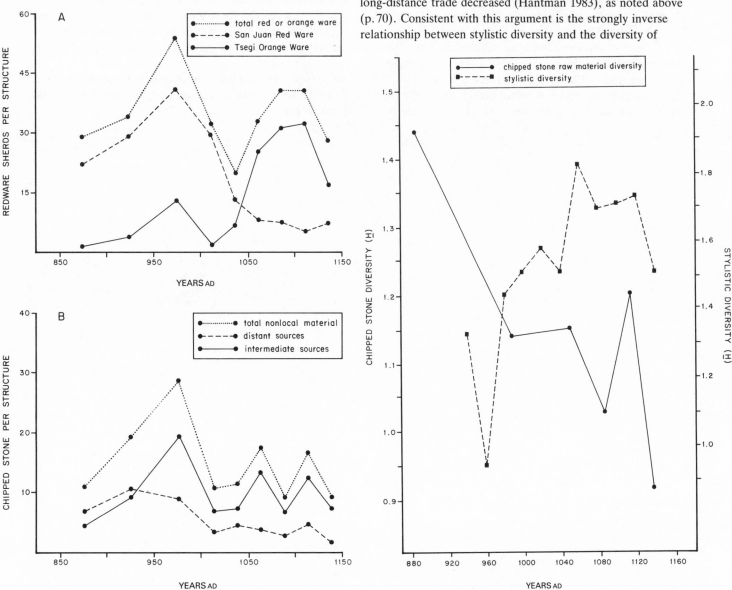

Fig. 7.5 Estimates of the intensity of (a) the exchange of red- or orange-ware ceramics and (b) the exchange of non-local raw materials for chipped stone in the study area (reprinted from S. Plog, ed., *Spatial Organization and Exchange*, with permission of Southern Illinois University Press).

Fig. 7.6 The relationship between stylistic diversity in decorative characteristics and the diversity in chipped-stone raw materials in the Black Mesa study area (reprinted from S. Plog, ed., *Spatial Organization and Exchange*, with permission of Southern Illinois University Press).

nonlocal raw materials on Black Mesa sites (Figure 7.6). Thus while some mechanisms were operating to increase integration *within* regions, thus increasing the use of nearby raw materials and decreasing the total diversity of materials used, some social ties or alliances also were established across broad geographic areas through other mechanisms, and those increasingly diverse ties were symbolized by various decorative characteristics.

The stylistic evidence of broad regional ties and the significant population immigration into the study area raise questions about correlations between culture change on Black Mesa and other regions of the northern Southwest, and the possible relationship between northern Black Mesa and the Chacoan network suggested by the distributions of Dogoszhi Black-on-white. The period of major population increase, as well as sharp changes in ceramic assemblages (S. Plog 1986a), coincides with the growth and expansion of the large regional system centered on Chaco Canyon. There is certainly no evidence that population movements occurred from the Chaco area to Black Mesa or even evidence of direct exchange ties between the two areas, but it is also likely that developments in the two areas have some common social and environmental causes, as LeBlanc (1986) has argued. Such direct contacts are not necessary, however, to propose some type of relationship between the growth of the Chaco network and change on Black Mesa (as well as other parts of the northern Southwest). As a result of the standard interpretive framework within which Southwestern archaeologists have operated, there unfortunately has been little consideration of the types of evidence which would support such a relationship or of the mechanisms which would lead to the creation and development of ties between the Black Mesa region and surrounding areas. There is now a need to place more emphasis on studies of regional social organization. As the above analysis suggests, such studies may require a broader perspective on possible causes of stylistic variation, including a willingness to consider the possibility that decorative variation may be iconographic, and new types of analyses that focus on patterns of attribute association as well as the contexts within which various decorative characteristics occur on sites.

Chapter 8

Style and iconography as legitimation in complex chiefdoms

Timothy Earle

Using two case studies, the Hawaiian and the Olmec chiefdoms, the author attempts to build a materialist understanding of iconographic construction and its use in the politics of chiefly societies. Earle shows how archaeologists can use stylistic analysis of certain classes of items to understand the way leaders legitimized systems of inequality and control, and how these styles were woven into the political structure of complex chiefdoms. He provides specific archaeological examples to substantiate the general observation that "early great art styles" must have had an organizing role in society and were actively part of the political realms during the rise of early civilizations.

Complex chiefdoms are associated with the emergence of "great styles." Gordon Willey, in his influential article "The early great styles and the rise of pre-Columbian civilizations" (1962), recognized the organizing role of iconography in both the Olmec and Chavin cultures. Both of these cases, and similar societies such as the Mississippian of the American Southeast (Muller 1984), late Neolithic of Britain (Bradley 1984), and the northern European Bronze Age (Kristiansen 1987), are characterized by broadly related styles that unite isolated and politically separate regions. Why these great styles developed and how they functioned in emergent civilizations are intriguing questions in the study of social complexity. This chapter examines the way iconography, and its stylized representation, serves to legitimize systems of inequality and control built into complex chiefdoms.

Before jumping into the analysis of style in complex chiefdoms, I will set up a materialist framework within which we may consider the changing nature of style and iconography in the evolution of human society. Style is quite simply patterned variation in appearance. To archaeologists, style has two conceptually different meanings (see Sackett 1977, 1982, and chapter 4, this volume; S. Plog 1980), a passive meaning and an active meaning. First, and most commonly, it is viewed as passive tradition. As people become socialized, they learn how properly to make and decorate objects. In Deetz's terms, each craftsman holds a mental template, "idea of the proper form of an object [that] exists in the mind of the maker" (1967: 45). Style is largely implicit, because the choice between alternative forms is determined by custom. For the archaeologists, stylistic differences such as these are useful to define "archaeological cultures" that retain unconsciously different behaviors.

Second, style is viewed as an active medium of communication by which individuals and social groups define relationships and associations (Wobst 1977; Conkey 1978a). Elements of style, as in objects used in ceremonial display, are chosen purposefully to signal social relationships and group membership. Thus style acts as a critical prop in social drama as it functions to form, maintain, and transfigure social relations.

The active meaning of style is deeply rooted in anthropological and archaeological inquiry. Going back to Boas, Benedict, and Kroeber, cultures have been viewed as patterned, imbued with meaning represented objectively in their arts and crafts. Iconography has continued to hold a central place in archaeological research both in North America and Europe. Recently studies of style have become popular in European archaeology. Hodder (1982a, chapter 5, this volume) insists that style is not arbitrary but results from the active selection of meaningful objects that can be understood only in their broader social context. Throughout these works is the assumption that arts and crafts make concrete the ways individuals in their social contexts perceive and order reality.

Simply recognizing the importance of ideology and active style in cultural systems should not obscure the inherent difficulties with such studies. Attempts to attach specific meaning to iconography are usually unconvincing, except in the exceptional cases where strong cultural continuity exists with the ethnographic present. Iconographies unique to individual cultures serve to identify cultural traditions, but they do little to explain cultural processes and the evolutionary significance of ideology.

In this chapter I will analyze the function of style as a critical aspect in cultural evolution. For this purpose, an active view of style is appropriate. While it may be impossible to recognize the specific meaning of prehistoric iconographies, it should be possible to recognize the formal and functional properties of ideological systems from the nature of their presentation, the context of their use, and the pattern of their distribution. We need not project ourselves back into past cultures except in explicit behavioral ways. Such work should also permit true cross-time and cross-cultural research. As it has been forcefully articulated by Abner Cohen,

> The analysis of symbolic forms in relation to symbolic functions which is the central problem of social anthropology can be greatly enhanced through comparing different cultural forms that are carried by different groups. Thus one aspect of our work is to reduce cultural heterogeneity to functional uniformities.
>
> (1974: 86)

Although the meaning of symbols may be culturally specific and unknowable archaeologically, the contexts of their use on specific material forms in specific social and political situations should show regular cross-cultural patterning. The rudimentary outlines for a general theory of ideology and style should place them within the broader context of cultural evolution.

I am not claiming this as a new approach to ideology and style as it goes back in archaeology to the seminal work of Flannery (1968), Drennan (1976), Wobst (1977), Conkey (1978a), and Stephen Plog (1980), among others. What I would like to do is to summarize briefly the potential contribution of this approach to style within an evolutionary framework worked out by Allen Johnson and myself (Johnson and Earle 1987). This evolutionary framework presents a developmental continuum condensing several evolutionary lines with distinct characteristics. Although any brief overview may appear unilinear, we have explicitly emphasized the environmental, technological, and historical factors which give rise to

alternative pathways to complexity. However, the driving force to evolution is evidently material in the cases that we examined – a cycle of population growth, technological development and intensification, warfare and exchange. These are conditions which require group action and leadership, and create opportunities for control and stratification. In our argument, we have tried to address the critical role played by ceremonialism and ideology at four levels of development – the family, the local group, the chiefdom, and the state.

Family-level societies are low density and informally organized. The subsistence economies typically combine hunting and gathering, with perhaps some horticulture. Most importantly, the family is the basic social and economic unit. Families associate opportunistically to form camps or hamlets with fewer than ten members which continually fragment and conjoin. Beyond the camps or hamlets, individuals establish broad interpersonal networks which provide reciprocal visiting rights important for trading, mate selection, and especially security from temporary local food shortage (see Wiessner 1982a). For the camp, relationships are close and familistic but especially beyond the camp reciprocal bonds are essential. In the absence of a formalized local group and with the need for personal external ties, it is reasonable to expect that stylized display would be fairly limited. The active projection of group identity is inappropriate where groups are informal and noncorporate. For example, Conkey (1978a) discounts stylistic types for most of the Lower Paleolithic when social groupings were probably small and biologically based. In family-level societies, active use of style may be appropriate for special objects used to establish and maintain the regional exchange web. The ground stone axes of Australia used in numerous social exchanges are a good ethnographic example (Sharp 1952); the Acheulian hand ax of the Lower Paleolithic may be another (Wobst 1976).

Local groups ("village"-level society) of several hundred form under conditions of higher population density and subsistence intensification that often result in warfare. The major changes appear as a response to competition. Especially important is the elaboration of corporate groups (clans and lineages) which act to restrict access to productive resources, and the elaboration of local territorial groups (villages or hamlet clusters) which defend resources. Beyond the local group, extensive regional ties are established for marriage, exchange, and security but especially for alliance in warfare. The network of interaction, although not politically centralized, can be organized by intense ceremonial interaction into what Newman (1957) calls a "regional collectivity."

Ceremonies and associated display objects function at two levels (see Rappaport 1967). First, at the level of the local group, participation in ceremonies defines membership in corporate groups and establishes personal rights of resource access. Local groups are closely identified with a tract of land; often an origin myth specifies a location from which the group's ancestors sprang, and the territory is the home of the ancestral spirits. The local group is identified ceremonially by special regalia that emphasize the group's separation, as signalled by distinctive cultural patterns. Archaeologically, the development of local groups can be seen in the regionalization of styles in domestic artifacts such as service vessels and projectile points. Conkey (1978a) identifies the Upper Paleolithic with an "explosion" in symbolic behavior as local styles in art and technology proliferate. Gilman (1984) explains this stylistic elaboration as a result of increased competition and the need to exclude populations from access to resources. The formulation of the local group creates a corporate structure, and symbolic systems help specify rights within the structure.

Second, at the level of the region, ceremonies define relationships among local groups. As Rappaport (1967) and Meggitt (1972) have argued, these highly visible ceremonies are used to advertise the power of the local group and its desirability as an ally and its peril as an enemy. At ceremonial occasions when neighboring local groups are invited to participate, people adorn themselves elaborately as with the feather headdresses and body paints of New Guinea. Elaborate gifts of valuables are also formally presented. These ceremonies are essential to the local group and its members to obtain allies for defense, mates, and exchange partners. To some degree, uniformity in items of display and exchange can be expected both because of trade in valuables, such as in the New Guinea exchange of shell, and because of the necessity for comparable measures of prestige (see Strathern 1971). Braun and Plog (1982) have described the regional integration of ceramic styles in the American Southwest and Midwest as representing such broad patterns of ceremonial integration. Although the use of ceramics as part of this display function seems somewhat inappropriate, the increasing development of "regional collectivities" with agricultural intensification is plausible.

With the initial evolution of social stratification and chiefdoms, new uses of symbolism and style categories develop. Chiefdoms are regionally organized societies in which comparatively large populations in the thousands or tens of thousands are organized within a single political unit. Typically the population consists of several communities integrated around a political center, where major rituals integrate the larger political unit and define rights within the polity. The regional organization of chiefdoms has led some researchers to suggest that style will become more uniform to the limits of the polity (Redman 1978: 205–06; Watson and LeBlanc 1973). As I will be arguing, this extension in the uniformity of regional style, while undoubtedly real, has been misunderstood and requires a rethinking of the function of style in chiefdoms.

At the local level, considerable stylistic variability may continue between communities in clothing and display items. At the regional level, however, iconography and elite styles become important to legitimize or "naturalize" the inherent inequality in these systems. Specific materials, objects, and symbols serve to identify the ruling elites with the supernatural. In her innovative analysis of Panamanian chiefdoms, Helms (1976) describes how the local chiefs established long-distance trade and visiting relationships with the chiefdoms of Colombia.

She argues that control of esoteric knowledge plays a critical role in establishing sanctified models for the stratified society. The extensive interchiefdom trade and shared political ideology thus serve to deliver rare and foreign objects linked symbolically to universal forces. Prestige goods obtained by chiefs through exchange then provide a new opportunity for control (Friedman and Rowlands 1978: 224). Exciting work on the function of style in stratified societies includes the recent analyses of Randsborg (1982), Kristiansen (1984, 1987), and Bradley (1984) for European chiefdoms; Upham, Lightfoot and Feinman (1981) and Hantman and Plog (1982) for the American Southwest; and Pollock (1983) and Wright (1984) for the complex chiefdoms of Mesopotamia.

In chiefdoms, and increasingly in states, it is possible to speak of ideology. Using Yengoyan's (1985: 332) definition, the basis of ideology is "the ability of a group of individuals to utilize cultural symbols for *certain willfully designed ends . . .*" In other words, material goods and their associated symbols are being used not to represent relationships but to mask relationships of inequality and domination as part of a religiously sanctioned world-view.

True states extend and solidify the organization of regional populations numbering into the hundreds of thousands and more. Especially important is the development of administrative bureaucracies and other special religious and military institutions. Local styles continue to be important to define community membership with implied rights to land; for example, distinctive community and ethnic dress is characteristic of closed corporate peasant communities. In fact the state may become covertly involved in emphasizing ethnic distinctions among commoners as a way to define a peasantry divided by tradition and in competition for stately favor. States also become involved in the semi-industrial manufacture of special goods with uniform styles that function both as status markers and as means of payment.

As I have argued elsewhere (D'Altroy and Earle 1985; Earle 1987), the controlled manufacture and distribution of a political currency is integral to state finance. This transformation is clearly visible in our recent research in the Mantaro valley of Peru (Earle and Costin 1986). From the pre-Inka to the Inka period, objects used to differentiate elite status among the local Wanka ethnic group changed dramatically. In the pre-Inka period, characterized by competing chiefdoms, elite status was marked by special ceramics and metals produced and distributed within the valley and by long-distance wealth objects including ocean shells and pottery. In the Inka period, the exclusive items marking elite status were ceramics, cloth, and metals in established state styles that were most probably produced and distributed by the state. A person's position locally, therefore, became dependent on a foreign symbolic system provided by the state. In addition, Inka ceramics were involved in special state ceremonies of generosity to local populations, and these styles are heavily concentrated at state facilities (Morris 1982).

After this cursory overview of ideology and style in

cultural evolution, I want to turn my attention to a consideration of the active use of style in complex chiefdoms. Complex chiefdoms (Earle 1978; Steponaitis 1978; Wright 1984; Johnson and Earle 1987) are regionally organized, stratified societies, retaining many of the characteristics of chiefdoms but anticipating the features of state societies. The sizes of the independent polities probably range into the tens of thousands organizing many separate local communities. A distinctive three-tiered hierarchy typically exists in the settlement system and its political organization. Strikingly new is an elite social class, carefully distinguished from commoners in rules of dress, marriage, and the like. Typically this aristocratic group is the owner of all productive resources which are allocated to commoners in return for labor and specific goods. Complex chiefdoms are organized by a special institution of leadership which is highly elaborated but remarkably undifferentiated internally (see Wright 1977). In other words, positions of leadership within the regional chiefdoms are carefully organized as a special hierarchical system (often with strong kin-based relationships). These positions, unlike state institutions, are however highly generalized, combining all aspects of leadership (religious, military, administrative, social, and economic). It is for this reason that complex chiefdoms are often called "theocracies," although this label overemphasizes the religious (rather than generalized) nature of their organization (Webster 1976).

Archaeological evidence of complex chiefdoms can be broken down into three main classes:

(1) a two-tiered settlement hierarchy, above the level of the local communities, with centers containing public space and often monumental architecture (Wright 1984);

(2) evidence for an elite social class, often distinguished by the concentration of special "wealth" objects in burials (see Peebles and Kus 1977) and by high labor investment in architecture (Arnold and Ford 1980; McGuire 1983); and

(3) as I discuss here, an interpolity symbolic system that delineates the ruling elites as divine, thus combining both religious and secular leadership.

In complex chiefdoms, iconography and associated style act to discriminate the ruling elite and to mark them as a people apart. Most important is their direct tie to divine forces of the universe characteristically manifest as high gods, not tied to a particular geographical location. As Helms (1976) has shown, competition for control of esoteric knowledge that identifies elites with universal forces is a central part of the political process. Trade in special objects and associated esoteric knowledge creates a broad commonality in elite iconography that cross-cuts chiefdoms across a broad area. Brown (J. Brown 1976), for example, has argued that the Southern Cult of Mississippian chiefdoms was a widespread symbolic representation of social eliteness, military power, and religious sanctity.

One purpose of this paper is to investigate the use of iconography in the complex chiefdoms of Hawai'i and the

Mesoamerican Olmec. On the basis of earlier discussions, I will move on to address the question of why broadly similar styles, frequently referred to as "cults" because of their religious iconography, can be so widespread? To preview the answer to this question, I will argue that the use of religious iconography to empower and sanctify political domination is a general characteristic of complex chiefdoms.

As I will now describe, elite style functioned in the complex chiefdoms of Hawai'i to identify a ruling aristocracy and to link it to the gods. The lesson was unmistakable – chiefs are divine and their rule is part of a natural order in the universe.

The Hawaiian chiefdoms were certainly among the most complex nonstate societies that existed in isolation from states down to the historic period (see Malo 1951 [1898]; Sahlins 1958; Goldman 1970; Hommon 1976; Earle 1978; Kirch 1984). The Hawaiian islands were colonized perhaps about AD 600 by a small Polynesian population which grew over the next thousand years. At first contact with the west (1778), each major island (Kaua'i, Oah'u, Mau'i, and Hawai'i) with 30,000 or more people was controlled by a separate chiefly line. The different chiefly lines were locked in intense rivalry with each other for control over the islands, but they were also intertwined by marriage and alliance and used a single ideology of legitimization.

Each chiefdom was organized hierarchically. At the top was the ruling paramount chief, supposedly the highest-ranked individual in the chiefdom and a living god. The paramount was the owner of all lands which he gave out as community estates to high-ranking chiefs who were closely aligned to him genealogically and politically. Because of the large size of the chiefdoms, two additional levels existed in the administrative hierarchy. Between the paramount and the community chiefs were district chiefs, close personal advisors to the paramount, who coordinated the delegation of quotas and collection of labor and goods. Below the community chiefs were land managers, typically lower-ranked chiefs, responsible for the daily administration of the chiefly estate.

In some ways, the Hawaiian chiefdoms seem almost to have been small states (see Hommon 1976). Especially important in this regard were marked social stratification (chiefs vs. commoners), elite ownership of all means of production, a military elite attached to the paramount, and an incipient bureaucracy with district advisors and community land managers. Conversely, I (Earle 1978) have argued that Hawaiian society was still fundamentally a chiefdom because positions of leadership were highly generalized. At all levels in the hierarchy, social, political, economic, and religious, authority was vested in the single body of a chiefly person (compare Wright 1984). This person could delegate certain duties to others, such as the paramount's advisors or the community chief's land manager, but these individuals were directly attached to the main elite person from whom they drew authority and power, and they did not constitute a separate administrative institution. In the complex chiefdoms, such as in

Hawai'i, no separate institutions of government or religion existed but a largely undifferentiated social elite organized by principles of ranking and kinship provided the same functions.

Perhaps the most important thing to remember about chiefs in Hawai'i is their divinity. Kamakau (1961) listed three kinds of gods: the local (or low) gods, the high gods, and the chiefs. The chief, according to his/her genealogical rank, was thought to hold or be characterized by considerable religious power (*mana*) and sanctity (*kapu*). The highest ranked chiefs held a level of sanctity called *kapu moe* that "demanded full prostration from subordinates below a prescribed rank in the presence of the Source or any intimate object belonging to him" (Goldman 1970: 217). The power associated with the chiefs (*kapu*) was greatly feared by those without sanctity (the commoners) and violation of the (*moe*) prescription was supposedly sanctioned by death.

The world of the Hawaiian chiefdoms was thus divided into an essential dichotomy: elite–commoner, sacred–profane, leader–led, owner–tiller. This basic material, structural, and ideological division was clearly visible in stylistic elements that proclaim participation in this social system. To consider style in the Hawaiian chiefdoms, I will briefly sketch the pattern among two classes of goods – the household goods used by most households and special elite goods used to demarcate status among chiefs.

The household inventory of commoners contained a wide range of implements and dress as described fully by Buck (1957). Items include bark cloth (*tapa*) used for clothing, beaters for preparing the *tapa*, boards and pounders for the plant taro, and an assortment of storage and serving vessels of gourd and wood. In comparison to simpler chiefdoms such as the Maori and Marquesas, these household objects are comparatively simple and unelaborated stylistically. Form appears to follow function, with some local variation in *tapa* decoration, *poi* pounders, and adze form. Although a systematic study of these collections is needed, an active use of style among Hawaiian commoners was apparently unelaborated.

This contrasts to a fairly elaborated use of special objects to denote status among the elites. Chiefs' distinctive clothing and adornment corresponded to rank. Most important were the articles of dress that included feathered cloak and helmet, neck pendants of carved whale teeth, and other ornamentation.

Most work has been done on the feathered helmets (*mahiole*) and cloaks (*'ahu'ula*) (Malo 1951 [1898]: 76–77; Brigham 1899, 1903, 1918; Buck 1944, 1957: 215–50; Kaeppler 1970, 1978, 1982; Cummins 1984; Earle 1987). The helmets, unique in style to the Hawaiian islands, consisted of a rigid woven frame onto which was attached a fine netting covered with brilliant yellow, red, black and green feathers. The style, associated with the high chiefs, comprised a full skull-covering from forehead to neck and around the ears. Starting perhaps 2 centimeters in at the forehead a medial crest arched over the helmet; this crest, often projecting forward, is highest in the front and lowers towards the neck (see Fig. 8.1). The feathers were applied in broad bands that emphasized the crest.

Virtually all cloaks are crescent-shaped, although they vary in length (shoulder-length to full-length) and in the feather type. Feathers are yellow, red, and black, and the designs are most commonly contrasting crescent-shaped figures (red on yellow background or yellow on red background). Often one large crescent is centered on the wearer's back and two others cross the wearer's front when the cloak is drawn together. The finest cloaks were full-length and brilliant yellow with contrasting red designs. The cloaks were made with a fine net base onto which were attached perhaps half a million bird feathers carefully collected for the chiefs and given to them in regular ceremonies (Kaeppler 1970).

The basic style of these objects was remarkably invariable across the Hawaiian chiefdoms. Thus the basic uniform, including helmet and cloak covered with the brilliant feathers, was found from Kaua'i to Hawai'i. The symbolism of dress, as I shall discuss in a moment, was essentially the same, although variation from island to island clearly indicated local manufacture. For example, the helmets of Kaua'i had broader and lower crests than those from Hawai'i (Kaeppler 1978: 67).

Cloaks, along with the matching helmets, could only be worn by high-ranked chiefs (community chiefs and higher) in

Fig. 8.1 Hawaiian chief with feather helmet and cloak symbolic of social position. Drawing by Webber, who accompanied Captain Cook on his third voyage, BL Add. Ms 15, 514.27; reproduced with permission of the British Library.

battle and at important display ceremonies (Earle 1987: Fig. 1). Variation among the helmets and cloaks was less related to individual polities than it was to chiefly status that cross-cut the chiefdoms. Therefore the largest cloaks of the very rare yellow *mamo* were said to be worn only by the paramount chiefs (Malo 1951 [1898]: 77). Smaller cloaks made of more common feathers were worn by lesser chiefs (King 1784: 136–37).

The symbolic tie between the dress of the high chiefs and the gods seems to be quite explicit and easily documented. Elsewhere in Polynesia, as in Hawai'i, feathers form the clothes of the gods. For example, in the chiefdoms of Tahiti, Henry describes how the highest-ranked chiefs "as descendants of the highest class of gods were alone entitled to wear the *'ura* feather girdle, which was supposed to be the costume of the gods" (1928: 229). Among the Hawaiian islands, gods were frequently represented as wicker bodies overlain with brilliant feathers. At least eight examples of these feathered images were collected during Cook's discovery voyage (Kaeppler 1978: Figs. 55–58). When Cook first arrived at Hawai'i, the paramount chief, Kalaniopu'u and his high chiefs in full feathered dress came out in a dramatic ceremonial greeting. On a double canoe accompanying this regal party were three large feathered images (see Kaeppler 1978: Fig. 64):

> In the first canoe was Terreeoboo [Kalaniopu'u] and his chiefs, dressed in feathered cloaks and helmets, and armed with spears and daggers; in the second, came the venerable Kaoo, the chief of the priests, and his brethren, with their idols displayed on red cloth. These idols were busts of a gigantic size, made of wicker work, and curiously covered with small feathers of various colors, wrought in the same manner with their cloaks.
>
> (King 1784: 16–17)

The feathered helmets of the high chiefs are also seen characteristically represented on god images of both wood and feathers. Figure 8.2 shows a feathered image with a projecting crest identical to the helmets. Kaeppler (1982: Figs 8, 9, 11–16, 19) illustrates ten wooden images with this same overarching crest, which she argues is an extension of the vertebral column symbolizing the genealogical linkage binding living chiefs to their godly ancestors.

The symbolism of the cloaks identifies the chiefs who wear them with the gods. The cloak's name *'ahu 'ula* means literally "red garment," red being the chiefly color of Polynesia and frequently linked symbolically with the gods (Buck 1944: 9). Red feathers were used in the cloaks, sometimes as background but more commonly as the design motif on the rarer yellow feathers. The cloak was worn to encircle the sacred (tabu) back of a chief. The primary motif on the cloaks was the crescent which arches over the chief's back as a rainbow. In mythic histories, a god's presence is shown by the overarching rainbow (Cummins 1984). Cummins explicitly ties the rainbow symbolism to *pio*, the marriage between brother and sister of the ruling line which is the ultimate source of all *mana* (sacred power) of the ruling chiefs. The use of the rainbow symbol on the cloaks was thus a clear association of the wearer with the

ruling senior lines and their direct claim to sacredness and godhood. The wearer as a god figure held obvious rights of control, natural to the social and religious order. His position was inviolate except in competition with other chiefs, themselves living gods.

What we see in the Hawaiian chiefdoms is a remarkably uniform style in a very special set of adornments. These objects of adornment shared a uniform ideology across a number of competing chiefdoms that were linked by alliance and marriage across the top and mutually reinforced by the symbolisms and associated ritual.

Elsewhere (Earle 1987) I have argued that the ruling lines controlled the manufacture and distribution of the cloaks. By delivering a cloak unto a chief, the paramount recognized the chief's sanctity and affirmed his economic rights. Distribution of rights in income estates and distribution of the cloaks were identical. In an illiterate, stateless society, the giving, receiving,

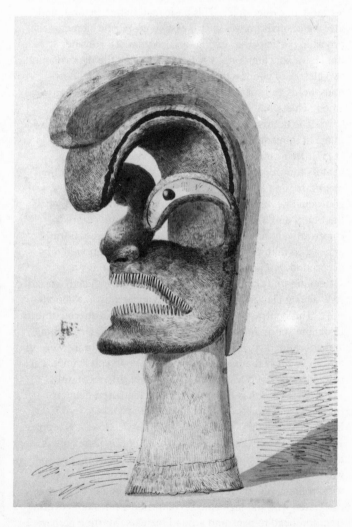

Fig. 8.2 Feather-covered wicker god from Hawai'i, after a drawing by Webber (James Cook, *Voyage to the Pacific Ocean . . . for making Discoveries in the Northern Hemisphere . . . 1776–1780, Atlas* [London: Strahan, 1784], Plate 67). Note the overarching crest similar to the helmet worn by a Hawaiian chief.

and wearing of the cloaks demonstrated the social and religious linkages among the chiefly elites and demonstrated what amounted to the contractual rights within the political and economic system.

What I will try now to demonstrate is that the use of critical symbolism in the prehistoric complex chiefdoms of the Olmec culture illustrates a similar use of an elite style. I argue that the use of this elite style across a broad geographical area and in a number of different contexts represents a system of legitimation.

The Olmec culture was a small group of complex chiefdoms located along the tropical Gulf coast of modern Mexico. The subsistence economy apparently combined shifting and permanent cultivation; Coe (1974) has argued ingeniously that control of limited natural levee soils, suitable for permanent cultivation, underlay Olmec political development.

The Olmec culture is seen by many as Mesoamerica's first civilization and the foundation for later developments (see especially Willey 1962). There is no question that the Olmec was a complex, regionally organized society (Heizer 1960; Drucker 1981). The largest centers such as La Venta contain both massive stone sculptures and mound constructions that represent large labor investments. Built on an island surrounded by marsh, La Venta consists of a carefully planned complex with a large central mound (100 feet tall), flanking mounds, plazas, ceremonial courts fenced with basaltic columns, and the large Olmec heads. The planned layout of La Venta along a clear central axis (8° west of north) suggests a symbolic ordering of spatial relationships in the ceremonies that must have taken place on this monumental stage.

As Heizer has estimated (1960), La Venta contained over a million man days of labor in construction which would have required mobilizing labor from a support area surrounding the center. Drucker (1981) summarizes the ample evidence for non-food-producing specialists involved in planning the centers, in organizing large labor crews, and in manufacturing large sculp-tures and wealth objects. Evidence for social stratification with a ruling elite is evident in the burial ritual and the iconography.

How can we characterize the Olmec culture? Sanders and Price (1968: 127–28) and I (Earle 1976) argue that the Olmec were organized as chiefdoms. Conversely, Heizer (1960) and Drucker (1981) argue for a simple state, with strong "theocratic" overtones. Although it is evident that the Olmec culture represents a form significantly more complex than simple, village-level chiefdoms (such as Drucker and Heizer were familiar with in North America), it is also evident that Olmec culture lacked the characteristic institutional elaboration (such as with true bureaucracies) that characterizes states. Social stratification and the highly generalized nature of the elites as both sacred and secular leaders make Olmec a particularly good example of complex chiefdoms. As already discussed complex chiefdoms are what used to be called "theocratic states"; how this looks iconographically should be clear in a moment.

As impressive as the spectacular Gulf coast development is the broad spread of Olmec "influence" throughout much of Mesoamerica. Sites located in Morelos (Chalcatzingo, Gualupita, Atlihuagan), Puebla (Las Bocas), the Basin of Mexico (Tlatilco, Tlapacayan), and even into Guerrero, Oaxaca, and coastal Guatemala contain portable objects and occasionally stone sculpture in Olmec style. Willey (1962) sees the Olmec as Mesoamerica's first "great style" defining a horizon across the culture area. The Olmec style certainly contained the symbols of a religious ideology that linked up much of Mesoamerica and can be seen as a foundation for the later developments.

But how can we explain this impressive spread of Olmec style? Three suggestions have been made.

(1) The Olmec culture may have been spread by military conquest. Certain impressive sites, such as Chalcatzingo in Morelos, have been interpreted as Olmec colonies (see, for example, discussion in Benson 1968). On the basis of iconography (see Drucker 1981), although warrior motifs are common, the clothing and paraphernalia of the defeated, subjugated people are Olmec, not foreign. The warrior theme thus fits better a picture of intense interchiefdom rivalry within the Olmec heartland such as characterizes the political dynamics of chiefdoms and the available Olmec settlement pattern data (Earle 1976). No evidence exists for a far-flung Olmec administrative system with roads and special military facilities. The Olmec elements away from the Gulf coast are selective (some monumental sculpture and personal items of status display), indicative of shared ideological concepts but not the displacement of highland people by lowland Olmec conquerors (Flannery 1968). Most such Olmec items in the highlands, for example, show definite evidence of local manufacture and interpretation (Grove 1984).

(2) The Olmec style may represent a religious cult that spread by proselytizing through Mesoamerica from its origins in the Gulf coast region. Certainly this explanation fits better the selective nature of shared style in elements of "religious" iconography. As Sanders and Price (1968: 120) pointed out, however, the idea of Olmec missionary groups spreading a cult is improbable because analogous situations of cults in the Old World do not appear until late into the Iron Age when states and mercantile trade unified large areas throughout Europe, the Middle East, and Africa. The religious aspects of the Olmec are apparent, but the nature of their spread and adoption would appear best explained by the third suggestion, which follows.

(3) In an influential paper, Flannery (1968) argued against either conquest or missionization. Instead he saw the local evolution of stratified societies, i.e. chiefdoms, and their linking up through elaborate systems of exchange, alliance, and intermarriage. Some have interpreted the most important lesson from Flannery as being that long-distance exchange and symbiosis were ultimately at the base of the ideological bonding; however, long-distance trade and ideological interrelation are in my estimation best seen as an outcome of an ultimately more interesting phenomenon of ceremonial legitimation.

At this point, I would like to step back a moment to review what we know as the character and distribution of the Olmec style in Mesoamerica. In the Gulf coast heartland area (see Fig. 8.3), representations of figures that combine human and feline elements are common. These figures are found as massive heads, semi-relief carvings, jade celts, serpentine mosaics, and decoration on special serving vessels (bowls, dishes, and bottles). In his article, "Olmec jaguars and Olmec kings," Coe (1972) argues that the Olmec iconography was associated with a royal cult which functioned to sanctify the ruling Olmec elites. Certainly the emphasis in the Olmec monumental art is on human and anthropomorphic forms (Fuente 1981). Much of the art may have been portraits of ruling chiefs (Grove 1981: 61). Individuals are represented with composite elements indicating a duality most probably associating the individuals with a divine source. Coe describes the direct tie between a naturalistic ruler and a feline in the Olmec wall paintings from Guerrero that he sees as making explicit the divinity, or at least the divine connection, of Olmec rulers. Working from an Aztec analogy, Coe concludes, "By means of a long-series of structural oppositions, the divine nature of the royal line and its total separation from (and superiority to) the common people are stated in vivid terms" (1972: 9). The Olmec ruler and, by extension, all Olmec lords were thus presented as god figures in a way analogous to the Hawaiian case.

What is at first puzzling and then becomes clear is the reason for the spread of Olmec iconography across Mesoamerica. Although motifs and general stylistic rendering were quite broadly shared across much of Mesoamerica, the actual pattern of distribution was spotty and realized in quite different contexts from place to place. At a few sites such as Chalcatzingo in the highlands of Morelos (see Fig. 8.3), the Olmec style was elaborated and linked to the distant Gulf coast heartland (Grove 1984; Guillen 1984; cf. Flannery 1968). The stylistic link is evident especially in the famous bas-relief stone carvings, elite burials with jade and greenstone wealth objects, and portraiture figurines probably representing rulers or their deified ancestors (Grove 1984: 49–68; 73–75, 87–88). The stone carving is very close to the lowland prototypes, suggesting to Grove that stone-carvers from the Gulf coast may actually have come in to do the work. The elite burials in crypts also follow an Olmec model. The two richest interments are on the main platform mound at Chalcatzingo; one individual wore jade earspools, necklace and a pelvic bead string, and the other had jade earspools, a turquoise mosaic, and hematite mirror. These objects were used in similar burial contexts in the Gulf coast region. Most of the archaeological assemblage from Chalcatzingo, however, is quite clearly of a local highland tradition (Grove 1984; Flannery 1968). Even the "Olmec" pieces are of local manufacture and show strong indications of local interpretation.

Chalcatzingo was not an Olmec site, but Olmec

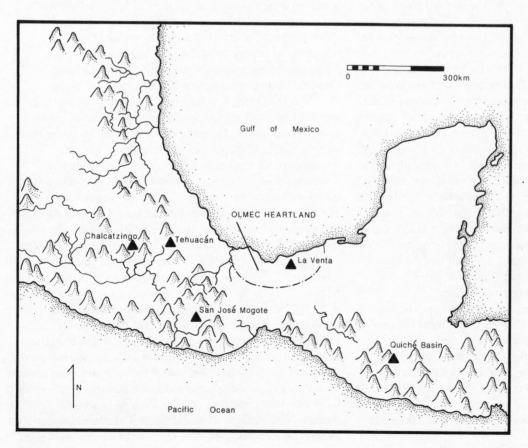

Fig. 8.3   Map of Mesoamerica showing the Olmec-period sites and areas discussed in the text.

iconography was used selectively, associated with public, ceremonial space and with elite burials. In an interesting analysis of a bas-relief sculpture with a female representation, Guillen (1984) suggests that elite marriage alliances existed between Chalcatzingo and the Gulf coast Olmec. The marriage would give the lowland Olmec access to the highland raw materials and the highlanders connection to the sacred kin lines of the Olmec.

In the region of Oaxaca the use of Olmec iconography was more limited, including the directional orientation of civic-ceremonial architecture at San José Mogote and the use of Olmec-style motifs (especially the "were-jaguar" and "fire-serpent") on special ceramic vessels. Pyne (1976) has shown that these Olmec motifs, with special ritual or cognitive significance, are *not* found associated with public architecture in Oaxaca but are found in residential contexts, especially in the houses of elites, identified by differential access to long-distance trade goods (spondylus, pearl oyster, mica, and magnetite). Interestingly, different houses and associated house clusters vary in the specific motif which is most common, suggesting that separate social lines were identified with different divine motifs.

In other regions, such as the Tehuacan valley of Puebla (Drennan and Nowack 1984), the Quiché basin of Guatemala (Brown 1984) and the eastern lowlands of the Peten (Blanton *et al.* 1981), no use of Olmec iconography has been recognized despite considerable archaeological work. In terms of distance, these areas are as close (or closer) to the Olmec heartland as other areas with definite Olmec connections.

The differential use of Olmec iconography outside of the Gulf coast region would appear to reflect the different levels of social complexity in the region. Where chiefdoms had already developed, the Olmec style was adopted to meet *existing* political needs for legitimation of the stratified and politically centralized organization (Drennan 1976; Blanton *et al.* 1981). In fact, the probable difference in complexity between the chiefdoms of Morelos and Oaxaca may be seen as determining quite different patterning of use of the Olmec style from its more public use at Chalcatzingo. However, regardless of distance from the Gulf coast, areas without Olmec connections were areas without established chiefdoms. Once established, the connections between the elites along the Gulf coast and in the highland areas would have provided important opportunities for control of long-distance trade (see Hirth 1978) and the associated esoteric knowledge that sanctified the principles of inequality. These long-distance trade relations would then have served as critical support for continued political power.

What I stress here is that style, as iconography, can be understood to function in broad social processes. Style proclaimed and justified, in the absence of written contracts, individual and group rights of resource access. In nonstratified societies, these rights derived from membership in local groups, which own land based on residence, defense, and ceremonial identification. In such a system, display artifacts, such as dress,

should be locally distinct, and all households should share access to them. Through the display of these goods, the group is proclaimed an entity with its members' rights to the estate.

In stratified societies, the unequal access to resources on which the chiefdoms depended was sanctified by the connection of the elites to universal, divine forces external to the local world of commoners. The Olmec rulers or the Hawaiian chief proclaimed connection through a special iconography to divine forces which sanctified their rule and legitimized their rights of control. Thus the Hawaiian feather cloak with its encircling rainbow announced the presence of a god, or at least his representative. The Hawaiian paramounts allocated to their immediate supporters both economic rights in communities and the cloaks that demonstrated the sanctity of those rights. In the Olmec, the anthropomorphic felines similarly represented the link between rulers and divine powers.

The Olmec stylistic connection between highland chiefdoms and the Gulf coast chiefdoms may have signified social and religious bonds based on marriage and alliance (Flannery 1968). Among the Hawaiian Islands, one island's ruling line (that of Kaua'i) was considered most sacred and all other ruling lines sought marriages with it. Alternatively, a religious system that defined a connection between chiefs and a universal divine force (symbolized by the feline) could have spread because of its unquestionable utility to local polities outside the Olmec core. Interregional connections were further reinforced by the exchange of special items such as the magnetite mirrors and jade celts that demarcated elite status. The amount of interconnectedness among the regional chiefdoms of Formative Mesoamerica is difficult to assess based on present evidence, but the reason for a broad interregional "great style" seems clear – legitimation of the chiefdoms.

Stylistic patterning, commonly studied by archaeologists, offers ways to investigate political and social processes at the very core of societal dynamics. It seems likely that cross-cultural and cross-time similarities in the specific patterns of stylistic identification and differentiation will be shown to articulate with broad evolutionary patterns in society. To do this, as archaeologists, we must be concerned with the specific uses of style as identified by the contexts of their appearance. This should not, however, concern us with identifying historically specific meaning but lead us to a concern with the functions of style and symbolic representations in human culture.

As the Hawaiian and Olmec cases inform us, style is a formal and an informal way to present meaning. In a society divided by classes and factions, style is actively constructed within the iconographic system. It is used to create and manipulate knowledge and thus to fashion consent as the necessary adjunct to power based on economic control. With this in mind, a processualist and materialistic orientation to prehistory should incorporate the functional aspects of style and iconography within its models developed to explain the evolution of social complexity.

Chapter 9

Interaction, imitation, and communication as expressed in style: the Ucayali experience

Warren R. DeBoer

In this lively ethnographic essay, the author discusses the group and personal aspects of style that are embodied in the forms of various things, such as projectile points, head-flattening, and decorative style. For his contextual stylistic presentation, DeBoer focuses on the decorative style of the modern Shipibo-Conibo group of the Ucayali Basin, Peru. By discussing the elements of the style with detailed design illustrations and the personal histories of the teaching, learning, and "artistic" performances for nine case studies, DeBoer conveys to us an understanding of the way in which designs are transferred and acquired among modern artists. From this, he is able to outline some of the processes of stylistic variability within the Shipibo-Conibo and between their neighbors, providing some conclusions about group and stylistic behavior useful to archaeological studies.

Introduction

I wear the shoes of Assiniboin. Your men follow us, they think I take you to Assiniboin country. It was true: his were not the shoes of Dakota, she had observed Dakota moccasins before this – knew the form and stitching and angles of decoration, and had seen how their shape was different from the footgear of Hidatsa.

(Kantor 1961: 85)

It is to be remembered that a person's footprints are as well known as his face.

(Marshall 1976: 188)

Much like a spoor, whether moccasined or bare-footed, style can communicate much to those who know how to read the message. In archaeology, an interest in style seems to be undergoing a much-needed renaissance (Hodder 1982b; Sackett 1982; S. Plog 1980, 1983; Wiessner 1983, 1984). Such a development is not surprising given the fact that so much of the archaeological record, at least for the last 30,000 years or so, consists of stylized artifacts. In wringing meaning from style, however, archaeologists are at a disadvantage: they were never the intended receivers of the messages style may carry.

In the following essay, I wish to review my own experience in coming to grips with style as revealed, often reluctantly, among the Shipibo-Conibo Indians of the Ucayali Basin in the Peruvian Amazon.[1] First, however, some conceptual and empirical groundwork must be laid.

Certain concepts govern my approach to style. I regard style to be the communicational aspect of form. Note that in this working definition, style is a communicational aspect, embodied in form, but not form itself. Communication is a relationship, a context, not a thing. I raise this point only to avoid wasted arguments as to whether a particular artifact, or a particular attribute, is utilitarian or stylistic in character. Such a thing-oriented opposition misleads us entirely. The proper question is purely contextual. Edge-angles on scrapers can be simultaneously utilitarian and stylistic. So can the size of projectile points (see the recent exchange between Sackett [1985a] and Wiessner [1985]).

As a second guiding principle, it should be recognized that style is "delightfully multidimensional" (Wobst 1977). It does many things at many levels and scales simultaneously. Depending on the knowledge of the audience, style may signal personal, family, village, or ethnic identity as it is defined in local, regional, national, or international arenas. Among the Shipibo-Conibo, stylistic productions are constantly evaluated according to their propriety and beauty. Among the neighboring Campa, a Shipibo-Conibo pot is a rare and much-esteemed trade item. In Moyobamba, several hundred kilometers from the Ucayali, Shipibo-Conibo textiles are flown in from Pucallpa so that local folk can parade as "real" Indians in the annual "tourist day" productions sponsored by the Chamber of Commerce. In New York City, both on Madison Avenue and on the Upper West Side, art dealers regularly advertise Shipibo-Conibo ceramics and textiles as treasured vestiges of a pristine and primitive world. Such pristineness and primitiveness, of course, never existed, even in the prehistoric world.

Style is also multimediated. It need not be restricted to any single class of material goods. Archaeologists may wish that ceramics, lithics, or other durable residues carry the full communicational burden from the past, but there is no reason to believe this to be the case. Among the Shipibo-Conibo, a distinctive decorative style not only adorns ceramics, but a virtually complete artifactual environment. Cotton textiles are painted and embroidered, always in the Shipibo-Conibo style. Wooden clubs, house posts, turtle carapaces, calabashes, and dug-out canoes are incised, and skin is painted. The Shipibo-Conibo provide an excellent example of decorative redundancy of the kind that so impressed Boas (1955) in his masterful study of primitive art.

The multimediated nature of the Shipibo-Conibo style is not restricted to physical objects. As Gebhart-Sayer (1984) has tried to convey, the Shipibo-Conibo view their decorative style as an objectified representation, or precipitate, of a spirit world that only arduously trained shamans (usually males) are capable of contacting. Such contact is facilitated by an appropriate mix of hallucinogenic drugs and spirit-endowed songs. For the Shipibo-Conibo, songs, visions, and designs are one and the same. For the archaeologists, however, songs and visions are poorly fossilized, and only designs in durable media will be left to study.

As multidimensional and multimediated communication, style is perforce reactive and always sensitive to context. It is never purely an "isochrestic" (Sackett 1982) epiphenomenon of people just doing what they're supposed to do. This point is particularly critical in the case of ethnoarchaeological inquiry. Perhaps the archaeological record can be treated as consisting of mute and non-reactive artifacts, but artifacts involved in on-going behavior are rarely so lifeless. They constantly change in response to all sorts of stimuli, including the presence of the tourist, missionary, and ethnoarchaeologist. This "uncertainty principle," in which observer and observed are mutually

influencing, is a fact of life. On the part of the observer, it is an illusion to pretend to be totally unobtrusive. Such an illusion is especially unexpected among anthropologists, as if the very presence of a professional observer does not destroy the myth of an ahistorical, and therefore uncontaminated, living past. When art is commissioned, as I and others have commissioned art among the Shipibo-Conibo, the product is directed, in large part, toward us. Having suggested that Shipibo-Conibo artists draw designs with magic markers on white paper, as I did in 1975, just how guilty should I feel now that magic markers are a valued trade item along the Ucayali? Other examples of this point in action have been given elsewhere (DeBoer 1984). Here one more case can be raised.

Based on observations in the 1960s, Lathrap (1976) has detailed the simplifying and economizing effects that a nascent but growing tourist market had on Shipibo-Conibo ceramics. To the visiting tourist, interested in weekend exposure to the primitive world, Shipibo-Conibo potters responded by producing vessels that look "primitive," thereby satisfying market expectations, and that can be packed away easily in a suitcase, thereby meeting the conditions of air travel, whether to Lima or Los Angeles (also see DeBoer 1983). As documented by Lathrap, this "trade ware" violates many of the decorative and size canons of the traditional ceramic style and is compartmentalized effectively from the Shipibo-Conibo's own standards by which pottery is evaluated. By the late 1970s, however, Gebhart-Sayer (1984) was to observe that pottery produced for sale did not necessarily suffer from the symptoms diagnosed by Lathrap over a decade earlier. Highly elaborate and traditionally "correct" ceramics were being produced for sale by potters in Caimito and other communities on the Ucayali. "Buyers," however, now included a sophisticated clientele of art dealers and anthropologists intent on collecting the "real thing." Both Lathrap and Gebhart-Sayer are right, but their contexts differ. Change has taken place. In this sense, longitudinal "re-studies" neither test nor refute, but only track ever-changing circumstances and experiences. Furthermore, there is no reason to assume that the reactive and conditional nature of style is something peculiarly restricted to capitalist or earlier "World system" contexts. People and style have never been without history.

Let us now look at some of the stylistic correlates and agents of this history as traced in the Ucayali Basin.

Style at work in the Ucayali Basin

The Ucayali is a large southern tributary of the Amazon that meanders northward through the lowland tropical forests flanking the eastern base of the Peruvian Andes (Fig. 9.1A). In recent geological time, the Ucayali has been an aggrading river that has formed a wide floodplain that is characterized by fertile, annually renewed soils and that supports a rich and diverse riverine and riparian fauna. The earliest historic accounts and the prehistoric archaeological record clearly indicate that the floodplain supported large, complexly organized, and competing polities (Lathrap 1970; Myers 1974;

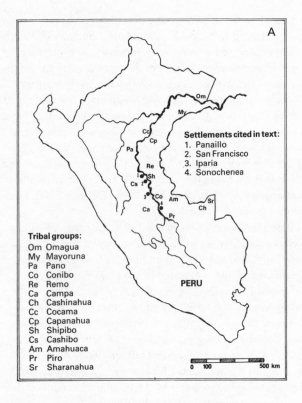

Tribal groups:
Om Omagua
My Mayoruna
Pa Pano
Co Conibo
Re Remo
Ca Campa
Ch Cashinahua
Cc Cocama
Cp Capanahua
Sh Shipibo
Cs Cashibo
Am Amahuaca
Pr Piro
Sr Sharanahua

Settlements cited in text:
1. Panaillo
2. San Francisco
3. Iparia
4. Sonochenea

PERU

0   100   500 km

DeBoer 1981). In contrast, the interfluves or off-river regions can be characterized as a kaleidoscopic mosaic of smaller and often less sedentary "tribal" groups. Between this polarity of Ucayali mainstream and backwoods – a polarity that has a solid ecological basis and that in the world view of the mainstream groups forms a symbolic opposition between culture and nature, or civilization and savagery (Roe 1982) – are occupants of major Ucayali tributaries on which limited floodplain agriculture and canoe travel are still possible. These three ecotypes, along with language distributions, are plotted schematically in Fig. 9.1B.

The map shown in Fig 9.1B holds historical information. Following the methodology pioneered by Sapir (1916) and others, Lathrap (1970) has presented an elegant and cogent historical scenario based upon distributional, linguistic, and archaeological evidence. Within the Ucayali Basin, Arawakan speakers such as the Piro and Campa occupy upstream or interfluvial zones. Arawakan languages, of course, have a far-flung distribution throughout the Amazon Basin, and glottochronological estimates suggest that the divergence of Piro and Campa from proto-Arawak must be measured in millennia (Noble 1965). Both the mainstream and interfluves of the Ucayali heartland are dominated by Panoan speakers. Linguistic evidence suggests that a major diversification and radiation of Panoan languages took place about a thousand years ago (d'Ans 1973). This estimated time-depth accords well with the archaeological facts. The Cumancaya ceramic style of about AD 900 (Raymond, DeBoer, and Roe 1975) is a reasonable antecedent for most of the ceramic assemblages produced by contemporary Panoan-speakers (Fig. 9.2). As a third and final ingredient, Tupian-speakers such as the Cocama and Omagua stand out as a recent, virtually protohistoric, penetration into the Ucayali Basin. The dating and nature of this penetration are confirmed by both linguistic and archaeological data (Weber 1975). In short, the map of Fig. 9.1B can be read as a form of horizontal stratigraphy in which Arawakan, Panoan, and Tupian speakers successively have had

LANGUAGE AND ECOTYPE

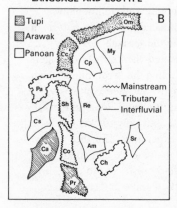

Tupi
Arawak
Panoan

Mainstream
Tributary
Interfluvial

TATTOOING AND HEAD-FLATTENING

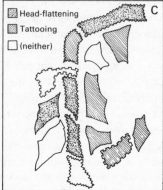

Head-flattening
Tattooing
(neither)

ELABORATE PROJECTILES

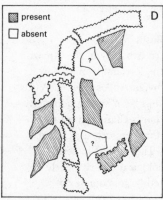

present
absent

DECORATIVE STYLE

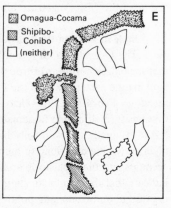

Omagua-Cocama
Shipibo-Conibo
(neither)

Fig. 9.1 Distribution of peoples, languages, and assorted classes of material culture in the Greater Ucayali Basin of the Upper Amazon, eastern Peru.

A. Distribution of ethnic groups. Numbered circles pertain to Shipibo-Conibo settlements examined in text.

B. Linguistic affiliation and ecotype. Ecotype is defined according to location on the Amazon-Ucayali mainstream, on a major tributary, or in the interfluves.

C. Distribution of two common forms of body mutilation, tattooing and head-flattening.

D. Occurrence of elaborately decorated projectiles, either arrow or, as among the Mayoruna, spear points.

E. Distribution of the two major polychrome decorative styles, Omagua-Cocama and Shipibo-Conibo.

(Major sources for C–E are Tessmann 1930 and Steward and Metraux 1948.)

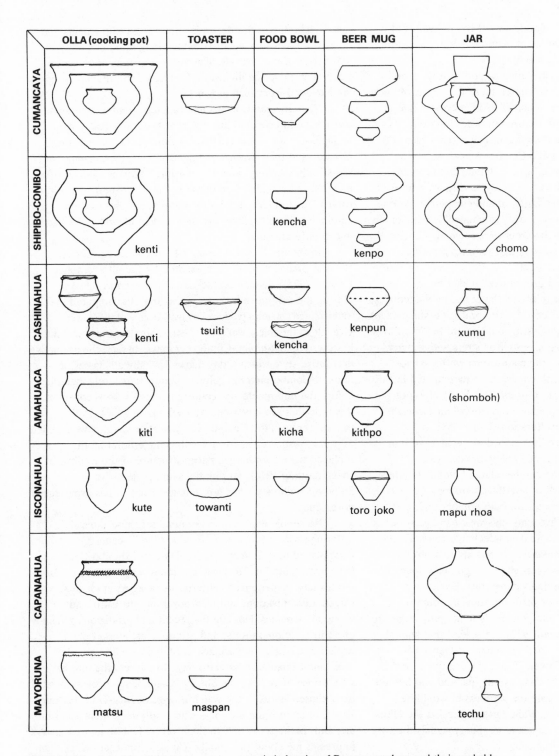

Fig. 9.2 Major vessel forms in contemporary ceramic industries of Panoan-speakers and their probable derivation from Cumancaya prototypes (*ca* AD 900). The chart is based on the following sources: for Cumancaya, Raymond, DeBoer, and Roe 1975; for the Shipibo-Conibo, Lathrap 1970 and DeBoer and Lathrap 1979; for the Cashinahua, Kensinger 1975; for the Amahuaca, Dole 1974; for the Isconahua, the Malkin Collection in the American Museum of Natural History, New York; and for the Capanahua and Mayoruna, ceramics on display in the SIL Museum, Yarinacocha, Peru.

their day on the productive floodplains of the Ucayali. Let us now see how certain categories of material culture map onto time and space in the Ucayali Basin.

Fig. 9.1C plots the distribution of body tattooing and frontal head-flattening. I have chosen these two forms of body mutilation because they are essentially somatic styles that, unlike moccasins, cannot be changed in order to deceive. Two patterns stand out. Taking the sequent mainstream groups of Omagua, Cocama, and Shipibo-Conibo, we can note a respective alteration between head-flattening and tattooing. This alternating pattern almost certainly constitutes a form of iconologic signaling in which adjacent and competing riverine groups distingush themselves in a stylistic indelible manner. In contrast, east-bank interfluvial groups are seemingly obsessed with body tattooing, an obsession that requires separate explanation. From at least the late seventeenth century until the early 1940s, mainstream groups have raided these backwoods groups in order to obtain slaves and nubile females. As will be seen shortly, the legacy of this practice is still evident in recently collected genealogies. I would regard the interfluvial penchant for body-tattooing as a stylistic strategy that marks resistance to abduction into the mainstream world. Almost certainly, the west-bank Cashibo also have participated in this strategy. Their recent adoption of the Shipibo-Conibo practice of head-flattening can be explained in terms of an especially well-understood case of acculturation (Gray 1953).

Elaborately decorated and shaped projectiles, such as arrow or spear points used in the killing of large game, including humans, constitute another class of material culture that is an apparent hallmark of interfluvial groups (Fig. 9.1D). The Cashibo are a case in point. In both ethnohistoric and more recent ethnographic accounts, this west-bank group is famed for its large, salient, and death-dealing arrows. To the Shipibo-Conibo, these ostentatious arrows are just further proof that the Cashibo are incorrigible savages who, much like beasts, are dumb, but potentially dangerous. From the perspective of the Cashibo or other interfluvial groups, however, these prominent and potentially lethal projectiles are "displays of power" (Lowman 1973) of the kind that animal ecologists would subsume under the general category of aposomatic display (e.g., Emlen 1973: 105). An unadorned arrow may kill a tapir, but a flamboyantly painted and barbed arrow is more likely to increase the wariness of would-be raiders from the mainstream. While tattooing resists the ethnic counterfeiting of the body, imposing weaponry signals the very real risks involved in body-snatching.

Finally let us turn to a hallmark of the mainstream world, namely polychrome decorative styles executed in mineral pigments colored black, red, and white. In recent times, there have been two such major styles that, named after the major protagonists, can be called the Omagua-Cocama and Shipibo-Conibo styles (Fig. 9.1E). These decorative styles would seem to be a virtual monopoly of the mainstream. Elsewhere (Lathrap 1973; DeBoer and Lathrap 1979; DeBoer 1984), it has been pointed out that the proper execution of

these decorative styles depends upon access to pigments and other resources that are distributed along hundreds of kilometers of the Ucayali. This access depends upon canoe travel along riverine highways; foot-based interfluvial groups are excluded from such networks.

The Omagua-Cocama and Shipibo-Conibo decorative styles have interrelated but different histories. Today the Omagua-Cocama style is virtually extinct. Its bearers, the Cocama and their downriver linguistic kin, the Omagua, are, stylistically speaking, almost "invisible" Indians (Stocks 1978); many have been absorbed ethnically into the *mestizo* world of rural Peru. In marked contrast, the Shipibo and Conibo continue to flaunt stylistically their Indian identity. The past tells a different story.

In the fourteenth century AD, the Omagua-Cocama style, as archaeologically represented by Caimito ceramics (Weber 1975), dominated the Lower and Central Ucayali. During the seventeenth century, the Spanish compared the multicolored ceramics produced by the Cocama of the Lower Ucayali to the finest wares of Castile. Similar praise was not bestowed upon Shipibo-Conibo ceramics. In fact, the distinctive decorative style which today marks virtually all classes of Shipibo-Conibo material culture cannot be securely identified before the mid-nineteenth century (see the vessels collected at this time that are illustrated by Dellenbach 1932). In the present century, the Omagua-Cocama style has rapidly declined to a pale vestige of its former self. Simple floral motifs have replaced the elaborate geometric structure of the traditional style (Lathrap 1970). During the same period, the Shipibo-Conibo style has not only persisted, it has experienced florescence.

No simple explanation accounts for these radically differing stylistic trajectories in which the Cocama have downplayed their Indian identity while the Shipibo-Conibo have accentuated it. No facile economic account suffices. Both groups have experienced centuries of ravaging epidemics, forced missionization, and incorporation into European economic schemes. Nor can the recent and prodigious demands of an international tourist and primitive-art market alone explain the strange persistence of Shipibo-Conibo art. A satisfying explanation will also have to address the internal significance of art. For the Shipibo-Conibo, style communicates their chosen status to the watchful eyes of Inca-God (Harner 1974), to unknowing outsiders who avidly seek their beautiful art, and, perhaps overall, to themselves. One thing that always impresses me about the Shipibo-Conibo, and that makes them such a wonderful people to work with, is their self-acknowledged superiority. No one else can make such beautiful and grace-giving designs.

At least in terms of archaeological nomenclature, however, I have probably committed an egregious sin by equating people with style. In fact, as indicated in Fig. 9.1E, genes, cognates, and stylistic motifs do not form perfectly impermeable packages. In the last century and during the early decades of this century, the Panoan-speaking Pano painted their pots in a manner that is clearly derived from the Omagua-Cocama style (Tessmann 1930: color plate VI). This case of cross-language stylistic acculturation perhaps can be explained by the long-term coresidence of the Pano and Cocama in Jesuit and later Franciscan missions. If we question the notion that propinquity automatically breeds similarity, however, the Pano assimilation of the Omagua-Cocama style can be viewed more dynamically as an attempt, on the part of the Pano, to participate in the prestige of a mainstream style. This latter interpretation is more in accord with the case of the Piro. Just as the Pano adopted the Omagua-Cocama style, the Arawakan Piro have mimicked the decorative style of their downstream neighbors, the Panoan-speaking Conibo. In terms of rendition, color scheme, and overall elaboration, Piro versions of the Shipibo-Conibo style can be analyzed as bold, but none the less simplified and misconstrued copies. This situation can be summarized in terms of a dual comparison in which Pano are to Cocama as Piro are to Conibo. It is tempting to extend this comparison in order to account for the still poorly understood genesis of the Shipibo-Conibo style. As Lathrap (1970) has pointed out, Shipibo-Conibo art can be understood, in part, as the grafting of Omagua-Cocama color and modular width conventions onto the millennium-old Cumancaya design style. In all of these cases, a hierarchy of stylistic prestige seems to be at work, in which the gradient runs from the wide productive floodplains of the lowlands upstream into the valleys of the eastern Andean slopes.

Flattened heads, tattooed skin, embellished weapons, and pretty pots constitute a forest (and river) of messages that communicate much about a geopolitical landscape in which boundaries can be accentuated or blurred. Up to this point, however, I have treated these material messages as normative statements: frontal head-flattening occurs or it does not; an artist paints in the Shipibo-Conibo style or she does not. It is now time to step inside these messages, to see how they are learned in the first place, and then how they are used to communicate within the boundaries. My example will be the Shipibo-Conibo style as it is produced by the Shipibo and Conibo themselves.

The Shipibo-Conibo style has been scrutinized from a number of different standpoints and is the subject of a large and growing literature (Vossen 1969; Roe 1976, 1980, 1981; DeBoer and Moore 1982; Lathrap 1983; Gebhart-Sayer 1984). Fig. 9.3A presents a fine example of the style as painted on a large beer mug in the village of San Francisco de Yarinacocha in 1971. Note the thick-lined primary design, customarily repeated in registers around the circumference of the vessel. This primary design is bordered by, and hence predetermines, thinner secondary lines. Finally remaining space is filled with thin-lined tertiary work, composed of scroll- or key-shaped elements. This mature example of Shipibo-Conibo art was produced by a woman whose mother was an Amahuaca abducted into the mainstream world. Fig. 9.3B-D are also examples of the Shipibo-Conibo art, although obviously less mature. They are produced by young girls who have not yet fully

mastered the underlying principles and technical complexities of the adult style. One basic opening question is how one gets fom Fig. 9.3B-D to Fig. 9.3A.

Learning Shipibo-Conibo art

One way to understand an art style is to learn to make it or, from a more common and distant anthropological perspective, to observe how artists themselves learn to make it. Learning and producing a style must be distinguished from consuming that style. For example, Marlena, a Pano who has had long and intimate contact with the Shipibo and their art, and who, in fact, is a *comadre* to a fully competent Shipibo artist, does not know where to begin when asked to make a Shipibo design. She does about as well as avid collectors of Shipibo-Conibo art in New York City. She is clearly less adept than most anthropologists who have studied Shipibo-Conibo art.

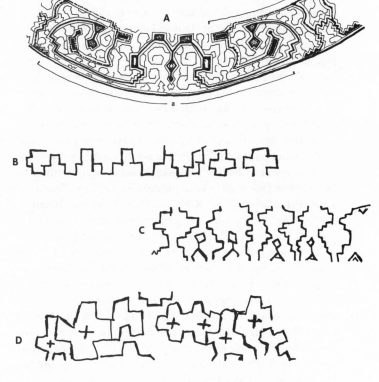

Fig. 9.3 A. A portion of a band design made by an adult artist, San Francisco de Yarinacocha. The design is painted in black (solid) and red (stippled) pigments over the white-slipped upper body of a *kenpo*, or beer mug. The design is composed of two major motifs (*shate*), 'a' and 'b,' which are repeated according to the scheme "abab" to complete the band. These major motifs are bordered by thinner secondary lines (*beshecan quetana*); remaining space is filled with fine-lined scrolls and key-shaped elements (*beshecan quene*). In the figure captions below, the following abbreviations are used: B = black; R = red; W = white; I = incised; B + R/W = black and red over white, etc.)
B–D. Designs painted in B/W by 7-year-old artists from Panaillo (B–C) and San Francisco de Yarinacocha (D). Note the prominence of either isolated or concatenated cross-shaped elements (*caros*).

Learning to make art is an active, on-going, and long-term process that always involves both imitative and creative components. Among the Shipibo-Conibo, the imitative component is evident in two common teaching practices. In one, the child adds the virtually predetermined secondary lines to a design made by her mother or other tutor. In the second, the child paints directly over a design that an adult has incised lightly in the plastic surface of an unfired ceramic vessel. Neither of these common tutoring strategies, however, ever leads to a perfect cross-generational transmission of individual design styles. As Lathrap (1983: 27) tersely and wryly comments, artists are not xerox machines.

In order to better understand both the imitative and creative aspects of art acquisition, I undertook a study of designs produced by Shipibo-Conibo children during the summer of 1975. Ideally such a study should be based on longitudinal observations that monitor the development of individual artists. Given the short duration of my field work, however, I adopted the expedient compromise of collecting designs made by a cross-sectional sample of variously aged children. The two most obvious and useful results of this investigation can be summarized quickly; details are given in Fig. 9.4 and Table 9.1.[2]

The first noteworthy result is that the truly bewildering variety of adult Shipibo-Conibo artistic productions, in which no two designs even approach identity, can be traced back to relatively simple ontogenetic antecedents in which surprisingly few design elements and operations are successively mastered by the maturing child-artist. Before age 5, children's drawings can be aptly described as "scribbling" and seem to conform to the scribbling stage postulated for child art in "First World" settings (Lindstrom 1957; Kellogg 1969; but also see Alland 1983). After age 5, distinctive properties of Shipibo-Conibo style are fully anticipated. The most basic and ontogenetically prior element is an enclosed cross (*caros* – see Fig. 9.4-[1]). As is detailed in Fig. 9.4, much of the subsequent development of Shipibo-Conibo art can be understood in terms of this fundamental cross-shaped element as it is subjected progressively to various operations. By age 16, the female artist has ordinarily mastered the full repertoire of basic elements and operations that underlie the style. Her artistic performance, as revealed in skill or technique, may still be rudimentary, but her competence, or understanding of the style's underlying structure, is expected to be mature. This expectation takes cultural form in marriage in which a proper bride should be able to make appropriately decorated ceramics and textiles for her new husband. Expectations, however, are inherently normative, and there are cases, sometimes scandalous, of Shipibo-Conibo women who never become good, or even adequate, artists.

The second major implication of this inquiry into children's art is of a more universal nature in that it deals with the processes by which pan-human capabilities unfold in predictable ways, even while being directed toward culturally specific goals. As is shown in Table 9.1, the sequence in which

Caption to Fig. 9.4

9.4 A primer for the ontogeny of Shipibo-Conibo art.

The figures are abstracted and schematized renditions of drawings commissioned from child artists in the villages of Panaillo and San Francisco during the summer of 1975. Children were asked to draw on 8½" by 11" paper with black and red magic markers, each color represented by two markers with differing line thicknesses. Red, black, and the differing thicknesses are features of the Shipibo-Conibo art style. These solicited drawings were supplemented by examples of children's art which the author collected during fieldwork in 1969 and 1971. (The age distribution of all design elements and operations is given in Table 9.1.)

(1) Cross, or *caros* in Shipibo-Conibo, a fundamental and ontogenetically early element.

(2) Cross subjected to translation which, following Shepard (1963): 269) involves moving the element in one direction without change in orientation.

(3) Crosses subjected to concatenation. Such concatenated crosses form one version of a design which the Shipibo-Conibo call *ronin quene*, or "great boa" design.

(4) A cross bearing secondary bordering lines (*beshecan quetana*) and tertiary filler work (*beshecan quene*). Secondary and tertiary work typically incorporates thinner lines than the primary design and may be executed in a different color.

(5) Cross with a square filler element, or *toro*. The square may also be colored in (*beroa*) or stippled (*chacha*). Three renditions of an X-shaped filler element (*ashta*) are also shown.

(6) Formation of Compound I from two crosses. The crosses may be modified as shown, forming curved designs (*maya*).

(7) Three versions of Compound II.

(8) Derivation of central line, or *natana*, by connecting *ashta* within the context of Compound I.

(9) Derivation of common motifs through division along an axis of symmetry followed by reflection. Both operations entail a commitment to bilateral symmetry which the Shipibo-Conibo gloss as *beibana quene*, or literally "face-to-face designs."

(10) Decorative field generated through the horizontal and vertical translation of crosses. Although bounded in practice, the field can be imagined as an infinite lattice.

(11) A modular section of an infinite field formed by translating Compound II in both horizontal and vertical directions. The stippled background of this design is itself a common motif. The visual play between design and ground is called by the Shipibo-Conibo *rabe quene*.

(12) Three common motifs latent in a field of translated crosses. One (heavy dark line) is based on the primary design, two (stippled) on the ground.

(13) Band designs derived from the field shown in 12.

(14) Row of translated crosses with square fillers that is given a diagonal orientation and then subjected to progressively narrowing banding. Diagonality, which opens up all kinds of new design possibilities, is called by the Shipibo-Conibo *intaina*.

(15) Diagonal Compounds II and derived band designs.

(16) Diagonal Compounds II and derived ground (stippled) and band designs.

(17) Merged diagonal Compounds II and derived band design.

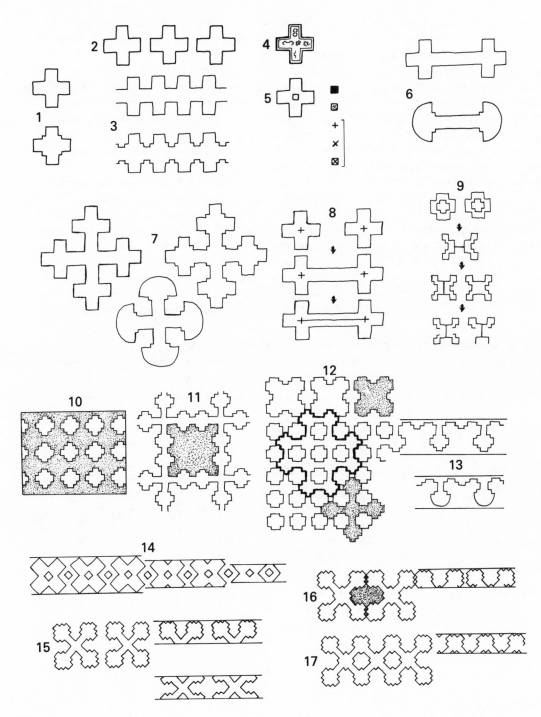

Fig. 9.4

children master design elements and operations is highly patterned. As was indicated previously, the basic cross is mastered first. This element is then successively submitted to a number of increasingly complex operations that entail concatenation, repetition, compounding – first in one, then in two dimensions – and finally various partitioning and orientational transformations. The strength of this sequential pattern suggests that a powerful maturational program of the kind famously diagnosed by Piaget (1970) is at work. Although of interest, this finding will not be further explored here, as my immediate concern is not how the Shipibo-Conibo are like all other human beings, but rather how they and their art become distinctively Shipibo-Conibo.

It is now time to turn from this rather formal and anonymous account of how Shipibo-Conibo art is learned to concrete and individual cases of how this art expresses social relations in the adult world.

Women at work within the Shipibo-Conibo style

Among the Shipibo-Conibo, women are the artists, potters, and weavers. Only in male-dominated shamanic ideology do men control art (Gebhart-Sayer 1984). In everyday practice, when men carve designs into a wooden club or canoe paddle, they carefully follow a template drawn in pencil or pigment by a woman. At age 8, male and female children are almost equally versatile in the making of *quenea*, or designs. By age 10, males pretend almost complete ignorance about the world of art.

The following cases of female art in action are selected with purpose. First, each artist must be represented by at least ten designs. Ten is not a large number, but is a reasonable cut-off given the fact that I assiduously attempted to collect at least all ceramic designs available at the time of observation. Second, I have concentrated on coresidential artists, i.e., artists who live either within the same house or within the same compound. A compound ordinarily consists of matrilineally related households arranged around a common plaza. The

Table 9.1.   Age distribution of elements and operations of the Shipibo-Conibo design style

Age range	5–7		8–9		10–11		12–15	
	no.	%	no.	%	no.	%	no.	%
Cross (*caros*)	25	*60*	22	*80*	20	*90*	21	*100*
Concatenation	13	*40*	14	*50*	4	*20*	2	*10*
Translation	4	*10*	8	*30*	7	*30*	14	*70*
Secondary work (*quetana*)	17	*40*	18	*60*	13	*60*	15	*70*
Thickness contrast	7	*20*	13	*40*	9	*40*	8	*40*
Color contrast	16	*40*	20	*70*	19	*90*	21	*100*
Tertiary work (*beshecan sharan*)	5	*10*	2	*10*	4	*20*	7	*30*
Square (*toro*)	7	*20*	21	*70*	10	*50*	13	*60*
X (*ashta*)	6	*10*	14	*50*	8	*40*	13	*60*
Placement of square or X inside cross	7	*20*	21	*70*	10	*50*	13	*60*
Compound I	4	*10*	13	*40*	8	*40*	8	*40*
Curvilinear designs (*maya*)	2	*x*	1	*x*	9	*40*	7	*30*
Compound II	1	*x*	1	*x*	3	*10*	5	*20*
Use of solid fill (*beroa*)	1	*x*	2	*10*	8	*40*	3	*10*
Use of stippled fill (*chacha*)	1	*x*	1	*x*	4	*20*	1	*x*
Natana	1	*x*	2	*10*	5	*20*	10	*50*
Design–ground complementation (*rabe quene*)	–	–	5	*20*	7	*30*	14	*70*
Truncation of infinite field	–	–	4	*10*	7	*30*	14	*70*
Band borders	–	–	2	*10*	5	*20*	8	*40*
Division along axis of symmetry	–	–	1	*x*	7	*30*	6	*30*
Reflection (*beibana quene*)	–	–	–	–	3	*10*	5	*20*
Merging of adjacent elements	–	–	–	–	1	*x*	2	*10*
Lineation	–	–	–	–	3	*10*	3	*10*
Diagonality (*intaina*)	–	–	–	–	3	*10*	6	*30*
Number of drawings involved	42		29		22		21	

Shipibo-Conibo terms in italics. Percentages (also in italics) given to nearest 10 per cent; x indicates presence at less than 5 per cent.

rationale for this choice is based on archaeological considerations. Compounds are ordinarily represented by spatially discrete middens (DeBoer and Lathrap 1979).

In appraising the following case studies, I have kept several factors in mind:

(1) The size of the settlement. Other things being equal, it can be expected that small hamlets consisting of two or three artists provide less artistic stimulus than large settlements composed of dozens of artists.

(2) Social origin and learning route. Is the artist raised and taught to make art within her natal community, or is she an "outsider," either immigrant from another Shipibo-Conibo community or abducted from a non-Shipibo-Conibo group? In all these cases, from whom is Shipibo-Conibo art actually learned?

(3) Psychodynamic factors. All primates probably learn better in warm and supportive social environments. What effect does the nature or degree of familial harmony have on artistic transmission?

My information concerning factor (1) is relatively precise. Knowledge concerning factor (2) is adequate, although not nearly as precise. My understanding of factor (3) is primarily impressionistic, based as it is on relatively short-term observations of how people got along during the time of my visit.

Case 1: Three sisters of Iparia

At the time of my visit in 1971, Iparia, a west-bank community on the Upper Ucayali, had a population of some 150 *mestizos* and a smaller contingent of 20 Conibo. The Conibo *barrio* was separated from the *mestizo* section of town by a hundred meter walk along a jungle path. Relations between these two *barrios* were strained and decidedly asymmetric. Conibo women regularly were abused, verbally and otherwise, by *mestizo* men, and the pilfering of Conibo goods and gardens was endemic. This predatory relationship was only partially suspended when a relatively prosperous and prestigious *gringo* archaeologist visited Iparia and chose to live with the Indians.

The Conibo *barrio* consisted of three houses, each occupied by one of the three sisters and her children. During my two-week stay, husbands were absent: one was working in lumbering; one was visiting Pucallpa; and one hadn't been seen for a couple of years, and his whereabouts were uncertain. The three sisters, although nominally Conibo, were born of an Amahuaca mother who was captured earlier in this century in a Conibo raid. None of these sisters had learned to make art from her Amahuaca mother. Rather the oldest daughter had learned to make proper Shipibo-Conibo art from a Conibo mentor (now deceased) and, in turn, this daughter had trained her two younger sisters. Representative designs produced by these three sisters of Iparia are illustrated in Fig. 9.5.

Fig. 9.5 presents a homogeneous set of designs that is distinctively "Iparian." The primary design is thin-lined and lithely executed. *Maya quenea*, or curved designs, are conspi-

cuous. Red-filled and rectangularly shaped *toro* are also common to the three artists. Secondary and tertiary work is executed consistently with needle-incision. Other similarities can be noted by any observer who ponders the designs for a while.

The three sisters of Iparia, whose Amahuaca pedigree is tainting, whose position in the Shipibo-Conibo world is marginal, and whose backs are against the wall in a *mestizo*-dominated situation, still produce designs that are fully in the fold of the Shipibo-Conibo style. Within this fold, however, these artists produce a bounded and easily recognized substyle.

Case 2: The mother and daughter of Sonochenea

Sonochenea is a two-house hamlet located at the southern extremity of Conibo-land. The two adjacent houses

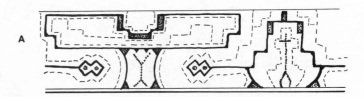

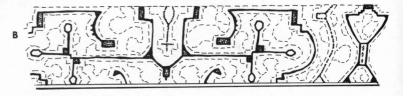

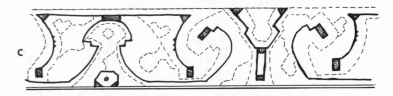

Fig. 9.5 Designs from Iparia.

A. House 1, *oso* (white) *kencha*, B + R + I/W

B. House 1, *oso kencha*, B + R + I/W

C. House 2, *kenpo*, B + R + I/W

D. House 3, *kenpo* with rattle base, B + R + I/W.

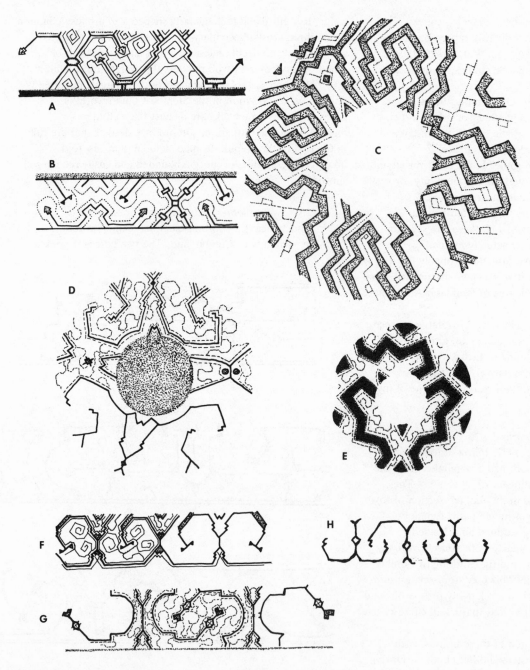

Fig. 9.6 Designs from Sonochenea.

A. House 1, *oso kencha*, B + R/W

B. House 1, neck of *chomo*, B + R/W

C. House 1, body of *chomo* (top view), B + R/W

D. House 2, *oso kencha* (bottom view), B + R + I/W

E. House 2, *oso kencha* (top view), B + R + I/W

F. House 2, *oso kencha*, B + R/W

G. House 2, *oso kencha*, B + R + I/W

H. House 2, neck of *chomo*, B/W; design first incised by the mother with a needle, then painted over in
   black by the 9-year-old daughter.

are occupied by mother and daughter respectively. Unlike in Iparia, husbands are present, and pestering *mestizos*, if not equally irksome archaeologists, are two hours distant (here and below I lapse into the present tense of 1971 field notes).

From a proper Shipibo-Conibo point of view, the hamlet of Sonochenea is a scandalous case of miscegenation. The mother is an abducted Amahuaca; her daughter married a Campa. During normal day-to-day activities, these ethnic distinctions are politely ignored; at night, after the proper doses of *masato* or manioc beer, the visiting *gringo* finds out what the Conibo, Amahuaca, and Campa – armed with wounding words and bluffing machetes – really think of each other. If I understand the trilingual exchange and accompanying gesticulations correctly, the answer is "not much." As shown in Fig. 9.6, however, the mother and daughter of this turmoil-ridden hamlet continue to produce handsome designs that are faithfully Shipibo-Conibo in style.

There is continuity between the designs of mother and daughter. Both artists make thick band designs (*canoa*) that are delightfully asymmetric (Fig. 9.6C, E). Both frequently use a primary motif that consists of a pointed central element flanked by symmetric "wings," or *pechi* (Fig. 9.6A, D, F). In contrast

to Iparia, however there are also consistent differences between the two women. The mother tends to use red-colored secondary work and often deletes tertiary work altogether (Fig. 9.6B-C). When tertiary work is added, it emphasizes scrolls (Fig. 9.6A). In only one of twelve cases does the daughter use such scroll-based tertiary work (Fig. 9.6F). In contrast to her mother, the daughter regularly uses incision to execute both secondary and tertiary work, and her tertiary work favors key-shaped elements (Fig. 9.6D-E, G). Unlike the nice little stylistic front presented by Iparia, Sonochenea suggests more internal differentiation. It is quite likely that this differentiation expresses the interpersonal stresses at work within the small and isolated Sonochenea homestead.

Case 3: An outsider from Panaillo

Panaillo is located on the west bank of the Central Ucayali, virtually across from the mouth of the Callaria. The community, which has been the subject of a major cultural ecological study (Bergman 1974), is much larger and more internally heterogeneous than the tiny matrilocal hamlets of Iparia and Sonochenea. During my visit in 1975, Panaillo had a population well in excess of 100 individuals. A partial

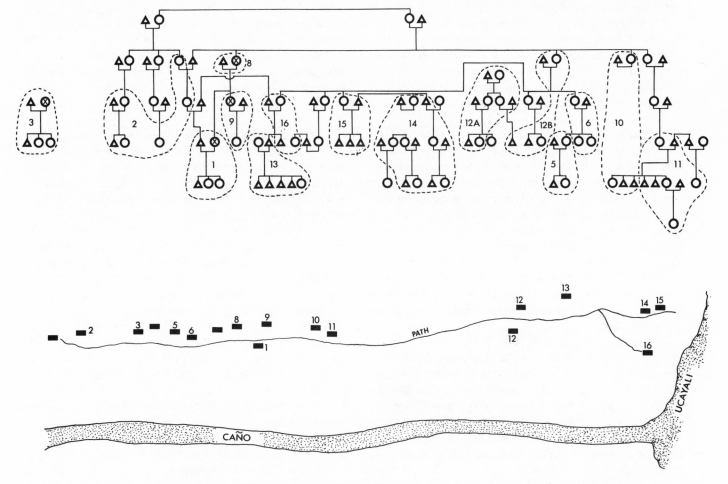

Fig. 9.7 A partial genealogy of the settlement of Panaillo. Dashed lines enclose residents of the same house. The location of these houses is shown in the schematic map at the bottom. Artists discussed in the text are marked with an X.

genealogy for this community is given in Fig. 9.7. In this genealogy and accompanying map, note the common practice of adoption. Also note the matrilocal bias in residential patterns. Finally, note the obvious "outlier" of household 3, a household that has no kinship ties to the rest of Panaillo. In the following discussion, I shall call the artist and potter of household 3, reasonably enough, artist 3.

Artist 3 was born, raised, learned to make art, and still has kin on the Pisqui, a major west-bank tributary of the Central Ucayali. In my brief two-week visit, I was unable to determine what factors prompted her move to Panaillo. Mainstream Shipibo refer to their cultural and linguistic brethen on the Pisqui with the somewhat condescending locative term "Pisquibo." Roe (1981) has outlined the micro-stylistic distinctions that separate Pisquibo from mainstream Shipibo art. Artist 3 lends some support to Roe's diagnosis. She produces the terminal "hammer-head" element (Fig. 9.8A) that Roe identifies as a Pisquibo characteristic. In addition, artist 3 still obtains her pigments from the Pisqui, and her maroon reds are readily distinguishable from the lighter reds that typify mainstream-derived iron oxides. Beyond these distinctions, however, artist 3 produces perfectly acceptable Shipibo-Conibo art that is perhaps simpler than the Panaillo norm, but hardly out-of-place (Fig. 9.8A-C). Her designs certainly do not mark her, in any major sense, as an "outsider." In this regard, it may be significant to note that artist 3, although without local kin, is an affable and popular person who gets along well with her Panaillo neighbors. Friendship, unlike kinship, is a relationship that has not received much attention from anthropologists.

Case 4: A mother and two daughters from Panaillo

The mother (artist 8 in Fig. 9.7) is part of the kinship core of Panaillo. She and her sisters are, in a real sense, the founding matriarchs of the present Panaillo community. At the time of my visit, the mother was an elderly woman, well into her 60s. Her eyesight was failing, and her painting hand was unsteady. She still produced thick and bold designs with a sense of authority (Fig. 9.8D), but her finer-lined work intimated compositional disarray (Fig. 9.8E). Throughout Panaillo, this mother was recognized as an accomplished artist whose day had passed. Let us now see how two daughters, both of whom learned art from their mother, represent this legacy of artistic accomplishment.

The younger daughter (artist 1 in Fig. 9.7) produces art that is highly diverse in its degree of elaboration but that is rather uniformly based on compound II as defined earlier in this paper (Fig. 9.8F-G). Major similarities to the mother can be noted. As is evident in a comparison of Fig. 9.8D and F, both artists may dispense with secondary work and produce a primary design that appears to be laid over a continuous lattice of key-shaped tertiary work. Whether painting pots, skirts, or paper samplers, both artists tend to employ bordering bands of varying intricacy (Fig. 9.8D-F). Differences can also be noted. For instance, the serrated primary design shown in Fig. 9.8F

reflects a stylistic fad that was sweeping through the Shipibo-Conibo world in 1975. This vogue was said to have started in Tintaboya on the Lower Ucayali and, I suspect, is based on a jagged stitch produced by a sewing-machine. This stylistic innovation, readily adopted by the daughter and other young artists, never influenced the art of the mother.

As an additional observation, I should point out that the younger daughter headed one of the most acculturated households in Panaillo. Her husband ran the town store, where bottled beer, canned tuna, kerosene, cigarettes, and brassieres could be purchased. A material culture inventory of this house-store would include transistor radios, kerosene lamps and stoves, a battery-run record player, a reasonable collection of pop records, xeroxed portions of various anthropological works dealing with the Shipibo-Conibo (presumably bestowed by visiting anthropologists), and innumerable Playboy-type center-folds. Yet despite this flood of late-twentieth-century flotsam, the daughter continues to make reasonably refined Shipibo-Conibo art.

The older daughter (artist 9 in Fig. 9.7) stands apart, not residentially, but stylistically. Her husband is an alcoholic who, when tired of drinking elsewhere, comes home to drink some more. Despite this marital mess, artist 9 produces classic Shipibo-Conibo art. As shown in the skirt designs of Fig. 9.9, her style is simple, yet elegant, and proficiently executed. Similarities to mother and sister are unclear. In fact, I can find no formal stylistic basis for associating artist 9 with her kin, who also happen to be her neighbors. This triad, a mother and two daughters, does not form a readily identifiable micro-stylistic unit.

Case 5: Remo recruits at San Francisco de Yarinacocha

San Francisco de Yarinacocha is the Shipibo-Conibo "big time." Situated an hour north of the Peruvian city of Pucallpa, San Francisco is the largest, most tourist-visited, and most anthropologized of Shipibo-Conibo settlements. In 1975, the community numbered well over 700 individuals, split into nominal Catholic, Adventist, and Evangelical factions. Proximity to Pucallpa is the key factor in understanding this overblown and factionalized settlement. In Pucallpa, Shipibo men find work, and Shipibo women sell crafts. In addition, the swelling urban population of Pucallpa provides a ready market for bananas, manioc, maize, and other produce from Shipibo-Conibo gardens. Throughout Shipibo-Conibo-land, San Francisco is regarded simultaneously as corrupt, exciting, and opportunity laden. As recently as 1975, however, San Francisco art was still blatantly, perhaps flauntingly, traditional in character.

Fig. 9.10 gives a partial genealogy for the northern sector of San Francisco. Our first case consists of two artists, a mother and daughter, who live in house 13. As seen in Fig. 9.10, these artists have very tenuous kinship links with the San Francisco community. The mother in question is, in fact, the daughter of a Remo woman, long since deceased, who was captured in a Shipibo raid. The living artist did not learn art from her Remo mother, but rather from a Shipibo mentor. As shown in Fig. 9.11A-D, this training was sufficient for her to produce clearly recognizable, if simple, and sometimes slovenly executed (Fig. 9.11C) Shipibo-Conibo designs. Care must be taken, however, in assessing this case, for at the time of observation the mother of house 13 was an old woman whose artistic heyday had passed. Her middle-aged daughter, however, produced the same simple and repetitive designs (Fig. 9.11E). In fact, the mother and daughter often worked jointly in decorating ceramics. The mother would begin a primary design, the daughter would finish it. Both then would alternate in adding secondary and tertiary work. Among the Shipibo-Conibo, such decorative cooperation between adults is relatively rare. Ordinarily copying or "filling-in the blanks" is a strategy reserved for teaching young children (e.g., Fig. 9.6H). As is suggested by house 13, the wide adoption of such replicative techniques by adult artists would dramatically change the nature of stylistic patterning found in Shipibo-Conibo art.

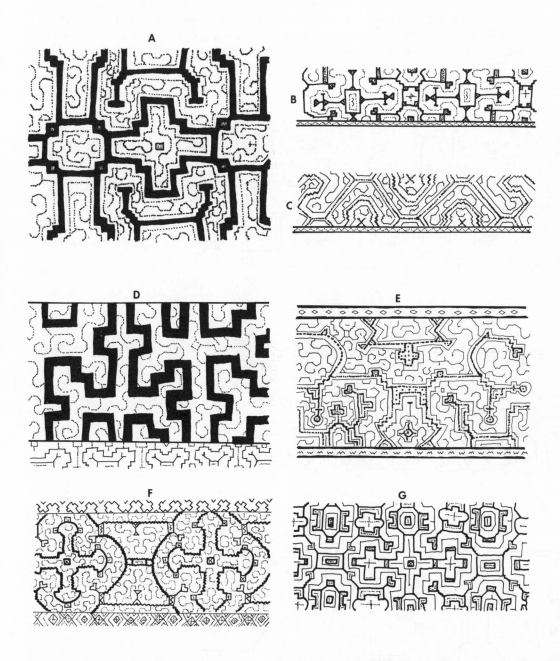

Fig. 9.8 Designs from Panaillo.

A–C. House 3, paper samplers, all B + R/W

D–E. House 8, paper samplers, all B + R/W

F–G. House 1, paper samplers, all B + R/W.

Case 6: Daughters, biological and adopted, from San Francisco

Our next case deals with Shipibo artists (those from houses 14 and 15) whose kinship ties with the rest of San Francisco are based on a single affinal link. The mother comes from Pacacha. Her biological daughter has married into San Francisco. The adopted daughter, like her adoptive mother, comes from Pacacha. The mother was the main art teacher for both daughters. Let us see how designs map onto this triad of artists.

The mother is an accomplished artist (Fig. 9.11F-G). In contrast, her biological daughter produces highly simplified, almost schematized, designs. In particular, there is a tendency to reduce tertiary work to a series of awkwardly spaced U-shaped elements (Fig. 9.11H-I). By Shipibo-Conibo standards, this daughter is an untalented artist and a disappointment to her mother. In fact, one of the mother's motives in adopting a daughter was to recruit a more promising art student. Indeed the adopted daughter proved to be such a student. As shown in Fig. 9.11J-K, her designs are elaborate and skillfully executed. In particular, this adopted daughter carries on the mother's penchant for using key-shaped tertiary work and a distinctive filler composition consisting of v- or w-shaped elements (compare Fig. 9.11F with 9.11J-K). This case clearly demonstrates that stylistic transmission is not a matter of pedigree.

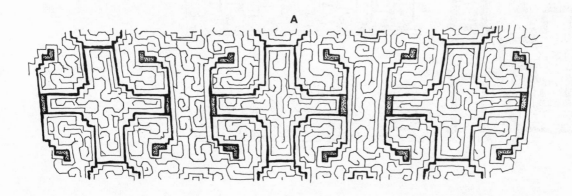

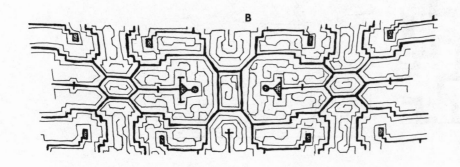

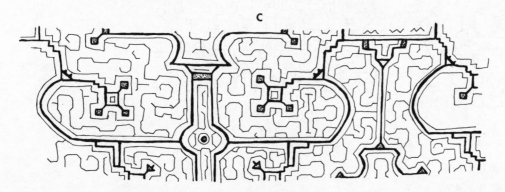

Fig. 9.9 Skirt designs painted by artist of House 9, Panaillo, all B + R/W.

Case 7: More bad artists from San Francisco

This and the remaining two cases deal with the same artists studied and reported upon by Roe (1980). Over a period of years, Roe and I spent many months living in the houses of these artists, while we recorded our archaeological collections from the Upper Ucayali. Many of the following observations reinforce Roe's analysis; however, there are also differences in viewpoint and emphasis. Following Roe (1980: 50), who often used fictive names for individual artists, I will use the even more anonymous system of numbers keyed to houses as they are plotted in Fig. 9.10.

This case pertains to house 1. The mother is a virilocally resident "outsider" who has but distant kinship links with the rest of the San Francisco community. She has married into a matrilocal fortress of mothers and daughters, represented by houses 2, 3, 5, and 6 as plotted in Fig. 9.10. As shown in Fig. 9.12A-D, her designs are simple and rudimentary, consisting of monotonously repeating motifs. Tertiary work is minimized. When this artist attempts something more elaborate, the result is incomplete and disturbed, as if a threshold of imagination or creativity has been crossed (Fig. 9.12D).

Her art-producing daughters continue this uninspired tradition. Fig. 9.12E illustrates a design produced by the older

daughter at age 12; by age 16, her designs obviously have matured, but they still display the simplicity and repetitiveness of the mother's style (Fig. 9.12F-G). There is no evidence at hand to suggest that the younger daughter will escape these stylistic confines (Fig. 9.12H).

I was thus surprised when Roe presented clear evidence that the older daughter indeed has escaped these confines. The design illustrated by Roe (1980: Fig. 10) is more elaborate than any I collected from this daughter. I am not convinced, however, by Roe's argument that this stylistic "leap" (which took place between 1975 and 1978) represents a case of rapid enculturation to the more masterful art produced in neighboring households. Of equal importance is the fact that this daughter married in 1975, shortly before her stylistic transformation. As pointed out earlier, a Shipibo-Conibo bride is expected to be an artist. The ethnoarchaeological lesson is clear: observations across time and across changed social conditions are not equivalent.

Case 8: Two sisters, as different as can be, from San Francisco

The older sister is a splendid and widely admired Shipibo artist and potter. As shown in Fig. 9.13A-C, her designs are

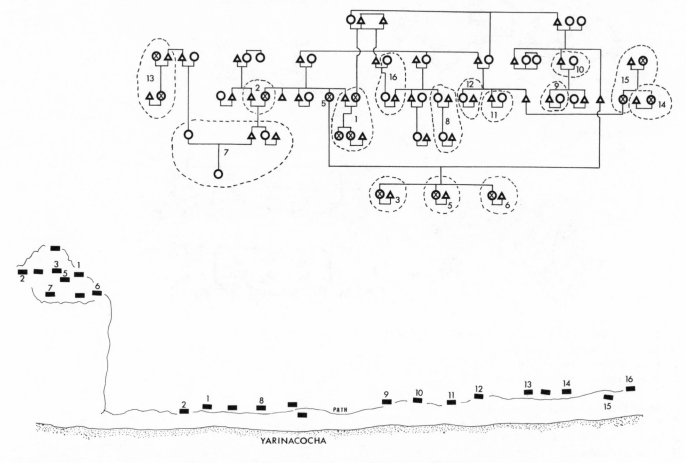

Fig. 9.10 A partial genealogy of the northern sector of San Francisco de Yarinacocha. Dashed lines enclose residents of the same house. The location of these houses is shown in the schematic map at the bottom. Both the 1971 (shoreline) and 1975 (inland) location of houses 1 and 2 is given. Artists discussed in the text are marked with an X.

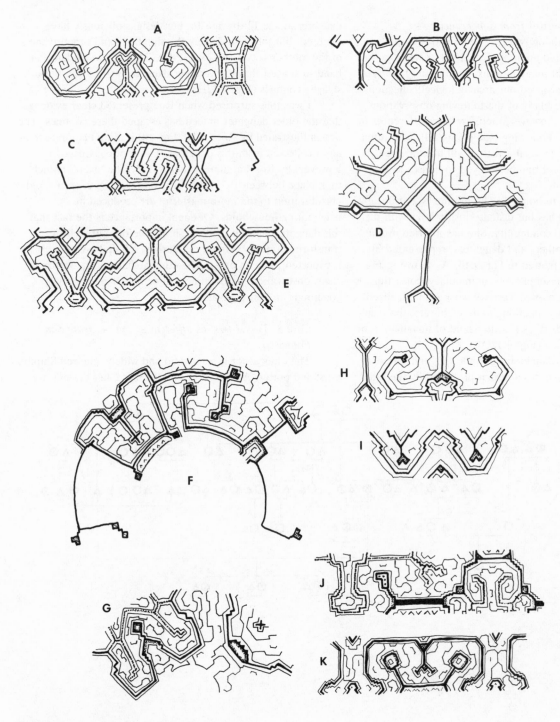

Fig. 9.11 Designs from San Francisco de Yarinacocha.

A. House 13 mother, *kenpo*, B + R/W
B. House 13 mother, *kencha*, W/R
C. House 13 mother, neck of *chomo*, B + R/W
D. House 13 mother, *kencha* (bottom view), W/R
E. House 13 daughter, neck of *chomo*, B + R/W
F. House 15 mother, neck of *chomo*, B + R/W
G. House 15 mother, *oso kencha*, B + R/W
H. House 15 daughter, neck of *chomo*, B + R/W
I. House 15 daughter, neck of *chomo*, B + R/W
J. House 14, *kenpo*, B + R/W
K. House 14, neck of *chomo*, B + R/W.

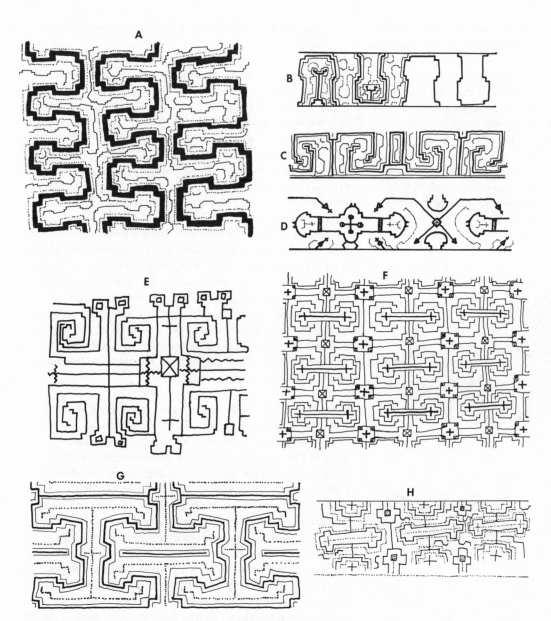

Fig. 9.12 Designs from house 1, San Francisco de Yarinacocha.

A. mother, paper sampler (1975), B + R/W

B. mother, neck of *chomo* (1971), B + R/W

C. mother, *kenpo* (1975), B/W

D. mother, neck of *chomo* (1971), B + R/W

E. older daughter, paper sampler (1971), B/W

F. older daughter, cloth sampler (1975), B + R/W

G. older daughter, skirt design (1975), B + R/W

H. younger daughter, paper sampler (1975), B + R/W.

diverse, complex, and consummately executed. In marked contrast, the younger sister produces simple, coarse, and even downright disgraceful renditions of the Shipibo-Conibo style (Fig. 9.13D–G). For once, there are clear reasons for this difference. The younger sister learned to make art from her mother, now deceased. The older and more artistically accomplished sister did not. Her artistic apprenticeship included lengthy stays at Shipibo-Conibo communities on Imariacocha as well as influences from the famed Conibo artist, Wasemea (Lathrap 1976). Learning from different teachers, these two sisters, living in neighboring houses, definitely do not form a micro-stylistic unit. Let us now look at the daughters of the more artistically accomplished sister.

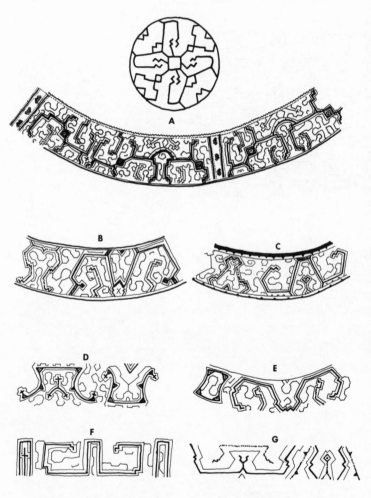

Fig. 9.13 Designs from San Francisco de Yarinacocha.

A. House 5 mother, *kenpo ani* (big *kenpo*), bottom (W/R) and body (B + R/W) designs

B–C. House 5 mother, *shrania* (pitcher), both B + R/W

D. House 2, neck of *chomo*, B + R/W

E. House 2, *kenpo*, B + R/W

F. House 2, *kenpo*, B/W

G. House 2, neck of *chomo*, B + R/W.

Case 9: Three daughters trained by an accomplished artist-mother

The oldest daughter is an accomplished artist (Fig. 9.14A, B); her designs resemble those of her mother in a number of ways, including use of broad-lined w-shaped elements (compare Fig. 9.13A with 9.14A). The second daughter also produces art fully within the maternal fold (Fig. 9.14C). The youngest daughter presents a more problematical case.

The designs I collected from this third daughter tend toward the simple and repetitive (Fig. 9.14D-E). Once again, however, Roe (1980: Fig. 6) shows that my sample is not representative of the artist's capability, and once again, I suspect that biographical conditions may be involved. This youngest daughter is married to a Shipibo school-teacher, and both spend considerable amounts of time teaching Spanish and the Peruvian national "line" to Conibo children on the Upper Ucayali. This couple is particularly adept at switching roles as they are defined simultaneously in national and strictly Shipibo-Conibo terms. The daughter *qua* wife is also adept at style-shifting, producing the simplified designs of Fig. 9.14D-E on some occasions, the elegant specimen figured by Roe on another. Clearly artistic performance by one artist may be highly variable and conditional.

What then can be made of these nine cases? On the one hand, each artist and her art are, of course, unique. On the other hand, all artists produce art that is unmistakably Shipibo-Conibo in style. Between these extremes, in which comparison is either impossible or unnecessary, are there patterns of artistic variability? In order to address this question, I have summarized the preceding artistic "profiles" in Fig. 9.15. The following discussion is keyed to this figure.

An immediate issue is the extent to which students resemble teachers. Our small sample includes seventeen teacher-student dyads. In eleven of these seventeen dyadic relations, artistic resemblance between student and teacher is fairly obvious and extends to specific elements and motifs, compositional themes, or overall decorative elaboration. As the popular saying and song would have it, "two out of three ain't bad," and these results could be used to support a largely imitational mode of design acquisition. This is a happy conclusion for those ethnoarchaeologists and "ceramic sociologists" who would like to have coresidential units and their associated middens mapping onto detectable micro-stylistic packages. These results do not support the largely negative verdict of Lathrap (1983) who argues that the Shipibo-Conibo evidence totally undermines any assumption of isomorphism between coresidence and stylistic homogeneity.

From another standpoint, however, a skeptic, whether of particularist or nomothetic persuasion, might be very uneasy with any theory that accounts for only two-thirds of all observations. Such healthy skepticism immediately directs us to the exceptions. In other words, what makes certain artists exceptional?

In the case of Sonochenea, the artist-daughter lives in a

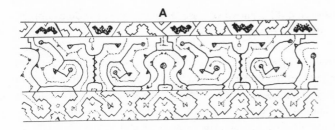

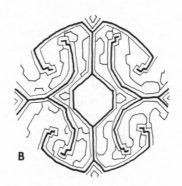

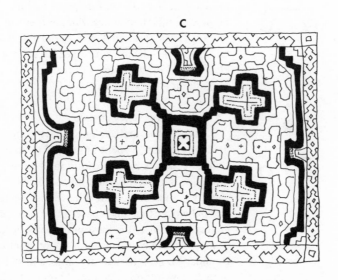

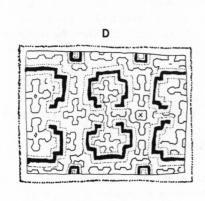

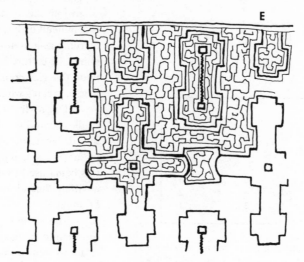

Fig. 9.14 Designs from San Francisco de Yarinacocha.

A. House 6, paper sampler, B + R/W

B. House 6, *kencha*, W/R

C. House 3, paper sampler, B + R/W

D. House 5 daughter, paper sampler, B + R/W

E. House 5 daughter, skirt design, B/W.

tiny social world beset by internal rifts. In case 4, from Panaillo, the older daughter produces a truly exceptional art, as if this almost substitutes for a hopeless marital situation. In case 6, from San Francisco, another common and pan-human dilemma is faced. Simply put, the biological daughter has no artistic talent; in this case, the problem of artistic succession is handled through adoption. In case 7, also from San Francisco, the older daughter is making valiant efforts to escape the narrow stylistic confines presented by her mother-teacher. In

somewhat different ways, cases 8 and 9 also provide examples of stylistic "escape."

As is shown in Fig. 9.15, settlement size and the social origin of artists do not appear to have any stunningly significant impact on the fidelity of design transmission. Whether small or large, Shipibo-Conibo settlements are always part of the larger Shipibo-Conibo artistic world. Inter-village visitation is commonplace, and stylistic fashions or innovations can spread almost instantaneously throughout Shipibo-Conibo-land. Furthermore, the fidelity of stylistic transmission does not seem particularly sensitive to the social origins of the artist. Whether she was recruited into the Shipibo-Conibo fold through birth or abduction apparently has little effect on adult artistic production. If anything, foreigners by birth are more faithfully Shipibo-Conibo in practice. Put another way, ethnic boundaries in the Ucayali basin are highly permeable with repect to bodies, but almost inviolable with respect to style. For further elaborations of this point, the reader is referred to the studies by Lathrap (1983) and Roe (1980).

Summary: styles of style

With style, archaeologists have come full-circle. As a graduate student, I spent innumerable hours seriating highly stylized ceramics housed within the bowels of the Lowie Museum, Berkeley. Seriation was possible because style was viewed as something that, other things being equal, changed gradually over time and space. Over time, style changes gradually because it is transmitted imperfectly; over space, it changes gradually because it is adopted imperfectly. Boundaries, i.e., marked disruptions in stylistic gradients, represent migration or cultural borders. I, for one, am reluctant to give up this traditional view of style. There is much to recommend it, based as it is upon a simple and elegant learning-as-imitation model. In fact, what we think we know about the culture history of the Ucayali Basin is predicated upon this viewpoint. To a large extent, this view, for better or worse, creates what we think we know about world prehistory.

During the heyday of the "new archaeology," stylistic studies geared toward cultural historical reconstructions fell into disfavor. In fact, in some circles, style became a virtual pariah, a residual category of little interest, unless, of course, it was being used to show that the new archaeology could do anything that social anthropology could do, even document kinship.

The circle is complete, not in that archaeologists have returned to treating style merely as an index of space–time relations, but in that style is reasserting itself forcefully as a focal and even unifying theme within an ever-expanding archaeological agenda. Far from being a residual category, style now threatens to become all-encompassing, even omniscient. This over-zealous developement places an excessive interpretive burden upon style. A major task facing archaeologists is to pare this hypertrophied notion of style to manageable and useful size.

Two recent attempts at beginning this paring and focusing

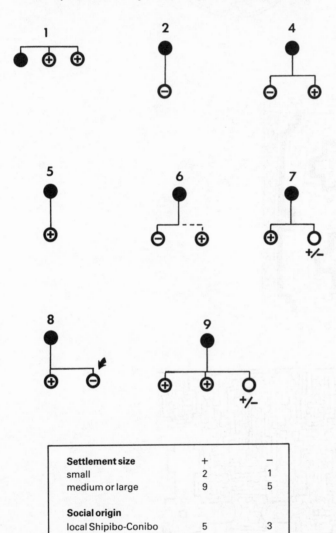

Settlement size	+	−
small	2	1
medium or large	9	5
Social origin		
local Shipibo-Conibo	5	3
non-local Shipibo-Conibo	3	2
non-Shipibo-Conibo	3	1

Fig. 9.15 A diagrammatic summary of the preceding cases (case 3, consisting of an individual artist, is excluded). Solid circles refer to teachers, open circles to students. A plus sign indicates a student whose art closely resembles that of her teacher; a minus sign indicates lack of such resemblance. Plus/minus refers to a student who shifts styles, alternately producing art that resembles, or differs significantly, from her teacher's art. The arrow in case 8 indicates that the student did not learn art primarily from her mother, but rather from unidentified outside sources. The table at the bottom plots the frequency of cases of resemblance or dissimilarity against settlement size and social origin of the artists.

task are provided by Hodder (1982b) and Wiessner (1983, 1984). Both authors properly eschew any notion of style that would have it be nothing more than a passive reflector of behavior. Both emphasize the active and strategic role of style in forging or breaking, exposing or masking social relations. For Hodder, the key factor in understanding the specific role played by style is the nature of social relations, specifically whether such relations are cooperative and emulative or, in contrast, competitive and distancing. For Wiessner, the signal concept is "social comparison," i.e., the process in which each individual assesses a social environment and then strategically "asserts" his or her separate identity within a group while simultaneously "emblematizing" group membership (compare Bateson's famed "schismogenesis," as rendered in Lathrap 1983). The ways in which Hodder and Wiessner approach style can be exemplified and partially evaluated in terms of the Ucayali experience.

Within the Ucayali Basin, two major axes of stylistic variability stand out. These axes map precisely onto the regional ecology. The first axis follows the Ucayali floodplain proper, the most productive and historically most contested zone within the Basin. The second axis is normal to the first and runs from the ecologically privileged mainstream to the more extensive, but considerably less productive, interfluvial hinterland.

Along the mainstream axis, the floodplain narrows and productive potential decreases as one moves upstream. A gradient of stylistic prestige also seems to run against the current. The Pano copy the decorative style of the Cocama; the Piro emulate the design style of their downstream neighbors, the Conibo. It is likely, although still poorly documented, that the genesis of the Shipibo-Conibo style can be understood similarly as an attempt to assimilate the flamboyant and prestigious polychrome style produced and carried upstream into the Ucayali world by the Cocama.

Relations among mainstream groups always have been, at least implicitly, competitive. The ethnohistoric record clearly indicates that geopolitical relations among mainstream polities were complex and ever-changing, oscillating between periods of nervous alliance and open, death-dealing hostility. Yet in spite of a highly nervous political landscape that is composed of clear enemies and untrusted allies, the stylistic gradient remains intact: prestige continues to run upstream; emulation continues to be directed downstream. Along the mainstream axis, stylistic phenomena appear to be relatively immune to the cooperation/competition dichotomy upon which Hodder places such singular significance. Rather, competition and stylistic emulation, not differentiation, would seem to be the rule.

The second axis running at right-angles to the mainstream tells a somewhat different story. Along this axis, gradients are replaced by relatively sharp breaks; one is either on the floodplain or not. Only in the case of the more substantial tributaries (such as the Pisqui, home of the Pisquibo), can one speak of transitions. The abruptness of the break between

mainstream and backwoods is further accentuated in mainstream ideology; one is civilized or one is not. In terms of stylized material culture, the dichotomy is expressed blatantly. Mainstream groups produce elaborate and complex art; by comparison, backwoods groups display a severely limited decorative repertoire. But this is not to say that backwoods folk are uncreative stylists whose aesthetics are limited by an impoverished interfluvial environment. For these folk, style is doing different things and is expressed accordingly in different ways. Bodies are tattooed in order to mark group membership in a permanent manner, thereby discouraging abduction into the mainstream world. Arrows and other weaponry are elaborated far beyond utilitarian needs in order to project and amplify an image of ferocity to mainstream raiders. The term "competition" does not convey adequately the sense of these stylistic decisions; tattooed bodies and fierce-looking arrows are viewed more appropriately as desperate, and often futile, stylistic expressions on the part of kidnapped, pillaged, and otherwise tyrannized peoples.

Finally, there are the Shipibo-Conibo themselves. The Shipibo-Conibo create a distinctive decorative style that is complex, that takes a long time to learn well, and that has clear-cut boundaries. Only the Piro have succeeded in partially penetrating these boundaries. For the Shipibo-Conibo, style is acting clearly as an emblem, in Wiessner's sense. Their style demarcates and signals their separate identity to others, to themselves, and to their gods.

For an emblem that is so unmistakably clear, the Shipibo-Conibo style encompasses an astonishing amount of variability. No two artists ever produce identical designs. The style is complex enough to ensure endless novelty. Style is played with, experimented with, admired, secretly ridiculed, but never copied slavishly. There is always plenty of room for individual artistic expression or, as Wiessner would say, "assertive" style.

But what factors prompt how style will be asserted? Our small sample of cases suggests an unremarkable answer to this question. In a majority of cases, students resemble teachers, usually their mothers. More interesting and germane to Wiessner's analysis, however, is that in fully one-third of all cases, such fidelity in artistic transmission is not evident. Often in these latter cases, the artist seems to be flaunting stylistically her opposition to, or separation from, an unhappy or abusive family situation, or other painful or embarrassing social circumstances. In other words, learning may lead to similarity or difference depending on context.

For the archaeologist, the Shipibo-Conibo case is instructive. Style operates simultaneously at many levels and in many contexts. This complexity cannot be flattened out to a single dimension without losing much information. At an external level, style can be a fixture that sharply marks ethnicity and that remains surprisingly impermeable to the in-flow of bodies from foreign groups. Such a crisply defined boundary separates the Shipibo-Conibo from their "backwoods" neighbors. In a different context within the same external level, style boundaries may be less abrupt and, given shifting boundaries over the time periods monitored by archaeologists, could mimic a clinal distribution. Such is the case of upstream stylistic emulation proposed for the Shipibo-Conibo and Piro. At a more narrowly focused and internal level, style can be a sensitive indicator of social position and individual experience. Among the Shipibo-Conibo, the compound of related women – which would have evident spatial correlates in the archaeological record – more often than not provides the context in which style is learned and in which adult stylistic production is carried out. As shown in several cases, however, the compound does not lead automatically to a micro-style with clear-cut boundaries. The matter is more complicated. Artists are not mechanical copycats but active and creative producers, and their production can be governed by an attempt to be different. In fact, slavish imitation is likely to mark an unskilled or socially marginal artist.

To get at these complex and multiple workings of style is a challenging and awesome task. There are no shortcuts. Archaeologists have to become intimately familiar with the style in question and how this style is situated in the full richness of contexts revealed in the archaeological record.

Notes

1. My experience has been informed by many teachers, colleagues, informants, friends, and hosts. The Shipibo-Conibo always put up with me, even though I knew so little about how to live and was pestering them persistently about self-evident or silly matters. There is an old academic adage that stealing from one source is plagiarism, from two research. The present research leans heavily on the combined efforts of the whole "Ucayali crew" assembled and then launched into the tropical forest by Donald Lathrap. We all continue to work under his spell, and, all too often, our fieldwork merely adds footnotes to his vision. To two members of the crew, I must acknowledge a special debt. From Cumancaya to Calgary, Scott Raymond and Peter Roe have been valued friends and intellectual irritants.

2. The present discussion of children's art is highly condensed from a paper originally prepared a decade ago (DeBoer 1975).

Chapter 10

Is there a unity to style?

Polly Wiessner

In this concluding chapter, the author draws upon all the chapters in the volume to make a case for a unity to style. She draws out the important theme that much research is now being directed toward answering the question, "what kind of information can we get from style?" Following on from her own previous approaches to style, Wiessner here argues for the communicative role of style, for style as non-verbal communication, and that stylistic comparison – as a behavioral process – mirrors social comparison. She discusses the different categories of style in use by the authors in this volume, and suggests that they are based on different criteria. Thus, she sees these approaches not as mutually exclusive, but as all raising questions about the particular sources of variation or levels at which style is at work.

This observation that there are different categories of style reinforces the author's belief that style, in fact, can be seen from a unified perspective as a means of non-verbal communication to negotiate identity. On the one hand, this kind of a concluding and integrating chapter is optimistic in the way that Wiessner draws on the differing postures of other contributors to make stylistic analysis viable and to present concepts of style that "make sense." On the other hand, the way in which the author must weave from among the many different contributions illustrates that the archaeological uses of style are diverse, complex, multi-faceted, and remain challenging. This chapter demands that readers consider carefully whether there is a unity to style.

Perhaps what is most striking to any reader of this volume is the diversity of the approaches to style that are taken by the contributors. The work of Conkey and of Davis provides a thorough discussion of the history of the use of style in

archaeology and in art history. There is much of value in these two chapters on the contribution as well as limitations of stylistic approaches used in archaeological inquiry. The chapters by Hodder, DeBoer, Earle, Macdonald, Sackett, and Plog concentrate on quite different issues. Amongst other things, they follow an interesting trend of breaking away from the question of "What is style?" and turning to the question "What kind of information can we get from stylistic studies?" The chapters by Conkey and Davis provide a critical understanding of the past in stylistic studies, and those chapters that reexamine the kind of information we can get from style open up new pathways for stylistic studies in the future. Here I would like to lend some unity to the volume by discussing the question "What is style?" and then draw on the diversity of the book to discuss the papers of DeBoer, Plog, Macdonald, Earle, Sackett, and Hodder in light of the question "What kinds of information can we derive from style?"

First of all, I feel that the question "What is style?" can only be answered from the viewpoint of "What is stylistic behavior?" Although it would be ideal to have a definition of style that would allow us to identify stylistic attributes in artifacts, to separate the stylistic from the functional from the technological, I doubt this will ever be possible due to the very nature of style, alas. Hodder's is one of the few chapters with an explicit discussion of what style is and he begins with the common definition that style is a "way of doing." In this he reminds us that the starting point of style is as a way of doing, or perhaps more appropriately, "doing something in a certain way." "A way of doing" alone, however, is too broad a view of style, for if principles and practices of a society, such as freedom of speech or the right to bury the dead, are considered as style, then style includes essentially all behavior and becomes a meaningless category. What is missing here is the communicative role that is so central to style, that style is a means of communication based on doing something in a certain way. I read this implication in Hodder's subsequent discussion of style: style is interpretive but it is the communicative aspects of style that inspire interpretation. Style is not power but a medium of communication that can legitimize power. If style is to be of use in archaeological analyses, it is necessary then to concentrate on the communicative aspects of style as "a way of doing" in addition to recognizing that style, amongst other things, is a part of non-verbal rather than verbal behavior. This is not to reduce style to communication, but to draw out the central aspect of style that is of use to archaeologists. It is not to say that other aspects of style cannot be defined and developed. If style is seen from the perspective of non-verbal rather than verbal communication, then many of the problems that archaeologists have with style can be elucidated. Let us take a look at style in this perspective.

Style as non-verbal communication

First of all, in non-verbal behavior many communicative signals are derived from functional counterparts, making communication closely intertwined with function. To give some basic examples often cited in ethology: sticking out one's tongue in rejection and mockery is thought to be derived from infants sticking out their tongues to reject food; kissing from kiss-feeding; and stamping one's feet in anger from aggressive approach (Eibl-Eibesfeldt 1989). Likewise, stylistic signals are frequently derived from functional elements.

A good ethnographic example would be the ceremonial axes of highland New Guinea. Before steel axes were introduced, stone work-axes were highly valued as the stone could only be obtained through trade in many areas and it took hours and hours of hard work to grind a blank into a functional axe blade. Axes were essential tools for forest clearance, as well as important weapons in battle, and thus were used in many payments, such as bridewealth and compensations. From the functional axes, ceremonial counterparts were derived. These were worn in men's belts during "sing-sings" (dances), pig exchanges, and other public rituals and events. Ceremonial axes had blades of finer quality than work axes and were largely a decorative symbol of wealth and strength. They were more fragile and could not be used to chop wood although they could be used to give somebody a good clout should a fight arise. Among the Melpa, axes had finely plaited hafting and clusters of bamboo rings attached to them and they were sometimes decorated with leaves and grasses, thus being both decoration and something to be decorated (Strathern and Strathern 1971).

Different highland groups developed their own styles of ceremonial axes. Thus a form that was designed primarily for communication about status had evolved from a functional tool.

Because many signals are derived from functional counterparts it is characteristic of non-verbal behavior that certain actions or ways of doing things take on a primarily functional role, a communicative role, or both, depending on context. For instance, one may stand close to somebody touching him or her either as an expression of affection and affiliation or to get a better view in a crowd. One may squint to keep out sharp sunlight or as part of a facial expression to convey some emotion. The same applies to material culture – artifacts may be made in a certain way for functional reasons, communicative reasons, or both. However, the fact that functional and communicative aspects of form may be interrelated does not remove the need to determine which parts of an object are important functionally and which communicatively in certain contexts. Such an understanding is critical to any interpretation.

I will return to style and function later, but first let us consider one more attribute of non-verbal communication, namely that non-verbal communication does not have the freedom of verbal communication and usually has restricted areas about which it gives information. Take facial expressions, for example. In all cultures, facial expressions are used primarily to express or mask emotions, and proxemics are used to express relative relations between people and groups. Just as it seems quite natural that proxemics express interpersonal affiliative relationships, it is not surprising that style, as communication through a way of doing things, is used to express identity. There are only limited criteria by which an identity can be attached to someone: by his natural physical appearance, by what he does, or how he does it. It appears that in all cultures people not only use ways of doing things to project their identity to others, but doing something in a new or different way spurs two questions: "Why are they doing it that way?" and "Who are they that they are doing it in such a way?" So automatic and universally found is this reaction that it suggests a deeply rooted perceptual bias for perceiving ways of doing things for both their functional efficiency and social meanings.

Finally, it should be noted here that although style has been considered for its efficiency in some studies (Wobst 1977), like other forms of non-verbal communication, style may not be the most efficient way to send a message in terms of cost, but it is often very effective. One factor that adds to its effectiveness is the fact that it can be a form of visual art and thus play on aesthetic perception in sending a message. Eibl-Eibesfeldt gives a good description of this quality of art and style:

> Art is the ability to put aesthetic perception in the service
> of communication and to use its attention binding
> structures and aesthetically rewarding nature as a means
> of conveying a message . . . when it is too easy for the
> observer to discover order, the object lacks effectiveness

and the same holds true when the object is too complex and regularity cannot be detected.

(Eibl-Eibesfeldt 1989: 673)

The contexts and ways in which style makes use of the aesthetic is a topic that deserves research in its own right. One excellent example of the role of aesthetic perception in style to project a positive image can be found in DeBoer's discussion (chapter 9, this volume) of Shipibo-Conibo ceramics.

Style and identity

While on the subject of identity, let us take a brief look at what is known about the process of identity formation because it is important to the understanding of stylistic behavior. In social psychology, the idea that the need to establish a self-image through comparing oneself to others and the desire to project this image in a positive way to others has been so strongly supported by evidence from different cultures that it is assumed to be a basic cognitive process in humans (Lemaine 1974; Tajfel 1978, 1982; Turner 1975). However, the many ways in which this may happen are recognized to be culturally and historically determined (Wetherell 1982). Through comparing themselves to others people evaluate their abilities in relative terms and develop a self-image.

Stylistic comparison mirrors social comparison. When people compare their ways of doing things with those of others, they also compare themselves with those others and decide whether to simulate, differentiate, emulate, etc.; they decide how to negotiate their relative identity. This concept is easy to grasp intuitively – when shopping for clothing or household furnishings, we avoid buying things that we associate with people we dislike or in some important way consider to be different than we are, and we gravitate towards things we associate with people we like and consider to be similar to us. A similar pattern of comparison was found among Kalahari San in an analysis of conversations about beadwork. Discussions of beadwork almost invariably led to discussions about the makers or wearers of certain styles. Positive comparisons centered around close kindred members and negative comparisons made references to more general groups of non-kin or affinal kin living at a distance (Wiessner 1984).

If the various points made in the above discussion are put together, this leaves us with the following working concept of style for archaeological studies: style is a form of non-verbal communication through doing something in a certain way that communicates information about relative identity.

Style and function

What does this working definition then imply for other views of style presented in this volume and for the categories of style presented here and elsewhere? First of all, the fact that function and communication are intertwined in most forms of non-verbal communication supports Sackett's model (1982; chapter 4, this volume) of isochrestic variation for where style resides. Since many communicative signals are derived from

functional counterparts, style must reside in both functional and decorative attributes.

Sackett's argument for a passive style also has some validity. Everything has to be done in some way and not every action is executed or interpreted with great significance attached to it. Many ways of doing are acquired gradually by enculturation, are not subject to regular stylistic and social comparison, and thus play a background role in communication. In everyday life, many ways of doing are ignored and only when somebody departs from standard procedure are questions of what, why, and who raised. At the other end of the spectrum are ways of doing to which great social and symbolic significance are attached. These are subject to active comparison and can be of major importance in communication, thus constituting an "active" style. Styles may change from passive to active if the role of the artifact changes or if social conditions bring about a need for increased communication.

I basically agree then with the concepts that Sackett presents in his papers. Where I have trouble with Sackett's ideas or papers is in his linking "isochrestic variation," a model for where style resides, with "passive style." Whether style resides in functional or decorative attributes should have absolutely no relation to whether or not it is used actively. In this issue lies the crux of our disagreement over stylistic variation in Kalahari San projectile points (Sackett 1985a; Wiessner 1985).

Categories of style

Now let us take a look at the categories of style presented in the literature: Sackett's isochrestic and iconological style (Sackett 1982), my emblematic and assertive style (Wiessner 1983) and Macdonald's "panache and protocol" (chapter 6, this volume). How do these categories fit with the views presented above? Can these categories be made to coincide with one another? Are these categories worthwhile in stylistic studies?

If one takes a close look at these three classifications of style, it becomes apparent that they are based on three different sets of criteria, each of which is a critical source of variation in style. Sackett's classification is based primarily on whether style plays an active or passive role in communication. As Sackett makes clear in this volume (chapter 4), iconological variation is essentially active style and isochrestic variation, passive style. Determining how actively or passively style is used in communication is probably the first step that must be taken in stylistic analyses. Passively used style is not subject to frequent or intensive comparison and thus social boundaries reflected by it may not keep up with changing social relations. Conversely, if the role of an artifact switches from a passive to an active one, then changes in stylistic boundaries may take place with little corresponding social change. This occurs with Kalahari projectile points after the introduction of metal (Wiessner 1985).

My categories of emblemic and assertive style are based on quite different criteria (Wiessner 1983), with by far the most important of these being specificity of referent. All styles have social referents, some having very specific ones (such as an emblem that represents a football team) and others (such as styles of clothing) much more vague associations. Styles with distinct referents are those that I call emblemic and those with more vague associations I call assertive. Styles without distinct referents that work through association are by no means the same as passive styles. They may be both active and effective means of communication giving powerful aesthetic impressions and stirring strong feelings through associations.

Specificity of referent has an important effect on the nature of stylistic and social comparison and how easily styles are adopted by others. Specificity of referent can and often does change as styles are used in new contexts and take on new meanings. One example can be seen in Hodder's description of Johnny Rotten and his present use of the swastika compared to its use in the past. Another modern example is the change in the context in which blue jeans have been worn during this century and the corresponding associations made with them. Blue jeans or dungarees began as workmen's clothing and were associated with practicality and work. In the 1960s they were adopted as one of many symbols of the youth revolution and in the 1970s and 1980s they were readapted as designer jeans, taking on a much wider, more varied and more vague set of associations.

Macdonald classifies style into panache or protocol on the basis of the level at which comparison occurs. This is a different criterion from that which Sackett and I have used. As with activeness or passiveness of style, the level at which comparisons are made is also an important source of variation in style. Comparison at the individual level will result in different stylistic distributions and rates of change from those at the group level. Conditions and contexts which bring out the use of style to negotiate individual or group identity will be mentioned later. The above three classifications then are based on different criteria, each of which is an important source of variation in style, and may be affected by different conditions, require different methods of analysis, and yield different kinds of information.

For these reasons, it may be best to move away from classification of style and see style from a unified perspective as a means of non-verbal communication to negotiate identity. Then at the beginning of stylistic analysis, the following three questions can be asked: does an attribute bearing style appear to play an active or passive role in communication? is it more likely to have had a distinct or vague referent? does it appear to express individual identity, group identity, or both?

What kinds of information are contained in style?

If style is non-verbal communication about identity through a way of doing, for archaeologists, it must be seen as communication during history and prehistory. The task of the archaeologist is to use all available historical and contextual information to assist in determining what was being communicated in the past. Five of the chapters in this volume –

Plog's, Macdonald's, Earle's, DeBoer's, and Hodder's – see style as communication in the past and ask the question of what style was used to express. Interestingly, each chapter uses style to derive somewhat different but related kinds of information about the past. Here I would like to discuss some of the ideas presented in these chapters as they greatly expand on traditional uses of style in archaeology.

Style, social boundaries and interaction

Aside from the use of style to establish chronology, the use of style to obtain information on prehistoric groups, boundaries, and interaction has been the most common use of style in archaeology. DeBoer and Davis (chapters 10 and 3, this volume) both give interesting discussions of style and social boundaries, but here I would like to concentrate on Plog's analysis (chapter 7) as it is an interesting archaeological re-analysis of style through time. Plog recognizes that the problem of many stylistic analyses lies in our simplistic assumptions about style: in particular, in the failure to recognize that as social systems evolve in complexity, so do the determinants of style. It is in this light that he re-analyzes the material from the southwestern United States.

In Plog's discussion, he raises two important sources of variation mentioned above, the passive or active role of style and the distinctiveness of referent. First he argues that the very broad distributions of style found at the beginning of his study period could be the result of style in pottery playing a very passive role and that subsequent changes, such as increase in population density or growth in pottery production, could alter the role of style without necessarily being accompanied by major changes in social groups. The latter is certainly the case for stylistic changes in Kalahari San beaded headbands (Wiessner 1984).

Plog points out that changes in stylistic boundaries do not necessarily have to correspond to changes in areas inhabited by different cultures but could be related to the changing roles of style or to social distance between members of one society. In his case study, it becomes clear that it is usually not possible to determine the source of stylistic variation from patterns of similarity or differentiation alone. For this, one must make use of all available contextual and historical data, a point made by Davis (chapter 3, this volume).

Plog goes on to mention the second major source of stylistic variation mentioned above, specificity of referent. Through time, the Dogoszhi style appears to take on a more distinct referent, becoming "iconographic." He interprets this style as an internal marker of higher or different social status due to its association with ceremonial structures. He also finds that style becomes much less stable after AD 1000 with increasing diversity of attributes. Plog attributes these trends to the establishment of social ties across a broader region. This is indeed one possibility but it also may be due to the third source of variation discussed above, the level at which comparison takes place.

In the face of increasing population density, individuals

often feel the need to distinguish themselves from others and to express greater individuality (Wiessner 1984). This trend would be encouraged by new economic opportunities, including broader exchange ties. Thus, diversity could be generated by expansion of exchange ties, a growing need for individual expression, or some sort of interaction between the two. The appearance of a style with a more distinct referent in the Dogoszhi style, apparent increasing individual expression in style, and possibly a more active role for style in pottery raises the question of whether these were due to social change alone or whether there was a corresponding change in the way pottery was used. Since the Dogoszhi style is found on ceremonial sites the possibility of a new role for other styles of pottery must also be considered. With the realization that the determinants of style become more complex as social systems evolve (Plog, chapter 7, this volume), stylistic studies will break away from simplistic analyses involving one-to-one relations between style and social organization and make a much greater contribution to our understanding of social change in the past.

Style, the individual and society

Macdonald's chapter brings up one of the more interesting potential uses of style in archaeology, the separation of individual (panache) from group (protocol) expression to discover changing relations between the individual and groups in a society. Macdonald focuses primarily on methodological considerations to provide the tools for examining stylistic variability in archaeological data and separating that generated at the individual level from that generated at the group level. Here I would like to expand on the kinds of information we can get from style by looking at individual and group expression.

There is a good theoretical basis in identity theory for arguing that style should project information about both individual and group identity. As mentioned earlier, individuals in all cultures have been shown to possess a strong desire to create a self-image through social comparison and to project this to others in a positive way. Self-images have two components, a personal one and a social one. Social identity is important in that individuals are unable to form self-images in the absence of an identity derived from membership in one or more groups (Tajfel 1982). Conversely, an element of personal identity seems equally important and when put in situations of extreme conformity, individuals experience discomfort and strive to differentiate themselves from similar others (Fromkin 1972; Lemaine, Kasterztein, and Personnaz 1978). Social and personal identity may be "switched on" by certain situations. Since style is one medium of projecting identity, one would expect both personal and social identity to be expressed in style. In fact, a very large part of being stylish does seem to involve playing individual against group expression in innovative ways.

The relation of the individual to society is an issue that has been widely discussed in the social sciences. In pre-class societies as well as in class societies, the conflict between the individual and the group is one of the driving forces of social change. As Macdonald points out, certain social conditions such as individual competition may bring out panache (individual) as opposed to protocol (group) stylistic expression. I have suggested elsewhere (Wiessner 1988) some other conditions that might "switch on" a sense of individual or group expression. Situations that switch on group identity include fear, inter-group competition and aggression, need for cooperation to reach certain goals, and imposed political control requiring group action. Those situations that could switch on personal identity would be inter-individual competition, options for individual economic gain, and breakdown in the social order that would require individuals to seek solutions for their own problems, amongst others. Using data from changing house decorations in Vietnam, ceremonial dress at various occasions in New Guinea, and beadwork styles from Kalahari San, very simple analyses of increasing diversity have yielded some promising results (Wiessner 1988). In all three cases, changing or different relations between the individual and society do become apparent in analysis of the stylistic data.

DeBoer's chapter (chapter 9) gives a particularly interesting perspective on style and individual and group relations because of his study of the learning process in acquiring skills for Shipibo-Conibo pottery. Through studying the process of design acquisition in children he isolates a limited number of design elements that are used to express Shipibo-Conibo identity. Along with these elements is an organizing principle that these elements should be combined in innovative and aesthetically pleasing ways to conform to Shipibo-Conibo style. Since Shipibo-Conibo style is admired and thus expresses a positive group identity, women from other roots of origin and with different degrees of acculturation conform to the basic elements and principles of the style. Within this basic style, however, is great individual expression and variation. Through his study of individual artists and their social situations in different family compounds, DeBoer finds that individual stylistic differentiation within the family is often associated with the desire to "escape." In other words, women who do not gain a positive image from their family situation often try to express their own individual positive identity.

DeBoer mentions that the distinctive decorative style that marks virtually all classes of material culture today cannot be securely identified before the mid-nineteenth century and that since then it has flourished. It would be interesting to look at the florescence of Shipibo-Conibo style in terms of changing relations between the individual and society through time. From looking at changes in style through time and corresponding contextual conditions, it is often easier to identify sources of variation than in a static ethnoarchaeological perspective. As Plog's and Hodder's studies also show, when one sees what changes occur through time and what factors these are associated with, it is possible to get further insight into the sources of stylistic variation.

Although the individual may be difficult to recognize in

archaeological studies, increasing individual expression should not. With more sophisticated methods of analysis such as those discussed by Macdonald (chapter 6), the changing relations between the individual and society should be one of the more promising areas of stylistic studies.

Style, status and power

In his chapter (chapter 8), Earle brings up the use of style to mark social boundaries and distance within a group rather than between groups – in other words, the use of style to confer and support status. The emergence of great styles in civilizations has long been discussed by archaeologists, but few systematic studies have centered on the question, "What kinds of information can we get from styles marking social distance within a group?"

Style has a number of inherent properties that make it a very effective means of marking status positions and social boundaries within a hierarchy. First of all, as a means of visual communication, style can catch the observers' attention and make a deep aesthetic impression while simultaneously sending messages concerning status and power. Style can make use of extravagance and display in a way that perhaps no other means of communication can. It is not surprising then that, more often than not, styles conferring status and power have to do with objects requiring substantial wealth, labor, or appropriate social ties to acquire. Styles supporting status are thus often an effective, although hardly an efficient, means of transmitting information at a low cost, as the cloaks of half a million bird feathers worn by Hawaiian chiefs illustrate. In addition, styles in many artifacts have a permanence that other forms of communication lack, lending an impression of solidity to a position. Style also has the potential to convey several impressions at once, one modifying, supporting, or accentuating the other.

Styles acting to convey status and power may, in many cases, be easier to identify and interpret than those delimiting boundaries between groups. This is because, as Earle mentions, they are often highly symbolic with distinct referents, are actively used and are found only in certain contexts. In addition, they are often incorporated into luxury items.

Complex societies, of course, can have many different forms of organization and the nature of status positions can vary radically from one to another. From a regional perspective, Earle shows how style is used as communication to legitimize chiefdoms, thus facilitating interaction and exchange through leaders sharing common bonding through styles. This is one of many possible strategies to use style to confer and maintain power and there is a great need for ethnoarchaeological studies to make explicit how style is used in different social strategies. For example, styles associated with inherited and fixed status positions may exhibit less variation than those associated with attained ones. Competition for social status may be expressed through stylistic imitation and emulation, with those striving for status imitating those in high status positions and the latter differentiating to maintain the

social difference. Earle's chapter is one carefully worked out example of how style is used in social and political power struggles. Further studies in other complex societies will elucidate many others, particularly since in this area of negotiating identity it is possible to take fullest advantage of the attributes of style as a means of non-verbal communication.

Style and the nature of relationships

Plog's, Macdonald's, DeBoer's, and Earle's chapters (7, 6, 9 and 8) have discussed three kinds of information that we can get from style: information about groups, boundaries and interaction; that on changing relations between the individual and society; and that on status and social hierarchies. Given that data are adequate for such analyses and that it is possible to get some control over sources of variation such as activeness of style, specificity of referent and level of comparison, still we get no more than a skeleton of the relationships that may have existed in the past. We may find indications of changing social boundaries, of increasing or decreasing group or individual expression, or of the existence and development of status positions, but still we will know little of the nature of these relations. DeBoer's chapter gives us an excellent idea of the multiplicity of relationships that can be expressed in style. It is here that Hodder's approach (chapter 5) has much to add to our understanding of the symbolism behind style and thereby puts some skin and flesh onto the skeleton of social relationships.

There are essentially two levels at which stylistic studies can proceed. The first involves the analysis of style according to expression of similarities versus differences, simplicity and uniformity versus complexity and diversity, with little attention being paid to underlying symbolism. The second level involves trying to understand the meaning of the symbolism behind style to grasp the underlying nature of social relationships. The latter is made possible by some of the properties of style discussed by Hodder: the relative nature of style in that it relates an individual event to a greater whole and to the interpretive and multivalent aspects of style.

Let us first look at the interpretive and multivalent quality of style. In choosing styles, people consciously or subconsciously play on symbols to express relative identity. This could not be more evident than in Hodder's discussion of Johnny Rotten and Boy George. The intricate meanings, implications, and associations attached to symbols make it possible to express relationships far more complex than those of mere similarity and difference. In addition, as mentioned earlier, style – as a form of visual art – can play on aesthetic perception to be a particularly effective means of communication. The extent to which style makes use of aesthetic perception, of course, will depend on how actively it is used in communication.

The interpretive quality of style may stem from several related factors. The first is the perceptual bias in humans to interpret ways of doing things for their social and functional meanings, an observation also made by Sackett and Hodder.

The second is style's role as a visual art that makes use of aesthetic perception, which in turn challenges the observer to seek multiple meanings. Art in many tribal societies, as well as in the works of such artists as Escher, conceals several aspects in one item, so that once one aspect is discovered, the observer is challenged to go on and see what else might be found.

Finally, style in the service of communication about identity makes use of ambiguity to facilitate certain social strategies. In many social interactions, it is most effective to avoid laying one's cards on the table, but rather to convey ambiguity and raise questions about one's identity, leaving room for the creation of a wide variety of relationships. It is thus essential in any attempts to interpret the symbolism behind style that the multivalent and ambiguous quality of style be recognized.

Another of the salient properties of style is that it is relative. This, I would argue, comes from the process underlying stylistic development and stylistic change, that of social and stylistic comparison. In choosing styles individuals compare themselves to others in the society or the society as a whole and communicate stylistically their position relative to that of others. They relate their individual or group identity to that of the greater society. In any society, there is a limited number of central relations of importance such as cooperation, competition, or separation and tension between the sexes, egalitarian, or competitive or structured status relations between individuals, and so on. There are also accompanying central metaphors to express these. Comparison relates back to these central relations and metaphors and as a result they appear again and again in different classes of data. Analyses of different sets of archaeological data, then, should lead back to these central relations and metaphors, giving some basis for accepting or refuting symbolic interpretations of one data set.

In principle, then, style should contain information on the nature of relationships within and between groups if the symbols that style plays upon can be interpreted. In this respect I fully agree with Hodder's overall point that there is much more than objective facts to be obtained from stylistic analyses. However, his argument that "archaeological analyses of style would benefit, first, from rejection of an 'objective', quantitative and descriptive approach" (Hodder, chapter 5, this volume: 50) could eventually lead to little more than writing fairy tales about the past. Meaningful interpretation of stylistic symbolism involves far more than intuitively reconstructing the "wholes" of a past society as Hodder does in his discussion.

Even in an ethnographic study with full information on history and context available, it can be very difficult to discover the symbolic meanings underlying style. When asked what something means, informants can often not say, but only convey a certain feeling associated with a style because much of stylistic symbolism works on association. Other symbols may once have had a distinct referent that became generalized or lost over generations of reproduction. Dreary as it is, the only solution seems to be careful descriptions and analysis – such as

in the work of Plog and DeBoer – of as many different classes of artifacts as possible, the linking of these with information on economy, exchange, politics, settlement patterns, etc., and in the end, an attempt at interpretation of meaning underlying central symbols and metaphor.

To illustrate this, let us take a look at Hodder's example:

> I have argued (Hodder 1987) that in the Neolithic women were seen as both the creators and destroyers of social life, as both creative and dangerous. It could be further suggested that, since evidence from cemeteries such as Nitra (Sherratt 1982) implies that older men often fulfilled dominant social roles, the link between women and the domestic family unit set up a conflict between women as producers and reproducers of the individual family entity and wider social and political constructs dominated by men.
>
> (chapter 5, above: 50)

For the sake of argument, let me suggest another interpretation. In many tribal societies, ancestor worship is based on the idea that reciprocal obligations do not end with death, but that it is necessary to maintain relations with the spirits of the dead similar to those with the living to keep up balance and harmony in a society. The association of women in the domestic context with symbols of death then does not necessarily mean that women are the destroyers of social life, but could represent women's role in perpetuating relations with the ancestors.

In addition, the role of women as producers and reproducers in the private realm and that of men in the political and social or public realm does not necessarily imply conflict. This division of labor may just as well be a solution to potential conflict. It is possible that the central conflict was between conflicting men's roles, that is, competition between individuals within the group to attain status on the one hand and competition between groups, which requires cooperation and group loyalty on the other. Women may have played a mediating role, acting as links between groups through marriage ties and as the ones who maintained ties with spirits of past generations.

Needless to say, my interpretation has no more validity than Hodder's. The point I am trying to make here is that only careful quantitative and descriptive analyses can lead us to accept one interpretation as being more plausible than the other. In this case, some relevant questions might be:

(1) What were the different sizes of social units marked by stylistic boundaries during different periods? Is there evidence of strong differentiation and perhaps competition between these? What was the settlement pattern within these units?
(2) Is there strong individual expression in either male or female items? In male items, is extravagance used, suggesting competition for status?

(3) Through time does individual expression in artifacts increase or decrease?

(4) Do symbols and styles in male and female realms show contrast and opposition?

These are just a few of several possible questions that might lend some degree of verification to one interpretation or another. If interpretation of symbols used in styles is to be of value to archaeology, then it must be founded in rigorous analysis of all available data and clearly tied to the results of these. If this is done, it may indeed be possible for archaeologists to provide interpretive insights into general symbols and metaphors of ways of doing, thinking, or being to which individual events were referred in the past.

In conclusion, style does have an underlying unity, although its manifestations and the relations it is used to negotiate are many. One can see this very clearly in an event such as a ceremonial dance in the highlands of New Guinea. All of the items worn by dancers have some meaning in communicating information about identity. Group boundaries are clearly delineated by styles of ceremonial dress, although the dress of neighboring groups shows mutual influence. The ability of dancers from one group to obtain similar ornaments of value simultaneously displays group wealth and strength. This representation is reinforced by the strong aesthetic impression conveyed by the line of dancers.

In contrast, individual variations in certain points of dress may express ingenuity, elegance, wealth, or status, which stands in opposition to group harmony. This tension may be felt by observers. Individual items of dress play very different roles in communication. Some items, such as frontal aprons, are rather standardized with little attention being paid to them other than that they are hung properly and move in rhythm to the dance. Other aspects, such as face paintings, may convey much more active messages. Some ornaments may bear decorations with distinct messages, such as a cluster of leaves in an armband as a signal to a girlfriend to enter the dance line next to her boyfriend. Other ornaments, such as large shells, may have no distinct meaning but only give an impression of greater size to the dancer, indirectly indicating power and strength. The amount of information contained in the various items of self-decoration is so great that Strathern and Strathern (1971) have devoted an entire book to the subject. An overall analysis of symbols would lead to one or two central metaphors: one involving strength, wealth, size, and power, and another involving the contradiction between the individual and the group so central to highland societies with fierce inter-individual and inter-group competition and aggression.

In leaving a ceremonial dance, one is struck by a number of impressions about style. The first is the unity of style as a means of communication about identity. The next is the vast amount of information on social relationships contained in style. The last, for an archaeologist, is a realization of the difficulties involved in obtaining this information from analysis of what, if anything, would be left as archaeological materials.

This volume as one of the first devoted solely to the subject of style, breaks away from traditional uses of style and explores the broad potential of stylistic studies within the limits of archaeological data.

REFERENCES CITED

Aberle, David 1960 The influence of linguistics on early culture and personality theory. In *Essays in the Science of Culture: In Honor of Leslie White*, edited by G. Dole and R. Carneiro, pp. 1–49. New York: Crowell-Collier

Ackerman, James S. 1963 Style. In *Art and Archaeology*, edited by James S. Ackerman and Rhys Carpenter, pp. 164–86. Englewood Cliffs, NJ: Prentice-Hall

Alexander, N. and E. McDill 1976 Selection and allocation within schools: some causes and consequences of curriculum placement. *American Sociological Review* 41: 963–80

Alland, Alexander, Jr. 1983 *Playing with Form*. New York: Columbia University Press

Alpers, Svetlana 1979 Style is what you make it: the visual arts once again. In *The Concept of Style*, edited by Berel Lang, pp. 95–117. Philadelphia: University of Pennsylvania Press

Alwin, D. 1976 Assessing school effects: some identities. *Sociology of Education* 49: 294–303

Arnold, J. and A. Ford 1980 A statistical examination of settlement patterns at Tikal, Guatemala. *American Antiquity* 45: 713–26

Bach, Kent 1970 Part of what a picture is. *British Journal of Aesthetics* 10: 119–37

Barthes, Roland 1983 *The Fashion System*, trans. M. Ward and R. Howard. New York: Hill and Wang

Bass, W., D. Evans and R. Jantz 1971 *The Leavenworth Site Cemetery: Archaeology and Physical Anthropology*. University of Kansas Publications in Anthropology, 2. Lawrence, KS

Baxandall, Michael 1972 *Painting and Experience in Fifteenth-Century Italy*. Oxford: Oxford University Press
    1979 The language of art history. *New Literary History* 10: 453–65
    1980 *The Limewood Sculptors of Renaissance Germany*. New Haven: Yale University Press

    1985 *Patterns of Intention: The Historical Explanation of Pictures*. New Haven: Yale University Press

Beals, Ralph L., George W. Brainerd, and Watson Smith 1945 *Archaeological Studies in Northeast Arizona*. University of California Publications in American Archaeology and Ethnology, 44. Berkeley, CA

Beckner, M. 1959 *The Biological Way of Thought*. New York: Columbia University Press

Bender, Barbara 1978 Gatherer-hunter to farmer: a social perspective. *World Archaeology* 10: 204–22

Benson, E. 1968 (editor) *Dumbarton Oaks Conference on the Olmec*. Washington, DC: Dumbarton Oaks

Bergman, Roland W. 1974 Shipibo subsistence in the Upper Amazon rainforest. Unpublished Ph.D. dissertation, University of Wisconsin, Madison

Bernal, I. 1968 View of Olmec culture. In *Dumbarton Oaks Conference on the Olmec*, edited by E. Benson, pp. 135–42. Washington, DC: Dumbarton Oaks

Bialostocki, Jan 1961 Das Modusproblem in den Bildenden Künsten. *Zeitschrift für Kunstgeschichte* 24: 128–41

Binford, Lewis R. 1962 Archaeology as anthropology. *American Antiquity* 28: 217–25
    1965 Archaeological systematics and the study of cultural process. *American Antiquity* 31: 204–10
    1972 *An Archaeological Perspective*. New York: Academic Press
    1973 Interassemblage variability – the Mousterian and the "functional" argument. In *The Explanation of Culture Change*, edited by C. Renfrew. London: Duckworth
    1986 An Alyawara day: making men's knives and beyond. *American Antiquity* 51: 547–62

Blalock, H. 1972 *Social Statistics*. New York: McGraw-Hill

Blanton, R., S. Kowalski, G. Feinman, and J. Appel 1981 *Ancient Mesoamerica*. Cambridge: Cambridge University Press

Blau, P. 1960 Structural effects. *American Sociological Review* 25: 178–93

Bloom, Harold 1973 *Anxiety of Influence*. New York: Oxford University Press

Boas, Franz 1955 *Primitive Art*. New York: Dover Publications

Bordes, F. and D. de Sonneville-Bordes 1970 The significance of variability in Palaeolithic assemblages. *World Archaeology* 2: 61–73

Bourdieu, Pierre 1977 *An Outline of a Theory of Practice*. Cambridge: Cambridge University Press

Brackenridge, H. 1962 *Views of Louisiana together with a Journal of a Voyage up the Missouri River in 1811*. Chicago: Quadrangle Books

Bradley, R. 1984. *The Social Foundations of Prehistoric Britain: Themes and Variations in the Archaeology of Power*. London: Longman

Braun, David P. 1977 Middle Woodland–early Late Woodland social change in the prehistoric central midwestern US. Unpublished Ph.D. dissertation, University of Michigan

1985 Absolute seriation: a time-series approach. In *For Concordance in Archaeological Analysis: Bridging Data Structure, Quantitative Technique, and Theory*, edited by C. Carr, pp. 509–39. Kansas City: Westport Publishers

Braun, David and Stephen Plog 1982 Evolution of "tribal" social networks: theory and prehistoric North American evidence. *American Antiquity* 47: 504–25

Bray, Tamara 1985 The past from an archaeological perspective. Manuscript on file, Department of Anthropology, State University of New York, Binghamton

Breternitz, David A. 1966 *An Appraisal of Tree-Ring Dated Pottery in the Southwest*. Anthropological Papers of the University of Arizona, 10

Brigham, W. 1899 *Hawaiian Feather Work*. Bernice P. Bishop Museum Memoir 1 (4). Honolulu: Bernice P. Bishop Museum Press

1903 Additional notes on Hawaiian feather work. *Bernice P. Bishop Museum Memoir* 1 (5): 437–53.

1918 Additional notes on Hawaiian feather work. *Bernice P. Bishop Museum Memoir* 7 (1): 1–64

Brown, J. 1976 The southern cult reconsidered. *Midcontinental Journal of Archaeology* 1:115–35

Brown, K. 1984 Hallucinogenic mushrooms, jade obsidian, and the Guatemalan highlands: what did the Olmec really want? In *Trade and Exchange in Early Mesoamerica*, edited by K. Hirth, p. 215–33. Albuquerque: University of New Mexico Press

Buck, P. 1944 The local evolution of Hawaiian feather capes and cloaks. *Journal of the Polynesian Society* 53: 1–16

1957 *Arts and Crafts of Hawaii*. Honolulu: Bernice P. Bishop Museum Press

Burgin, Victor 1986 The absence of presence: conceptualism and postmodernism. In *The End of Art Theory: Criticism and Postmodernity*, by Victor Burgin, pp. 29–50. Atlantic Highlands, NJ: Humanities Press International

Campbell, E. and N. Alexander 1965 Structural effects and interpersonal relationships. *American Journal of Sociology* 71: 284–89

Cashdan, Elizabeth 1985 Coping with risk: reciprocity among the Basawa of northern Botswana. *Man* 20: 454–74

Cauvin, J. 1972 *Religious néolithiques de Syro-Palestine*. Saint-André-de-Cruzières: Centre de Recherches d'Ecologie et de Préhistoire

1978 *Les Premiers Villages de Syrie-Palestine du IXème au VIIème millénaire*. Lyon: Maison de l'Orient Méditerranéen Ancien

Chibnick, M. 1985 The use of statistics in sociocultural anthropology. *Annual Review of Anthropology* 14: 135–57

Childe, V. Gordon 1949 Neolithic house types in temperate Europe. *Antiquity* 23: 129–40

Clark, Timothy 1973 *The Image of the People*. London: Thames and Hudson

1985 *The Painting of Modern Life*. New York: Knopf

Clarke, David L. 1968 *Analytical Archaeology*. London: Methuen

1973 Archaeology: the loss of innocence. *Antiquity* 47 (185): 6–18

1983 *Analytical Archaeology*, 2nd ed. New York: Columbia University Press

Clifford, James 1986 Introduction: partial truths. In *Writing Culture: The Poetics and Politics of Ethnography*, edited by James Clifford and George Marcus, pp. 1–26. Berkeley: University of California Press

Coe, M. 1972 Olmec jaguars and Olmec kings. In *Cult of the Feline*, edited by E. Benson, pp. 1–12. Washington, DC: Dumbarton Oaks

1974 Photogrammetry and the ecology of Olmec civilization. In *Aerial Photography in Archaeology*, edited by Evon Vogt, pp. 1–33. Cambridge, MA: Harvard University Press

Cohen, Abner 1974 *The Two-dimensional Man: An Essay on the Anthropology of Power and Symbolism in Complex Society*. London: Routledge & Kegan Paul

Cohen, J. and P. Cohen 1975 *Applied Multiple Regression Correlation Analysis for the Behavioral Sciences*. Hillsdale, NJ: Erlbaum

Collingwood, R. G. 1929 The history of historical cycles. *Antiquity* 1: 311–25, 435–46

1946 *The Idea of History*. Oxford: Oxford University Press

Colton, Harold S. 1939 *Prehistoric Culture Units and their Relationships in Northern Arizona*. Museum of Northern Arizona Bulletin, 17

1955 *Pottery Types of the Southwest*. Museum of Northern Arizona Ceramic Series, 3B

Colton, Harold S. and Lyndon L. Hargrave 1937 *Handbook of Northern Arizona Pottery Types*. Museum of Northern Arizona Bulletin, 11

Conkey, Margaret W. 1978a Style and information in cultural evolution: toward a predictive model for the Paleolithic. In *Social Archaeology*, edited by Charles L. Redman *et al.*, pp. 61–85. New York: Academic Press

1978b An analysis of design structure: variability among Magdalenian engraved bones from north coastal Spain. Unpublished Ph.D. dissertation, University of Chicago

1980 Context, structure, and efficacy in Paleolithic art and design. In *Symbol as Sense*, edited by M. L. Foster and S. H. Brandes, pp. 225–48. New York: Academic Press

1987 New approaches in the search for meaning? A review of research in Paleolithic "art." *Journal of Field Archaeology*, 14: 413–430.

1989 The use of diversity in stylistic analysis. In *Quantifying Diversity in Archaeology*, edited by G. T. Jones and R. Leonard, pp. 121–32. Cambridge: Cambridge University Press

Cowgill, G. 1977 The trouble with significance tests and what we can do about it. *American Antiquity* 42: 350–68

Csikszentmihalyi, M. and E. Rochberg-Halton 1981 *The Meaning of Things*. Cambridge: Cambridge University Press

Cummins, T. 1984 Kinshape: the design of the Hawaiian feather cloak. *Art History* 7: 1–20

D'Altroy, T. and T. Earle 1985 Staple finance and wealth finance in the Inka political economy. *Current Anthropology* 26:187–206

d'Ans, André-Marcel 1973 Reclasificación de las Lenguas Pano y Datos Glotochronológicos para la Etnohistoria de la Amazone Peruana. *Revista del Museo Nacional* 39: 349–69. Lima: Museo Nacional

Danson, Edward 1957 *An Archaeological Survey of West Central New Mexico and East Central Arizona*. Papers of the Peabody Museum of American Archaeology and Ethnology, 44 (1)

Danto, Arthur C. 1981 *The Transfiguration of the Commonplace*. New York: Columbia University Press

David, Nicholas, and Hilke Henning 1972 *The Ethnography of Pottery: A Fulani Case Seen in Archaeological Perspective*. Reading, MA: Addison-Wesley

Davis, Whitney 1982 The canonical tradition in ancient Egyptian art. *Res* 4: 20–46

    1986a Positivism and idealism in the study of Egyptian art. In *Proceedings of the Fourth International Congress of Egyptology, Munich 1985*, edited by Dietrich Wildung

    1986b The origins of image making. *Current Anthropology* 27: 193–215

    1986c Comments on Nathalie Franklin, "Stochastic vs. emblemic: an archaeologically useful method for the analysis of style in Australian rock art," *Rock Art Research* 3 (2): 124–25

    n.d. *Seeing through Culture: The Possibility of the History of Art*

Dean, Jeffrey S., Robert C. Euler, George J. Gumerman, Fred Plog, Richard H. Hevley, and Thor N. V. Karlstrom 1985 Human behavior, demography, and paleoenvironment on the Colorado Plateau. *American Antiquity* 50: 537–54

DeBoer, Warren R. 1975 The ontogeny of Shipibo art: variations on a cross. Paper presented at the 74th Annual Meeting of the American Anthropological Association, San Francisco

    1981 Buffer zones in the cultural ecology of aboriginal Amazonia: an ethnohistorical approach. *American Antiquity* 46(2): 364–77

    1983 The archaeological record as preserved death assemblage, in *Archaeological Hammers and Theories*, edited by James A. Moore and Arthur S. Keene, pp. 22–37. New York: Academic Press

    1984 The last pottery show: system and sense in ceramic studies, in *The Many Dimensions of Pottery*, edited by Sander E. van der Leeuw and Alison C. Pritchard. Amsterdam: Albert Egges van Griffen Instituut voor Prae- en Protohistorie, Universiteit van Amsterdam

DeBoer, Warren R., and Donald W. Lathrap 1979 The making and breaking of Shipibo-Conibo ceramics, in *Ethnoarchaeology: Implications of Ethnography for Archaeology*, edited by Carol Kramer, pp. 102–38. New York: Columbia University Press

DeBoer, Warren R., and James A. Moore 1982 The measurement and meaning of stylistic diversity, *Nawpa Pacha* 20: 147–62. Berkeley: Institute of Andean Studies

Deetz, James 1965 *The Dynamics of Stylistic Change in Arikara Ceramics*. Illinois Studies in Anthropology, 4. Urbana: University of Illinois Press

    1967 *Invitation to Archaeology*. Garden City, NY: Natural History Press

    1977 *In Small Things Forgotten*. Garden City, NY: Doubleday

Deetz, James, and Edwin Dethlefsen 1965 The Doppler effect and archaeology: a consideration of spatial aspects of seriation. *Southwestern Journal of Anthropology* 21: 196–206

Dellenbach, Marguerite 1932 Céramique des Xeberos (Pérou). *Journal de la Société des Américanistes* 24: 221–23

Derrida, Jacques 1970 Structure, sign, and play in the discourse of human sciences. In *Structuralist Controversy: the Languages of Criticism and the Sciences of Man*, edited by Richard Macksey and Eugenio Donato, pp. 244–72. Baltimore: Johns Hopkins University Press

    1974 *Of Grammatology*. Baltimore: Johns Hopkins University Press

DeWalt, B. and P. Pelto 1985 Microlevel/macrolevel linkages: an introduction to the issues and a framework for analysis. In *Micro and Macro Levels of Analysis in Anthropology: Issues in Theory and Research*, edited by B. DeWalt and P. Pelto, p. 1–21. Boulder, CO: Westview Press

Dickie, George 1974 *Art and the Aesthetic*. Ithaca, NY: Cornell University Press

Dohrn-Ihmig, M. 1973 Gruppen in der jungeren nordwestlichen Linearbandkeramik. *Archäologisches Korrespondenzblatt* 3: 279–87

Dole, Gertrude E. 1974 Types of Amahuaca pottery and techniques of its construction. *Ethnologische Zeitschrift Zürich* 1: 145–57

Donnan, Christopher 1978 *Moche Art of Peru*. Los Angeles: Museum of Cultural History, University of California

Doreian, P. and N. Hummon 1976 *Modeling social processes*. New York: Elsevier

Dougherty, Janet and James Fernandez 1981 Introduction. In Symbolism and Cognition, I (special issue), *American Ethnologist* (3): 413–21

Drennan, R. 1976 Religious and social evolution in Formative Mesoamerica. In *The Early Mesoamerican Village*, edited by Kent Flannery, pp. 345–68. New York: Academic Press

Drennan, R. and J. Nowack 1984 Exchange and sociopolitical development in the Tehuacan valley. In *Trade and Exchange in Early Mesoamerica*, edited by K. Hirth, pp. 147–56. Albuquerque: University of New Mexico Press

Drucker, P. 1981 On the nature of Olmec polity. In *The Olmec and their Neighbors*, edited by E. Benson, pp. 29–47. Washington, DC: Dumbarton Oaks

Drummond, Lee 1981 The serpent's children: semiotics of cultural genesis in Arawak and Trobriand myth. *American Ethnologist* 8 (3): 633–60

Dunnell, Robert 1978 Style and function: a fundamental dichotomy. *American Antiquity* 43: 192–202

    1980 Evolutionary theory and archaeology. In *Advances in Archaeological Method and Theory*, 3 (edited by M. B. Schiffer): 35–99. New York: Academic Press

    1982 Science, social science and common sense: the agonizing dilemma of modern archaeology. *Journal of Anthropological Research* 38(1): 1–25

    1986 Five decades of American archaeology. In *American Archaeology, Past and Future*, edited by D. J. Meltzer, D. D. Fowler, and J. A. Sabloff, pp. 23–49. Washington and London: Smithsonian Institution

Eagleton, Terry 1983 *Literary Theory*. Minneapolis: University of Minnesota Press

Earle, T. 1976 A nearest-neighbor analysis of two Formative settlement systems. In *The Early Mesoamerican Village*, edited by Kent Flannery, pp. 213–32. New York: Academic Press

    1978 *Economic and Social Organization of a Complex Chiefdom*. Anthropological Paper 63. Ann Arbor: Museum of Anthropology, University of Michigan

    1987 Specialization and the production of wealth: Hawaiian chiefdoms and the Inka empire. In *Specialization, Exchange and Complex Society*, edited by E. Brumfiel and T. Earle, p. 64–75. Cambridge: Cambridge University Press

Earle, T. and C. Costin 1986 Inca imperial conquest and changing patterns of household consumption in the Central Andes. Paper presented at the 6th Annual Meeting of the Society for Economic Anthropology (April), Urbana-Champaign, IL

Eco, Umberto 1976 *A Theory of Semiotics*. Bloomington, IN: Indiana University Press

Eibl-Eibesfeldt, Irenaus 1989 *Human Ethology*. Chicago: Aldine

Emlen, J. Merritt 1973 *Ecology: An Evolutionary Approach*. Reading, MA: Addison-Wesley

Fabian, Johannes 1983 *Time and the Other: How Anthropology Makes Its Object*. New York: Columbia University Press

Faris, James 1983 From form to content in the structural study of aesthetic systems. In *Structure and Cognition in Art*, edited by Dorothy Washburn, pp. 90–112. Cambridge: Cambridge University Press

Flannery, Kent V. 1967 Culture-history vs. culture-process. Review of *An Introduction to American Archaeology*, vol. 1: *North and*

Middle America, by Gordon R. Willey. *Scientific American*, vol. 217 (2): 119–22

1968 The Olmec and the valley of Oaxaca: a model for inter-regional interaction in Formative times. In *Dumbarton Oaks Conference on the Olmec*, edited by E. Benson, pp. 79–117. Washington, DC: Dumbarton Oaks

1972 The cultural evolution of civilizations. In *Annual Review of Ecology and Systematics*, 3: 399–426

1976 *The Mesoamerican Village*. New York: Academic Press

Ford, James A. 1952 *Measurements of some Prehistoric Design Developments in the Southeastern States*. Anthropological Papers of the American Museum of Natural History, 44, part 3

Foucault, Michel 1979 What is an author?, trans. Josué V. Harari. In *Textual Strategies: Perspectives in Post-Structuralist Criticism*, edited by Josué V. Harari, pp. 141–60. Ithaca: Cornell University Press

Franklin, Natalie R. 1986. Stochastic vs. emblemic: an archaeologically useful method for the analysis of style in Australian rock art. *Rock Art Research* 3(2): 121–24

Friedman, J. and M. J. Rowlands 1978 Notes towards an epigenetic model of the evolution of "civilization." In *The Evolution of Social Systems*, edited by J. Friedman and M. J. Rowlands, pp. 201–76. Pittsburgh: University of Pittsburgh Press

Friedrich, Margaret Hardin 1970 Design structure and social interaction. Archaeological implications of an ethnographic analysis. *American Antiquity* 35: 332–43

Fromkin, H. L. 1972 Feeling of interpersonal undistinctiveness: an unpleasant affective state. *Journal of Experimental Psychology*, 6: 178–85

Fuente, Beatriz de la 1981 Toward a concept of monumental Olmec art. In *The Olmec and Their Neighbors*, edited by E. Benson, p. 83–94. Washington, DC: Dumbarton Oaks

Gadamer, Hans Georg 1965 *Wahrheit und Methode*, 2nd ed., Tübingen: Mohr

Gebhart-Sayer, Angelika 1984 *The Cosmos Encoiled: Indian Art of the Peruvian Amazon*. New York: Center for Inter-American Relations

Giddens, Anthony 1979 *Central Problems in Social Theory*. Berkeley and Los Angeles: University of California Press

Gilman, Antonio 1984 Explaining the upper Paleolithic revolution. In *Marxist Perspectives in Archaeology*, edited by M. Spriggs, pp. 115–26. Cambridge: Cambridge University Press

Gladwin, W. and H. S. Gladwin 1935 *The Eastern Range of Red-on-Buff Culture*. Medallion Papers, 16. Globe, AZ: Gila Pueblo

Glassie, Henry 1975 *Folk Housing of Middle Virginia*. Knoxville, TN: University of Tennessee Press

Goldman, I. 1970 *Ancient Polynesian Society*. Chicago: Chicago University Press

Goldstein, L. 1980 *Mississippian Mortuary Practices: A Case Study of Two Cemeteries in the Lower Illinois Valley*. Northwestern University Archaeological Program Scientific Papers, 4. Evanston, IL

Gombrich, Ernst 1960 *Art and Illusion*. Princeton: Princeton University Press, Bollingen Series

1963 *Meditations on a Hobby Horse and Other Essays in the Theory of Art*. London: Phaidon

1968 Style. In *International Encyclopedia of the Social Sciences*, edited by David L. Sills, vol. 15, pp. 352–61

1972 *Symbolic Images*. New York: Phaidon

Goodman, Nelson

1940 On likeness of meaning. *Analysis* 1: 1–7

1972a *Languages of Art: An Approach to a Theory of Symbols*, rev. ed. Indianapolis: Bobbs-Merrill

1972b Seven strictures on similarity. In *Problems and Projects*, by N. Goodman, pp. 437–46. Indianapolis: Bobbs-Merrill

1978 The status of style. In *Ways of Worldmaking*, by N. Goodman, pp. 23–40. Indianapolis: Bobbs-Merrill

Grabar, Oleg 1973 *The Formation of Islamic Art*. New Haven: Yale University Press

Graves, Michael W. 1981 *Ethnoarchaeology of Kalinga Ceramic Design* (Ph.D. dissertation, University of Arizona). Ann Arbor: University Microfilms

1982 Breaking down ceramic variation: testing models of White Mountain Redware design style development. *Journal of Anthropological Archaeology* 1: 305–54

Gray, Gloria 1953 Bolivar Odicio, el Cashibo Civilizador. *Peru Indigena* 4: 146–54

Grinnel, G. 1891 Marriage among the Pawnee. *American Anthropologist* 4: 275–81

Grove, D. 1981 Olmec monuments: mutilation as a clue to meaning. In *The Olmec and Their Neighbors*, edited by E. Benson, M. Coe, and D. Grove, pp. 49–68. Washington, DC: Dumbarton Oaks

1984 *Chalcatzingo: Excavations on the Olmec Frontier*. New York: Thames and Hudson

Gruber, Jacob 1986 Archaeology, history and culture. In *American Archaeology, Past and Future*, edited by D. Meltzer, J. Sabloff, and D. Fowler, pp. 163–86. Washington, DC: Smithsonian Institution

Guillen, A. 1984 The possible role of a woman in Formative exchange. In *Trade and Exchange in Early Mesoamerica*, edited by K. Hirth, pp. 115–23. Albuquerque: University of New Mexico Press

Halland, R. 1977 Archaeological classification and ethnic groups: a case study from Sudanese Nubia. *Norwegian Archaeological Review* 10: 1–17

Handsman, Russell 1987 Stop making sense: toward an anti-catalogue of woodsplint basketry. In *A Key into the Language of Woodsplint Baskets*, edited by Ann McMullen and Russell G. Handsman, pp. 144–63. Washington, CT: American Indian Archaeological Institute

Hannan, M., J. Freeman and J. Meyer 1976 Specification of models for organizational effectiveness. *American Sociological Review* 41: 136–43

Hantman, Jeffrey L. 1980 Arizona D:11:215. In *Excavation on Black Mesa, 1979: a descriptive report*, edited by S. Powell, R. Layhe, and A. L. Klesert, pp. 211–17. (Center for Archaeological Investigations Research Paper 18.) Carbondale: Centre for Archaeological Investigations, Southern Illinois University

1983 *Stylistic Distributions and Social Networks in the Prehistoric Plateau Southwest* (Ph.D. dissertation, Arizona State University.) Ann Arbor: University Microfilms

Hantman, Jeffrey and Stephen Plog 1982 The relationship of stylistic similarity to patterns of material exchange. In *Contexts for Prehistoric Exchange*, edited by J. Ericson and T. Earle, pp. 237–63. New York: Academic Press

Harner, Michael J. 1974 Waiting for Inca-God. Paper presented at the Annual Meeting of the American Anthropological Association, Mexico City

Hebdige, Dick 1979 *Subculture: The Meaning of Style*. London: Methuen

Hegmon, Michelle 1986 Information exchange and integration on Black Mesa, Arizona, A.D. 931 to 1150. In *Spatial Organization and Exchange: Archaeological Survey on Northern Black Mesa*, edited by S. Plog, pp. 256–81. Carbondale: Southern Illinois University Press

Heizer, Robert 1960 Agriculture and the theocratic state in lowland southeastern Mexico. *American Antiquity* 26: 215–22

Helms, M. 1976. *Ancient Panama: Chiefs in Search of Power*. Austin: University of Texas Press

Hennig, Willi 1979 *Phylogenetic Systematics*, trans. D. D. Davis and R. Zangerl. Urbana: University of Illinois Press

Henry, T. 1928. *Ancient Tahiti*. Bernice P. Bishop Museum Bulletin, 48

Hermerén, Göran 1975 *Influence in Art and Literature*. Princeton, NJ: Princeton University Press

Hill, James N. 1966 A prehistoric community in Eastern Arizona. *Southwestern Journal of Anthropology* 22: 9–30

1970 *Broken K Pueblo: Prehistoric Social Organization in the American Southwest*. Anthropological Papers of the University of Arizona, 18. Tucson, AZ

1977 Individual variability in ceramics and the study of prehistoric social organization. In *The Individual in Prehistory*, edited by James N. Hill and Joel Gunn, pp. 55–108. New York: Academic Press

Hirth, K. 1978 Interregional trade and the formation of prehistoric gateway communities. *American Antiquity* 43: 35–45

Hodder, Ian 1977 The distribution of material culture items in the Baringo District, Western Kenya. *Man* 12: 239–69

1978 The maintenance of group identities in the Baringo District, Western Kenya. In *Social Organization and Settlement: Contributions from Anthropology, Archaeology and Geography*, edited by D. Green, C. Hasselgrove, and M. Spriggs, pp. 47–73. BAR International Series (suppl.), 47: Oxford

1979 Economic and social stress and material culture patterning. *American Antiquity* 44: 446–54

1982a *Symbolic and Structural Archaeology*. Cambridge: Cambridge University Press

1982b *Symbols in Action*. Cambridge: Cambridge University Press

1984a Burials, houses, women and men in the European Neolithic. In *Ideology, Power and Prehistory*, edited by D. Miller and C. Tilley, pp. 51–68. Cambridge: Cambridge University Press

1984b Archaeology in 1984. *Antiquity* 58: 25–32

1985 Post-processual archaeology. In *Advances in Archaeological Method and Theory*, edited by Michael B. Schiffer, vol. 8, pp. 1–26. New York: Academic Press

1987 Contextual archaeology: an interpretation of Catal Hüyük and a discussion of the origins of agriculture. *Bulletin of the Institute of Archaeology*, 24 (Jubilee Issue): 43–56

Hommon, R. 1976 *The Formulation of Primitive States in Pre-contact Hawaii*. (Ph.D. thesis, University of Arizona, Tucson AZ.) Ann Arbor: University Microfilms

Hosler, Dorothy 1986 The origins, technology and social construction of ancient West Mexican metallurgy. Unpublished Ph.D. dissertation, University of California, Santa Barbara

Jameson, Frederic 1984 Postmodernism or the cultural logic of late capitalism. *New Left Review* 146: 85–106

Johnson, A. and T. Earle 1987 *The Evolution of Human Society*. Stanford: Stanford University Press

Kaeppler, A. 1970 Feather cloaks, ship captains, and lords. *Bernice P. Bishop Museum Occasional Papers* 24: 180–91

1978 'Artificial Curiosities': An Exposition of Native Manufactures Collected on the Three Pacific Voyages of Captain James Cook, R.N. Honolulu: Bernice P. Bishop Museum Press

1982 A study of symbolism in Hawaiian images. In *Res 3*, Spring 1982, edited by R. Guidieri and F. Pellizzi, pp. 82–107. Cambridge, MA: Peabody Museum of Anthropology and Ethnology

Kamakau, S. 1961 *Ruling Chiefs of Hawaii*. Honolulu: Kamehameha Schools

Kantor, MacKinlay 1961 *Spirit Lake*. New York: Signet Books

Keesing, Roger 1974 Theories of culture. *Annual Review of Anthropology* 3: 73–98

Kellogg, Rhoda 1969 *Analyzing Children's Art*. Palo Alto: Mayfield Publishing Co.

Kensinger, Kenneth M. 1975 Studying the Cashinahua. In *The Cashinahua of Eastern Peru*, edited by Jane P. Dwyer. Providence, RI: Brown University, Haffenreffer Museum of Anthropology

King, J. 1784 *A Voyage to the Pacific Ocean*, vol. 3. London: H. Chamberlaine

Kintigh, K. 1982 A painless measure of archaeological diversity. Paper presented at the 47th Annual Meeting of the Society for American Archaeology, Minneapolis, MN

Kirch, P. 1984 *The Evolution of the Polynesian Chiefdom*. Cambridge: Cambridge University Press

Kluckhohn, Clyde 1939 The place of theory in anthropological studies. *Philosophy of Science* 6 (3): 238–344

1940 The conceptual structure in Middle American studies. In *Maya and Their Neighbors*, edited by C. L. Hay *et al.*, pp. 41–51. New York: Dover Publications

Kohl, Philip 1985 Symbolic cognitive archaeology: a new loss of innocence. *Dialectical Anthropology* 9: 105–17

Krieger, Alex 1944 The typological concept. *American Antiquity* 9 (3): 271–88

Kristeller, P.O. 1951–2 The modern system of the arts: a study in the history of aesthetics. *Journal of the History of Ideas*, 12: 17–46

Kristiansen, K. 1984 Ideology and material culture: an archaeological perspective. In *Marxist Perspectives in Archaeology*, edited by M. Spriggs, pp. 72–100. Cambridge: Cambridge University Press

1987 From stone to bronze: the evolution of social complexity in Northern Europe, 3200–1200 B.C. In *Specialization, Exchange and Complex Societies*, edited by E. Brumfiel and T. Earle, pp. 30–51. Cambridge: Cambridge University Press

Kroeber, Alfred 1948 *Anthropology*. New York: Harcourt, Brace

1956 *Toward Definition of the Nazca Style*. Berkeley: University of California Press

1957 *Styles and Civilizations*. Ithaca, NY: Cornell University Press

Kubler, George 1962 *The Shape of Time*. New Haven: Yale University Press

1979 Towards a reductive theory of visual style. In *The Concept of Style*, edited by Berel Lang, pp. 119–27. Philadelphia: University of Pennsylvania Press

1985 Polygenesis and diffusion. In *Collected Essays of George Kubler*, edited by T. F. Reese, pp. 251–55. New Haven: Yale University Press

La Capra, Dominick 1983 *Rethinking Intellectual History: Texts, Contexts, Language*. Ithaca, NY: Cornell University Press

Lathrap, Donald W. 1970 *The Upper Amazon*. New York: Praeger Publishers

1973 The antiquity and importance of long-distance trade relations in the moist tropics of pre-Columbian South America. *World Archaeology* 5 (2): 170–86

1976 Shipibo tourist art, in *Ethnic and Tourist Arts*, edited by Nelson H. H. Graburn, pp. 197–207. Berkeley: University of California Press

1983 Recent Shipibo-Conibo ceramics and their implications for archaeological interpretation. In *Structure and Cognition in Art*, edited by Dorothy K. Washburn, pp. 25–39. Cambridge: Cambridge University Press

Laville, H., J.-P. Rigaud, and J. R. Sackett 1980 *Rock Shelters of the Périgord*. New York/London: Academic Press

LeBlanc, Steven A. 1986 Aspects of Southwestern prehistory: A.D. 900–1400. In *Ripples in the Chichimec Sea*, edited by Frances Joan Mathien and Randall H. McGuire, pp. 105–34. Carbondale: Southern Illinois University Press

Lechtman, Heather 1977 Style in technology – some early thoughts. In *Material Culture. Styles, Organization, and Dynamics of Technology*, edited by H. Lechtman and R. S. Merrill (1975 Proceedings of the American Ethnological Society), pp. 3–20. St. Paul, MN: West Publishing

1984 Andean value systems and the development of prehistoric metallurgy. *Technology and Culture* 25 (1): 1–36

Lemaine, G. 1974 Social differentiation and social originality. *European Journal of Social Psychology* 4: 17–52

Lemaine, G., J. Kasterztein, and B. Personnaz 1978 Social differentiation. In *Differentiation Between Social Groups*, edited by H. Tajfel, pp. 269–99. New York: Academic Press

Lemmonier, P. 1986 The study of material culture today: toward an anthropology of technical systems. *Journal of Anthropological Archaeology* 5: 147–86

Leone, Mark 1972 Issues in contemporary archaeology. Introduction to *Contemporary Archaeology*, edited by M. Leone, pp. 14–27. Carbondale: Southern Illinois University Press

1973 Archaeology as the science of technology: Mormon town plans and fences. In *Research and Theory in Current Archaeology*, edited by Charles L. Redman, pp. 125–50. New York: John Wiley & Sons

1977 The role of primitive technology in 19th century American utopias. In *Material Culture: Style, Organization, and Dynamics of Technology*, edited by Heather Lechtman and Robert Merrill, pp. 87–107. St. Paul, MN: West Publishing

1982 Some opinions about recovering mind. *American Antiquity* 47: 742–60

Leone, Mark, Parker Potter, Jr., and Paul A. Shackel 1987 Toward a critical archaeology. In *Current Anthropology* 28 (3): 283–302

Leroi-Gourhan, André 1965 *Treasures of Prehistoric Art*. New York: Abrams

Lévi-Strauss, Claude 1982 *The Way of the Masks*, trans. Sylvia Modelski. Vancouver: Douglas and McIntyre

Levinson, Jerrold 1979 Defining art historically. *British Journal of Aesthetics* 19: 232–50

Lewis-Beck, M. 1980 *Applied Regression: An Introduction*. Sage University Papers on Quantitative Applications in the Social Sciences, 22. Beverly Hills: Sage Publications

Lewis-Williams, J. David 1981 *Believing and Seeing: Symbolic Meanings in Southern San Rock Art*. London: Academic Press

Lindstrom, Miriam 1957 *Children's Art*. Berkeley: University of California Press

Longacre, William A. 1963 Archaeology as anthropology: a case study. Unpublished Ph.D. dissertation, University of Chicago

1970 *Archaeology as Anthropology: A Case Study*. Anthropological Papers of the University of Arizona, 17. Tuscon, AZ

1981 Kalinga pottery: an ethnoarchaeological study. In *Patterns of the Past*, edited by I. Hodder, G. Isaac, and N. Hammond, pp. 49–66. New York: Cambridge University Press

Lowie, R. 1916 Societies of the Arikara Indians. *Anthropological Papers of the Museum of Natural History* 11: 647–78

Lowman, Cherry 1973 *Displays of Power: Art and War among the Marings of New Guinea*. New York: Museum of Primitive Art

Luquet, Georges Henri 1927 *Le Dessin Enfantin*. Paris: Alcan

Macdonald, W. 1985. Symbols and skin. Paper presented at the 50th Annual Meeting of the Society for American Archaeology, Denver, CO

Malo, D. 1951 (1898) *Hawaiian Antiquities*. Bernice P. Bishop Museum Special Publications, 2 (2nd ed.)

Maquet, J. 1979 *Introduction to Aesthetic Anthropology*, 2nd ed. Malibu, CA: Undeena Publications

Marshall, Lorna 1976 *The !Kung of Nyae Nyae*. Cambridge, MA: Harvard University Press

Martin, Paul S., and Fred Plog 1973 *The Archaeology of Arizona*. New York: Natural History Press

McGuire, Randall 1983 Breaking down cultural complexity: inequality and heterogeneity. In *Advances in Archaeological Method and Theory*, edited by M. Schiffer, vol. 6, pp. 91–141. New York: Academic Press

Meggitt, M. 1972 System and subsystem: the Te exchange cycle among the Mae Enga. *Human Ecology* 1: 111–23

Mellaart, J. 1967 *Catal Hüyük, A Neolithic Town in Anatolia*. London: Thames and Hudson

Meltzer, David 1981 A study of style and function in a class of tools. *Journal of Field Archaeology* 8: 313–26

Mercer, R. 1980 *Hambledon Hill: a Neolithic landscape*. Edinburgh: Edinburgh University Press

Miller, Daniel 1983 THINGS ain't what they used to be. *RAIN (Royal Anthropological Institute News)* 59: 5–7

Mitchell, W. J. T. 1986 *Iconology: Image, Text, Ideology*. Chicago: University of Chicago Press

Morris, C. 1982 The infrastructure of Inka control in the Peruvian Central Highlands. In *The Inca and Aztec 1400–1800: Anthropology and History*, edited by G. Collier, R. Rosaldo and J. Wirth, pp. 153–71. New York: Academic Press

Muller, J. 1977 Individual variation in art styles. In *The Individual in Prehistory*, edited by James N. Hill and Joel Gunn, pp. 23–39. New York: Academic Press

1984 The southern cult. Paper presented at the Cottonlandia Conference (September)

Munro, Thomas 1956 Style in the arts: a method of stylistic analysis. In *Toward Science in Aesthetics*, pp. 192–226. New York: Liberal Arts Press

1963 *Evolution in the Arts*. Cleveland: Cleveland Museum of Art

Murdock, G. 1949 *Social Structure*. New York: Macmillan

Myers, Thomas P. 1974 Spanish contacts and social change on the Ucayali River, Peru. *Ethnohistory* 21 (2): 135–58

Needham, Rodney 1983 Polythetic classification. In *Against the Tranquility of Axioms*, pp. 36–55. Berkeley: University of California Press

Neitzel, Jill 1985 Regional styles and organizational hierarchies: the view from Chaco Canyon. Paper presented at the 50th Annual Meeting of the Society for American Archaeology, Denver, CO

Newman, P. 1957. An intergroup collectivity among the Nootka. Unpublished M.A. thesis, University of Washington, Seattle

Noble, G. Kingsley 1965 *Proto-Arawakan and its Descendents*. Bloomington: Indiana University Research Center in Anthropology, Folklore, and Linguistics

Ong, Walter 1967 *The Presence of the Word*. New Haven: Yale University Press

1977 *Interfaces of the Word*. Ithaca, NY: Cornell University Press.

O'Shea, J. 1984 *Mortuary Variability: An Archaeological Investigation*. New York: Academic Press

Panofsky, Erwin 1939 *Studies in Iconology*. Oxford: Oxford University Press

1944 Renaissance and renascences. *Kenyon Review* 6: 201–36

1953 *Early Netherlandish Painting*. 2 vols. Cambridge, MA: Harvard University Press

1960 *Renaissance and Renascences in Western Art*. Stockholm: Almqvist and Wiksells

Peebles, C. and S. Kus 1977 Some archaeological correlates of ranked society. *American Antiquity* 42: 421–28

Piaget, Jean 1970 *Structuralism*, trans. Chaninah Maschler. New York: Harper & Row

Plog, Fred 1975 Demographic studies in Southwestern prehistory. In *Population Studies in Archaeology and Biological Anthropology: A Symposium*, edited by A. C. Swedlund, pp. 94–102. Memoirs of the Society for American Archaeology 30. Washington, DC: Society for American Archaeology

Plog, Stephen 1976 Measurement of prehistoric interaction between communities. In *The Early Mesoamerican Village*, edited by Kent V. Flannery, pp. 255–72. New York: Academic Press

1978 Social interaction and stylistic similarity: a reanalysis. In *Advances in Archaeological Method and Theory*, edited by M. B. Schiffer, vol. 1, pp. 143–82. New York: Academic Press

1980 *Stylistic Variation in Prehistoric Ceramics*. Cambridge: Cambridge University Press

1983 Analysis of style in artifacts. In *Annual Review of Anthropology*, 12 (edited by B. J. Siegel): 125–42

1986a Understanding culture change in the northern Southwest. In *Spatial Organization and Exchange: Archaeological Survey on Northern Black Mesa*, edited by S. Plog, pp. 310–36. Carbondale: Southern Illinois University Press

1986b Patterns of demographic growth and decline. In *Spatial Organization and Exchange: Archaeological Survey on Northern Black Mesa*, edited by S. Plog, pp. 224–55. Carbondale: Southern Illinois University Press

1986c Change in regional trade networks. In *Spatial Organization and Exchange: Archaeological Survey on Northern Black Mesa*, edited by S. Plog, pp. 282–309. Carbondale: Southern Illinois University Press

Plog, Stephen and Jeffrey Hantman 1986a Chronology construction and the study of culture change. Manuscript, Department of Anthropology, University of Virginia

1986b Multiple regression analysis as a dating method in the American Southwest. In *Spatial Organization and Exchange: Archaeological Survey on Northern Black Mesa*, edited by Stephen Plog, pp. 87–113. Carbondale: Southern Illinois University Press

Podro, Michael 1981 *The Critical Historians of Art*. New Haven: Yale University Press

Pollock, Susan 1983 Style and information: an analysis of Susiana ceramics. *Journal of Anthropological Archaeology* 2: 354–90

Pyne, N. 1976 The fire-serpent and were-jaguar in Formative Oaxaca. In *The Early Mesoamerican Village*, edited by K. Flannery, pp. 272–82. New York: Academic Press

Quick, P. 1986 *Proceedings of the Conference on the Reburial Issue*. Washington, DC: Society for American Archaeology

Randsborg, K. 1982 Rank, rights and resources: an archaeological perspective from Denmark. In *Ranking, Resources and Exchange*, edited by C. Renfrew and S. Shennan, pp. 132–39. Cambridge: Cambridge University Press

Rappaport, Ray 1967 *Pigs for the Ancestors*. New Haven: Yale University Press

Raymond, J. Scott, Warren R. DeBoer, and Peter G. Roe 1975 *Cumancaya: A Peruvian Ceramic Tradition*. Occasional Papers, 2. Calgary: Department of Archaeology, University of Calgary

Redman, C. 1977 The 'analytical individual' and prehistoric style variability. In *The Individual in Prehistory*, edited by James N. Hill and Joel Gunn, pp. 41–53. New York: Academic Press

1978 *The Rise of Civilization: From Early Farmer to Urban Society in the Ancient Near East*. San Francisco: W. H. Freeman & Co.

Renfrew, A. C. 1976 Megaliths, territories and populations. In *Accumulation and Continuity in Atlantic Europe*, edited by S. de Laet, pp. 198–220. Bruges: De Tempel

1978 Varna and the social context of early metallurgy. *Antiquity* 52: 199–203

Richardson, Jane and A. Kroeber 1940 *Three Centuries of Women's Dress Fashions: A Quantitative Analysis*. Anthropological Records, University of California, 5 (2). Berkeley: University of California Press

Richter, G. M. A. 1970 *The Sculpture and Sculptors of the Greeks*, 4th ed. New Haven: Yale University Press

Rick, J. W. 1980 *Prehistoric Hunters of the High Andes*. New York: Academic Press

Riegl, Alois 1985 *Late Roman Art Industry*, trans. R. Winkes. Archaeologia, 36. Rome: Giorgio Bretschneider

Roberts, Frank H. H., 1931 *The Ruins at Kiatuthlana*. Bureau of American Ethnology, Bulletin 100. Washington, DC: Government Printing Office

Robertson, Martin 1975 *A History of Greek Art*. 2 vols. Cambridge: Cambridge University Press

Robinson, Jenefer 1981 Style and significance in art history and art criticism. *Journal of Aesthetics and Art Criticism* 40: 6–14

Roe, Peter G. 1976 Archaism, form, and decoration: an ethnographic and archaeological case study from the Peruvian Montana. *Nawpa Pacha* 14: 73–94. Berkeley: Institute of Andean Studies

1980 Art and residence among the Shipibo Indians of Peru: a study in microacculturation. *American Anthropologist* 82: 42–71

1981 Aboriginal tourists and artistic exchange between the Pisquibo and Shipibo: trade ware in an ethnographic setting. In *Networks of the Past: Regional Interaction in Archaeology*, edited by Peter D. Francis, F. J. Kense, and P. G. Duke, pp. 61–84. Calgary: Archaeological Association of the University of Calgary

1982 *The Cosmic Zygote: Cosmology in the Amazon Basin*. New Brunswick: Rutgers University Press

Rowe, J. 1962 *Chavin Art: An Inquiry into its Form and Meaning*. New York: The Museum of Primitive Art

Rowntree, Lester B. 1987 Social theory and cityscape: a critique of the literary metaphor. Paper presented at the Annual Meeting of the Association of Pacific Coast Geographers, Davis, CA (available in Abstract form in the Association's *Yearbook*, vol. 50, pp. 138–9. Corvallis, OR: Oregon State University Press)

Sabloff, J. and G. Willey 1980 *A History of American Archaeology*, 2nd ed. San Francisco: W. H. Freeman & Co

Sackett, James R. 1973 Style, function and artifact variability in Palaeolithic assemblages. In *The Explanation of Culture Change*, edited by Colin Renfrew, pp. 317–25. London: Duckworth

1977 The meaning of style in archaeology. *American Antiquity* 42: 369–80

1982 Approaches to style in lithic archaeology. *Journal of Anthropological Archaeology* 1: 59–112

1983 From deMortillet to Bordes: a century of French palaeolithic research. In *Towards a History of Archaeology*, edited by G. Daniel, pp. 59–112. London: Thames and Hudson

1985a Style and ethnicity in the Kalahari: a reply to Wiessner. *American Antiquity* 50 (1): 154–59

1985b Style, ethnicity and stone tools. In *Status, Structure, and Stratification: Current Archaeological Reconstructions*, edited by M. Thompson, M. T. Marcia, and F. J. Kense, pp. 277–82. Proceedings of the Sixteenth Annual Chacmool Conference, The University of Calgary

1986a Style, function and assemblage variability: a reply to Binford. *American Antiquity* 51: 628–34

1986b Isochrestism and style: a clarification. *Journal of Anthropological Archaeology* 5: 266–77

1988 The Neuvic group: Upper Paleolithic open-air sites in the Périgord. In *Upper Pleistocene Prehistory of Western Eurasia*, edited by Harold Dibble and Anta Montet-White, pp. 61–84. Philadelphia: University Museum

1989 Statistics, attributes, and the dynamics of burin typology. To appear in *Alternative Applications in Lithic Analysis*, edited by Donald O. Henry and George H. Odell. *Archaeological Papers of the American Anthropological Association* 1

n.d. *The Archaeology of Solvieux: Excavations and Industries*. (Monumenta Archaeologica.) Los Angeles: The Institute of Archaeology, University of California

Sackett, J. R. and J. Gaussen 1976 Upper Paleolithic habitation structures in the Sud-Ouest of France. In *Les Structures d'Habitat au Paléolithique Supérieur*, edited by A. Leroi-Gourhan, pp. 55–83 (Colloque XIII. Nice: IXe Congrès de l'Union Internationale des Sciences Préhistoriques et Protohistoriques)

Sahlins, Marshall 1958 *Social Stratification in Polynesia*. Seattle: University of Washington Press

Salmon, Merrilee 1982 Models of explanation: two views. In *Theory and Explanation in Archaeology*, edited by C. Renfrew, M. Rowlands, and B. A. Seagraves, pp. 35–44. New York: Academic Press

Sanders, W. and B. Price 1968 *Mesoamerica: The Evolution of a Civilization*. New York: Random House

Sapir, Edward 1916 *Time Perspective in Aboriginal American Culture: A Study in Method*. Anthropological Series, 13. Memoirs of the Canadian Geological Survey, 90. Ottawa

Sass, Louis A. 1986 Anthropology's native problems: revisionism in the field. *Harpers* 272 (1632): 49–57

Sauerländer, Willibald 1983 From stilus to style: reflections on the fate of a notion. *Art History* 6: 253–70

Scarre, C. J. 1983 *Ancient France: Neolithic Societies and Their Landscapes 6000–2000 BC*. Edinburgh: Edinburgh University Press

Schäfer, Heinrich 1974 *Principles of Egyptian Art*, 4th ed. Translated by J. R. Baines. Oxford: Oxford University Press

Schapiro, Meyer 1953 Style. In *Anthropology Today*, edited by Alfred L. Kroeber, pp. 287–312. Chicago: Aldine Press

1979 *Modern Art*. New York: Braziller

Shanks, M. and Tilley, C. 1982 Ideology, symbolic power and ritual communication: a reinterpretation of neolithic mortuary practices. In *Symbolic and Structural Archaeology*, edited by I. Hodder, pp. 129–54. Cambridge: Cambridge University Press

1987 *Social Theory and Archaeology*. Oxford: Polity Press, in association with Basil Blackwell

Sharp, R. 1952 Steel axes for stone-age Australians. *Human Organization* 11: 17–22

Shaw, T. 1986 Archaeology and the politics of academic freedom. *Archaeological Review from Cambridge* 5 (1): 5–24

Shepard, Anna O. 1963 *Ceramics for the Archaeologist*. Washington, DC: Carnegie Institution

Sherratt, A. G. 1981 Plough and pastoralism: aspects of the secondary products revolution. In *Patterns of the Past*, edited by I. Hodder, G. Isaac and N. Hammond, pp. 261–306. Cambridge: Cambridge University Press

1982 Mobile resources: settlement and exchange in early agricultural Europe. In *Ranking, Resources and Exchange*, edited by A. C. Renfrew and S. Shennan, pp. 13–26l. Cambridge: Cambridge University Press

Sibley, Frank, N. 1959 Aesthetic concepts. *Philosophical Review* 68: 421–50

Simpson, George Gaylord 1961 *Principles of Animal Taxonomy*. New York: Columbia University Press

Sircello, Guy 1972 *Mind and Art*. Princeton, NJ: Princeton University Press

Smith, Cyril Stanley 1978 Structural hierarchy in science, art, and history. In *On Aesthetics in Science*, edited by Judith Wechsler, pp. 9–53. Cambridge, MA: Massachusetts Institute of Technology Press

Sneath, Peter H. A., and Robert R. Sokal 1973 *Principles of Numerical Taxonomy*, 2nd ed. San Francisco: W. H. Freeman & Co.

Sorokin, Pitrim A. 1937 *Social and Cultural Dynamics*, vol. 1: *Fluctuations of Forms in Art*. New York: American Book

Spaulding, Albert C. 1953 Review of *Measurements of some Prehistoric Design Developments in the Southeastern States*, by James A. Ford. *American Anthropologist* 55: 589–91

Sperber, Dan 1987 Culture and matter. Paper presented at "Symbolic, Structural and Semiotic Methods in Archaeology," a Conference, Bloomington, IN.

Spiro, Melford 1969 Discussion. In *Forms of Symbolic Action*, edited by Robert F. Spencer (Proceedings of the 1969 annual meeting of the American Ethnological Society), pp. 208–14. Seattle and London: University of Washington Press

Srejovic, D. 1972 *Europe's First Monumental Sculpture: New Discoveries at Lepenski Vir*. London: Thames and Hudson

Stadler, Ingrid 1982 The idea of art and its criticism: a rational reconstruction of a Kantian doctrine. In *Essays in Kant's Aesthetics*, edited by T. Cohen and P. Guyer, pp. 195–220. Chicago: University of Chicago Press

Steponaitis, Vincas 1978 Locational theory and complex chiefdoms: a Mississippian example. In *Mississippian Settlement Patterns*, edited by B. Smith, pp. 417–53. New York: Academic Press

Steward, Julian and F. M. Setzler 1983 Function and configuration in archaeology. In *American Antiquity* 1: 4–10

Steward, Julian H., and Alfred Metraux 1948 Tribes of the Peruvian and Ecuadorian Montana. In *Handbook of South American Indians*, edited by Julian H. Steward, vol. 3: Bulletin 143 of the Bureau of American Ethnology. Washington, DC: Smithsonian Institution

Stocks, Anthony W. 1978 The invisible Indians: a history of analysis of the relations of the Cocamilla Indians of Loreto, Peru to the state. Unpublished Ph.D. dissertation, University of Florida

Strathern, A. 1971 *The Rope of Moka*. Cambridge: Cambridge University Press

Strathern, A. and M. Strathern 1971 *Self-decoration in Mount Hagen*. London: Duckworth

Tagg, John 1985 Art history and difference. *Block*, 10, pp. 164–71

Tajfel, H. 1978 (editor) *Differentiation Between Social Groups*. New York: Academic Press

1982 Introduction. In *Social Identity and Intergroup Relations*, edited by H. Tajfel, pp. 1–11. Cambridge: Cambridge University Press

Tedlock, B. and D. Tedlock 1985 Text and textile: language and technology in the arts of the Quiché Maya. *Journal of Anthropological Research* 41: 121–46

Tessmann, Gunter 1930 *Die Indianer Nordost-Perus*. Hamburg: Friederichsen, De Gruyter & Co.

Thomas, D. 1976. *Figuring Anthropology*. New York: Holt, Rinehart & Winston

1978 The awful truth about statistics in anthropology. *American Antiquity* 43: 231–44

Tilley, C. 1982 Social formation, social structures and social change. In *Symbolic and Structural Archaeology*, edited by I. Hodder, pp. 26–38. Cambridge: Cambridge University Press

Toll, H. Wolcott 1985 *Pottery Production, Public Architecture, and the Chaco Anasazi system*. (Ph.D. dissertation, University of Colorado.) Ann Arbor: University Microfilms

Tringham, Ruth 1971 *Hunters, Fishers and Farmers of Eastern Europe, 6000–3000 BC*. London: Hutchinson University Library

Tukey, J. 1969. Analyzing data: sanctification or detective work? *The American Psychologist* 24: 83–91

Turner, J. 1975 Social comparison and social identity: some prospects for intergroup behavior. *European Journal of Social Psychology* 5: 5–34

Tversky, Amos, and I. Gati 1978 Studies in similarity. In *Cognition and Categorization*, edited by E. Rosch and B. Lloyd, pp. 79–98. Hillsdale, NJ: Erlbaum

Tylor, Edmund B. 1865 *Researches into the Early History of Mankind and the Development of Civilization*. London: John Murray

Upham, Steadman 1982 *Politics and Power*. New York: Academic Press

Upham, S., K. Lightfoot and G. Feinman 1981 Explaining socially determined ceramic distributions in the prehistoric plateau southwest. *American Antiquity* 46: 822–33

Vossen, Rudiger 1969 *Archäologische Interpretation und Ethnographischer Befund. Eine Analyse anhand rezenter Keramik des Westlichen Amazonasbeckens*. 2 vols. Munich: Komissionverlag Klaus Reiner

Walton, Kendall 1979 Style and the products and processes of art. In *The Concept of Style*, edited by Berel Lang, pp. 45–66. Philadelphia: University of Pennsylvania Press

Washburn, Dorothy K. 1977. *A Symmetry Analysis of Upper Gila Area Ceramic Design*. (Peabody Museum Papers, vol. 68). Cambridge: Harvard University Press

1983 *Structure and Cognition in Art*. Cambridge: Cambridge University Press

Wasley, William W. 1959 *Cultural Implications of Style Trends in Southwestern Prehistoric Pottery*. (Ph.D. dissertation, University of Arizona.) Ann Arbor: University Microfilms

Watson, P. J. 1986 Archaeological interpretation, 1985. In *American Archaeology, Past and Future*, edited by D. Meltzer, J. Sabloff, and D. Fowler, pp. 439–58. Washington, DC: Smithsonian Institution Press

Watson, P. J. and S. LeBlanc 1973 Excavation and analysis of Halafian materials from southeastern Turkey. Paper presented at the 72nd Annual Meeting of the American Anthropological Association, New Orleans

Weber, Ronald L. 1975 Caimito: an analysis of the late prehistoric culture of the Central Ucayali, eastern Peru. Unpublished Ph.D. dissertation, University of Illinois, Urbana

Webster, D. 1976 On theocracies. *American Anthropologist* 78: 818–28

Wedel, W. 1955 *Archaeological Materials in the Vicinity of Mobridge, South Dakota*. Bureau of American Ethnology Bulletin 157. Washington, DC: Smithsonian Institution

Weitz, Moris 1956 Family resemblances and generalizations concerning the arts. *American Philosophical Quarterly* 2: 219–28

Weltfish, G. 1965 *The Lost Universe*. New York: Basic Books

Wendorf, F., A. E. Marks, and J. L. Shiner 1977 Comments on archaeological classification and ethnic groupings. *Norwegian Archaeological Review* 10: 23–26

Wetherell, N. 1982 Cross-cultural studies of minimal groups: implications for the social identity theory of intergroup relations. In *Social Identity and Intergroup Relations*, edited by H. Tajfel, pp. 207–40. Cambridge: Cambridge University Press

Whallon, Robert 1968 Investigations of late prehistoric social organization in New York State. In *New Perspectives in Archaeology*, edited by S. R. and L. R. Binford, pp. 223–4. Chicago: Aldine Press

White, Leslie 1959 The concept of culture. *American Anthropologist* 68: 745–48

Whittle, A. 1985 *Neolithic Europe: A Survey*. Cambridge: Cambridge University Press

Wiessner, Polly 1982a Beyond willow smoke and dogs' tails: a comment on Binford's analysis of hunter-gatherer settlement systems. *American Antiquity* 47: 171–78

1982b Risk, reciprocity, and social influence on !Kung San economies. In *Politics and History in Band Societies*, edited by Eleanor Leacock and Richard Lee, pp. 61–84. Cambridge: Cambridge University Press

1983 Style and social information in Kalahari San projectile points. *American Antiquity* 49 (2): 253–76

1984 Reconsidering the behavioral basis for style: a case study among the Kalahari San. *Journal of Anthropological Archaeology* 3: 190–234

1985 Style or isochrestic variation? A reply to Sackett. *American Antiquity* 50 (1): 160–66

1988 Style and changing relations between the individual and society. In *The Meaning of Things: Material Culture and Symbolic Expression*, edited by Ian Hodder. London: Allen & Unwin

Willey, G. 1962 The early great styles and the rise of pre-Columbian civilizations. *American Anthropologist* 64: 1–14

Williams, Raymond 1961 *Culture and Society 1780–1950*. New York: Columbia University Press

Wilmsen, E. N. 1972 *Lindenmeier: A Pleistocene Hunting Society*. New York: Harper

1973 Interaction, spacing behavior, and the organization of hunting bands. *Journal of Anthropological Research* 29: 1–31

Wilmsen, E. N. and F. H. H. Roberts, Jr. 1978 Lindenmeier, 1934–1974. Concluding report on investigations. *Smithsonian Contributions to Anthropology*, 24. Washington, DC: Smithsonian Institution

Winters, H. 1969 *The Riverton Culture*. Illinois Archaeological Survey, Monograph 1. Springfield, IL

Wobst, H. Martin 1976 Locational relationships in Paleolithic society. *Journal of Human Evolution* 5: 49–58

1977 Stylistic behavior and information exchange. In *For the Director: Research Essays in Honor of James B. Griffin*, edited by Charles E. Cleland (Museum of Anthropology Anthropological Paper 61), pp. 317–42. Ann Arbor: Museum of Anthropology, University of Michigan

Wolff, Janet 1981 *The Social Production of Art*. New York: St. Martin's Press

Wölfflin, Heinrich 1932 *Principles of Art History*, 7th ed., trans. M. D. Hottinger. London: G. Bell and Sons

Wollheim, Richard 1968 *Art and Its Objects*. New York: Harper and Row

1974 Giovanni Morelli and the origins of scientific connoisseurship. In *On Art and the Mind*, by R. Wollheim, pp. 177–201. Cambridge, MA: Harvard University Press

1979 Pictorial style: two views. In *The Concept of Style*, edited by Berel Lang, pp. 129–45. Philadelphia: University of Pennsylvania Press

1980 *Art and its Objects*, 2nd ed. Cambridge: Cambridge University Press

Woodburn, J. 1980 Hunters and gatherers today and reconstruction of the past. In *Soviet and Western Anthropology*, edited by E. Gellner, pp. 95–118. London: Duckworth

Wright, J. 1977 Recent research on the origin of the state. *Annual Reviews of Anthropology* 6: 379–97

1984 Prestate political formations. In *On the Evolution of Complex Societies*, edited by T. Earle, pp. 41–77. Malibu: Undena

Wylie, M. Alison 1981 Positivism and the new archaeology. Unpublished Ph.D. dissertation, State University of New York, Binghamton

1982 Epistemological issues raised by a structuralist archaeology. In *Symbolic and Structural Archaeology*, edited by I. Hodder, pp. 39–46. Cambridge: Cambridge University Press

1985b Binford's second loss of innocence. Paper presented at the Binghamton Archaeology Conference, Binghamton, NY

Yengoyan, A. 1985 Digging for symbols: the archaeology of everyday material life. *Proceedings of the Prehistoric Society*, 51: 329–34

INDEX